THE
SPECTER
OF
MATERIALISM

THE SPECTER OF MATERIALISM

Petrus Liu

QUEER THEORY AND MARXISM IN THE AGE OF THE BEIJING CONSENSUS

Duke University Press Durham and London 2023

Project editor: Bird Williams
Designed by Aimee C. Harrison
Typeset in Untitled Serif and Helvetica Neue
by Westchester Publishing Services

Library of Congress Cataloging-in-Publication Data
Names: Liu, Petrus, author.
Title: The specter of materialism : queer theory and Marxism in
the age of the Beijing consensus / Petrus Liu.
Description: Durham : Duke University Press, 2023. | Includes
bibliographical references and index.
Identifiers: LCCN 2022029335 (print)
LCCN 2022029336 (ebook)
ISBN 9781478019428 (paperback)
ISBN 9781478016793 (hardcover)
ISBN 9781478024057 (ebook)
Subjects: LCSH: Queer theory—China. | Philosophy, Marxist—
China. | Homosexuality—Political aspects—China. | Queer
theory—China—History. | BISAC: SOCIAL SCIENCE / LGBTQ
Studies / Gay Studies | LITERARY CRITICISM / Semiotics
& Theory.
Classification: LCC HQ76.3. C6 L58 2023 (print)
LCC HQ 76.3.C6 (ebook)
DDC 306.7601—dc23/eng/20220804
LC recordavailable at https://lccn.loc.gov/2022029335
LC ebook record available at https://lccn.loc.gov/2022029336

Cover art: Wangechi Mutu, *Detail of Family Tree*, 2012. Detail of
13 individually framed, mixed-media collages on paper. Dimensions
variable. Courtesy of the artist and Vielmetter Los Angeles.

Duke University Press gratefully acknowledges the support of
Boston University's Center for the Humanities, which provided a
publication production award for this book.

FOR BRIAN

Contents

Acknowledgments

The Specter of Materialism would not have been possible without the support and guidance of many friends. I owe my greatest debts to Judith Butler, David L. Eng, Collen Lye, Christopher Nealon, Lisa Rofel, Carlos Rojas, and J. Keith Vincent, who provided not only sources of intellectual sustenance but also models of political integrity and commitment. I would also like to thank Zong-qi Cai, Steve Choe, Kirk Denton, Sarah Frederick, Yogita Goyal, Wenqing Kang, Mayumo Inoue, Lida Maxwell, Jasbir K. Puar, Hentyle Yapp, David Der-wei Wang, and the anonymous readers for their invaluable comments on previously published articles that became the kernel of this book.

I am grateful to Shoshana Adler, Paul Amar, Hongwei Bao, Pearl Brilmyer, Sophie Chamas, Jason Oliver Chang, Kyunghee Sabina Eo, Victor Fan, Liang Ge, Huang Yingying, Yoon Sun Lee, J. Daniel Luther, Colleen Lye, Masuda Hajimu, Janet Poole, Lisa Rofel, Carlos Rojas, Cathy Schlund-Vials, Jia Tan, Filippo Trentin, Zairong Xiang, and Shana Ye for inviting me to present my work in progress at the Berlin Institute for Cultural Inquiry; the Chinese University of Hong Kong; Duke University; King's College London; the National University of Singapore; the University of Pennsylvania; Renmin University; the University of California, Berkeley's Program in Critical Theory; the University of California, Santa Barbara; the University of Connecticut; the University of London; the University of Southern California; the University of Toronto; and panels at the American Comparative Literature Association, the Association for Asian Studies, the Association for Asian American Studies, the Modern Language Association, and the Marxist Literary Group conventions, where I also benefited from the critical intelligence of Anjali Arondekar, Crystal Bartolovich, Ericka Beckman, Michael Bourdaghs, Yomi Braester, Cai Yiping, Sealing Cheng, Debanuj DasGupta, Iyko Day, Kevin Floyd, Gail Hershatter, Susie Jolly, Heonik Kwon, Andrew Way Leong, Eng-Beng Lim, Song Hwee

Lim, Heather Love, Laikwan Pang, Geeta Patel, Kent Puckett, Shuang Shen, María Amelia Viteri, and Wei Wei.

At Boston University, I am fortunate to be surrounded by an amazing group of scholars in the Department of World Languages and Literatures, the Department of English, and the Women's, Gender, and Sexuality Studies Program. I would like to thank Cati Connell, Yuri Corrigan, Sean Desilets, Sarah Frederick, Abigail Gilman, Gisela Hoecherl-Alden, Sanjay Krishnan, Margaret Litvin, Jack Matthews, Roberta Micallef, Lee Monk, Erin Murphy, Anthony Petro, Carrie Preston, Inés García de la Puente, Takeo Rivera, Jennie Row, Peter Schwartz, Sunil Sharma, J. Keith Vincent, Will Waters, Yoon Sun Yang, and Catherine Yeh for sustaining this project with their wisdom and collegiality.

In many ways, *The Specter of Materialism* was written as a sequel to my 2015 book, *Queer Marxism in Two Chinas*, and I would like to thank those who have prompted me to rethink and rewrite its arguments: Michael Baas, Harlan D. Chambers, Todd Henry, Calvin Hui, Brandon Kemp, Tan Hoang Nguyen, J. Daniel Luther, Yün Peng, Megan Sinnott, E. K. Tan, Jia Tan, John Wei, and Alvin K. Wong. Many thanks to Daniel McNaughton for carefully copyediting an early version of the manuscript. At Duke University Press, I am once again fortunate to have the judicious Ken Wissoker at the helm of the project. Josh Gutterman Tranen, Lisl Hampton, and Bird Williams deftly managed the manuscript production.

The College of Arts and Sciences at Boston University supported this project with a research leave, with additional research and travel funds provided by the Women's, Gender, and Sexuality Studies Program, and with a publication subvention award provided by the Center for the Humanities. A multiyear research grant from the Ford Foundation furnished funding for two course releases. A visiting fellowship at the Berlin Institute for Cultural Inquiry deepened my thinking on gender and Marxism, and a National Humanities Center summer residency made it possible for me to collect important archival materials. The final stage of manuscript revision was supported by a fellowship at the Radcliffe Institute for Advanced Study at Harvard University in 2021–22.

Introduction

PERIODIZING THE

POST-1989 WORLD ORDER

The year 1990 is remembered by many as the annus mirabilis of queer theory. In addition to the publication of Judith Butler's *Gender Trouble*, David M. Halperin's *One Hundred Years of Homosexuality*, and Eve Kosofsky Sedgwick's *Epistemology of the Closet*, 1990 also saw Teresa de Lauretis's coinage of the term *queer theory* as the title of a conference at the University of California, Santa Cruz. But 1990 was also the year when a new economic relationship of mutual vassalage between the United States and China began to take shape, one that would eventually lead commentators to speculate, in the wake of the 2007–10 subprime mortgage crisis, that an alternative Chinese economic model called the *Beijing Consensus*—with its huge holdings of US government debt, productive capacity, and high savings rates—would enable the formerly socialist country to displace the United States as the center of global capitalism.[1] In 1989, while US academics were finalizing the inaugural texts of what would come to be known as queer theory, the rest of the world was in revolutionary fervor. With unprecedented spontaneity and scope, the 1989 Tiananmen Square demonstrations in China sent shock waves through the socialist world that catalyzed the dissolution of the Soviet Union and the Eastern bloc. In 1991 the US invasion of Iraq shattered any residual illusion that US-led capitalism could continue to expand without imperialism.

Belatedly, the crises of 1989–91 helped us realize that capitalism has always been racial capitalism—one that requires a geopolitical "outside" of differentially valued human populations and labor. If the global capitalist order seemed temporarily stable in the mid-twentieth century with a mass-consumption market backed up by US military hegemony, by the birth year of queer theory it had come undone by surges of antisystemic movements around the globe. The prolonged period of stagflation and decline in the rate of capitalist profit, which Robert Brenner identifies as having begun in 1965–73, induced a "flexible" mode of accumulation that relocated US capital to China and other low-wage sites for new rounds of expansion to counter the effects of underconsumption, rising production costs, and labor unrest.[2] As US workers demanded more codified protections from the modern welfare state, the flexible regime of post-Fordist production was able to counter the effects of declining profitability by turning workers in the global South into atom-ized and replaceable sources of value. With newly established subcontracting networks, US corporations outsourced the manufacturing of low-value-added products to China and transformed it into the "factory of the world."[3]

It turned out, however, that China was no ordinary factory. With its huge supply of low-cost, high-quality labor thanks to Mao Zedong-era investments in public health and mass literacy, a well-developed transportation and logis-tics infrastructure, a vast internal consumer market, and the technical know-how brought in by capitalists from Hong Kong and Taiwan, China quickly emerged as a core capitalist power in its own right and is now manufacturing products at all levels of the value chain.[4] Within a few decades of its market reforms, China became the largest single holder of US government debt and by 2020 had surpassed the United States as the world's largest recipient of foreign direct investment. In this process China has also reinvented itself from the victim of colonialism to a neocolonial power itself, boasting massive holdings in resource-rich countries in Africa and other parts of the global South. The Beijing Consensus represents global capitalism's latest mutation, with which materialist queer critics in North America have not yet caught up in their theorizations of the nexus of class- and gender-based oppression.

As both an economic beneficiary of late capitalism and a breeding ground for its new crises, China in the age of the Beijing Consensus has produced new forms of proletarianization and insurgency. After the 1989 Tiananmen Square massacre, the Chinese Communist Party under Deng Xiaoping adopted a new model of economic development designed to accelerate the accumulation of capital through the privatization of state-owned enterprises. To maintain competitiveness after China's accession to the World Trade Organization, the government sacked over forty million workers in state-owned enterprises and replaced them with migrant workers from rural China.[5] Massive labor strikes arose after the smashing of the "iron rice bowl" expelled workers from the circuit of production in China's industrial rustbelt (the northeast), while migrant workers in the export-oriented sunbelt (Guangdong) organized street protests and factory occupations against their treatment as second-class citizens.[6] As many of the displaced and dispossessed workers are women relegated to gender-specific sectors (*dagongmei*), these structural inequalities also inaugurated a renewed feminist (and, later, queer) politics that infused questions of gender and sexuality into the debates about China's neoliberal experiments. While gender- and sexuality-based minorities mobilize against the dispossessive logic of capital, other forms of organized resistance also enter the fray to reveal just how little consensus there is in the Beijing Consensus.

Despite the Chinese state's aggressive promoting of nationalism to fill the ideological vacuum left by the discrediting of Maoism, the "Chinese Dream" of the Xi Jinping era has failed to mask Beijing's exploitative and oppressive policies toward its various "souths": Hong Kong, Taiwan, Tibet, and Xinjiang (a point to which I return in chapter 4). Though diverse in causes, antisystemic movements in Hong Kong and Taiwan—from the 2014 Umbrella and Sunflower Movements to the 2019–20 Anti-Extradition Law Amendment Bill Movement—reveal social antagonisms that cannot be easily assimilated into China's "harmonious society" growth narrative. This punctuated history indicates that China's reintegration into the capitalist world economy is anything but a smooth or homogeneous process. Instead, it requires the subsumption or reordering of social relations—racialized, gendered, and sexual—that are not commonly recognized as relevant to capital accumulation. Indeed, what counts as "value" in capitalist dynamics is always governed by culturally informed assemblages of kinship, genders, and sexualities.[7] Moreover, as my analysis of China's agrarian hinterlands and engagement in Africa shows, these social relations are reproduced across geographic spaces that are excluded from generalized commodity circulation. The case of China demonstrates that capital, in its quest to produce value, requires spaces and populations that are racialized and gendered.

Through the study of China's postsocialist political economy in the age of the Beijing Consensus, *The Specter of Materialism* proposes a new theory of capital as the relentless drive to subsume and restructure relations of gender and sexuality in geopolitically segregated spaces. This book presents a history of labor struggles as well as the reconfiguration of gendered and sexual subjects—their bodily hexis, trajectories of desire, and scenes of identification—across transnational routes of accumulation and dispossession created by capital's "spatial fixes." With particular attention to capital's dispossessive power, my analysis reveals dimensions of social mediation that do not lend themselves to a multiculturalist analysis of identity-based discrimination.

The dilemmas and insurgencies of the Beijing Consensus have birthed new political discourses that are distinct from the liberal multiculturalist framework in the West. *The Specter of Materialism* is informed by new democracy theories formulated by Tiananmen dissidents, the scholarship on agrarian capitalism developed by the so-called New Left in China, Asian Marxist revisionist history of the Cold War, and queer Marxist writings associated with the inter-Asia cultural studies movement. Surprisingly, none of the foundational texts of US-based queer theory made any mention of the revolutions of 1989 or emergent forms of political radicalism from the East. Instead of giving us an updated vocabulary for political engagement and solidarity in these crisis-ridden force fields of world capitalism, queer theory—wittingly or unwittingly—promoted an image of the United States as the sole agent of its own fate.

For much of 1990s queer theory, the United States was not merely a self-contained society; it was a disembodied location. Claiming that the so-called Great Gay Migration—the postwar settlement of American GIs in coastal urban centers such as New York and San Francisco—invented a newfound homosexual identity that was not to be found anywhere else, queer theory adamantly denied the coevalness of China and America at precisely the historical moment of US capital's accelerated relocation to China in search of cheaper and more docile labor. Phrases such as "homosexuality as we understand it today" and "binary thought in the modern West" suffused early queer theory, fortifying an imaginary link among Plato's *Symposium*, the sexological writings of Magnus Hirschfeld, the Stonewall riots, and Henry James in a unilinear and self-referential history of sexuality. According to this view, homosexuality was a distinctly Western invention and a by-product of North Atlantic industrial capitalism. If homosexuals also exist in non-Western societies, they must be belated copies created by globalization or colonialism.

Queer theory's 1990s project of discovering a past historical consciousness as critique ended up naturalizing precisely what it was supposed to explain: the reproduction of power over time and in geographically discrete spaces. By divorcing the history of sexuality from the history of global capital, queer theory ended up substituting a liberal multiculturalist ethics of difference for a systemic analysis of the institutions and apparatuses that produce these exclusions in the first place. But the particular way China entered the world of global capital presents an opportunity for queer theory to develop a more analytically precise vocabulary (and politics) for deciphering the matrix of gendered life and political economy. As a novel form of capital accumulation that dispossesses nonnormative gender and sexual subjects, the Beijing Consensus reveals both the indispensability and the limits of concepts developed by Karl Marx's critique of political economy for contemporary queer thinking on matter, materiality, and materialism.

The Specter of Materialism argues that the emergence of queer theory was not a liberal achievement, as conventional explanations of the gradual consolidation of rights-based movements and nonnormative identities in the United States typically claim. Rather, it was part and parcel of crises brought about by the contradictory developments of capitalism on a global scale. As my analysis shows, US capital's accelerated relocation to China as a solution to underconsumption and rising labor costs created the conditions for China's own neoliberal transformations and new inequalities. Liberal queer theory's inability to devise effective responses to these global crises returns as the specter of materialism, manifesting itself as persistent calls for a materialist shift from questions of representation and performativity to those of dispossession, precarity, and the differential distribution of life chances. This materialist turn presents an opportunity to dialogue more fully with Marxist scholarship in the humanities, which has evolved from a 1980s-style ideology critique of false consciousness to the analysis of capitalism's dependency on "indispensably disposable" populations who are racialized and gendered.[8] Despite these shifts, materialist queer theory has reached an apparent impasse and finds itself continuously absorbed into the liberal project of diversity management, where the concept of class is read as a static form of social advantage among others. This theoretical and political weakness, I contend, stems from queer theory's incomplete understanding of capitalism's contemporary transformations, of which China has been at the center. Through the analysis of how relations of gender and sexuality have been reconfigured or subsumed to meet the needs of capital in new regimes of accumulation and dispossession, this book offers a history of collective struggles that are at once queer and labor based. In so doing, *The Specter of Materialism* develops a new framework for understanding the nexus between queerness and material life.

This approach to materialism, which combines both economic and cultural questions, necessarily challenges the premises of more commonly seen forms of queer anticapitalist analysis, which have largely focused on empowering multiply disadvantaged (for example, working-class and nonbinary) individuals. At best, the liberal project is directed at fairly redistributing the diminishing surpluses of capital within the United States instead of seeking capitalism's demise. By contrast, a materialist theory of how capital accumulation requires and produces the hierarchical differentiation of gendered bodies has the advantage of connecting queer struggles to a broader range of international social movements.[9] The case of China provides an indispensable perspective on the reordering of capital's relation to its "constitutive outsides." To expand this framework of materialist queer analysis, I offer a wide array of historical examples of the subsumption of social differences under capital's self-reproduction, from the creation of new gendered classes and the financialization of China's rural hinterlands to philosophical debates about the analytic distinction between sex and gender that occurred in the wake of socialism's collapse in the age of the Beijing Consensus.

The Beijing Consensus

Coined in the mid-1990s and popularized by Joshua Cooper Ramo in 2004, the concept of the Beijing Consensus articulates the belief that postreform China has invented a distinct model of development that has created high-speed economic growth without sacrificing national autonomy or repudiating the global necessity of socialism.[10] Supporters of the Beijing Consensus thesis regard China's investment in South-South Cooperation programs and multilateral treaties as an alternative to Washington's America First, unilateralist foreign policy. For some, the Beijing Consensus is a continuation of the anti-imperialist project of Bandung-era tricontinentalism and a reflection that China has achieved a socialist market economy with Chinese characteristics rather than capitalism.[11] Though it is common for Western observers to treat post-1978 China as a mere variant of global neoliberalism, Chinese intellectuals argue that China is a socialist and not a capitalist country, that it is still developing within the parameters of the 1949 revolution, and that its success is a product of China's revolutionary socialism, not a consequence of its integration into the world economy.[12]

Chinese commentators criticize the equation of China's prodigious ascent in the postreform era with neoliberalism in the United Kingdom and the United States, contending that this conflation is a faulty Eurocentric interpretation of global developments.[13] They emphasize that while certain features of contemporary China superficially resemble those of a dynamic late-capitalist economy, we cannot discount that this modernity was created by a revolutionary-socialist legacy and consequently contains elements that are poorly understood and theorized by international commentators. These elements, which I consider in greater detail in chapter 1, include the land-tenure system, the three rural issues (*sannong wenti*, namely, agriculture, rural areas, and the peasantry), and the absence of a recognizable bourgeoisie and private property rights. Whether China is still (or has ever been) socialist remains a question of utmost importance that is haunting the international Left, which is struggling to formulate effective responses to problems that defy the logics of the multiculturalist toolbox. It haunts China as well, for sure, presenting a political problem that Carlos Rojas and Ralph Litzinger aptly describe as the "ghost protocol" of three mutually imbricated sets of spectral aspirations: the promises of capitalism (the ghosts of global capital), the institutional legacy of the Maoist regime (shades of Mao), and the spirit of Marxist resistance (specters of Marx).[14]

By contrast, international commentators use the term *Beijing Consensus* to characterize present-day China, alongside Russia and Iran, as the site of "authoritarian capitalism."[15] To many working in gender and sexual justice movements, the Beijing Consensus represents a form of "debt-trap diplomacy" that focuses on infrastructure deals, energy projects, and extractive industries in Africa, Latin America, and other parts of the global South as a means of expanding its capitalist power, often with devasting consequences for women and gender minorities.[16] My aim is not to adjudicate on these debates about whether China is socialist or capitalist, neocolonial or liberationist. Rather, my interest lies in theorizing the reasons these debates are imbricated in and persistently displaced by questions of gender and sexuality. Reading these narratives dialectically, I make a critical return to Marx's concept of real and formal subsumption to develop a stronger form of materialist queer theory.

Materialism, Dispossession, and the Subsumption of Labor

What is materialism? And how does it serve as a critical philosophy for global queer Marxism to move beyond the critique of surface inequalities? In the United States, the prevailing model for discussion about social justice centers on a liberal language of tolerance, respect, inclusion, and diversity, with the primary goal of creating equal educational and employment opportunities for historically underrepresented minorities. While we owe many of the most successful political agendas in recent decades to liberal critiques, the inclusion/exclusion logic focuses on reforming the culture of the stakeholders and construes the problem as the perpetuation of stereotypes at the level of thought. The concept of inclusivity sometimes obscures the material conditions underlying the systemic reproduction of social inequalities, while naturalizing an abstract notion of democracy that treats the speaking subjects as equal partners without interrogating the power relations that limit access to dialogue and condition its form.

The ubiquitous mantra "Antiracism begins with education!" is an example of the fantasy that racism, sexism, heterosexism, and assorted phobias are mere mental attitudes that devalue certain populations and cause social harm and that once we remove these attitudes by reeducating those sufficiently privileged to attend a university, we also remove all problems in society.[17] Instead of the mental attitudes of the privileged, the starting point of a materialist analysis is the agency of the oppressed. As Marx writes in the famous eleventh thesis on Ludwig Feuerbach—"the philosophers have only *interpreted* the world in various ways; the point, however, is to *change* it"—a materialist analysis shifts the conversation from a matter of language policing to the conditions of possibility for political action.[18] Before we can reform language (prejudicial or respectful, in the classroom or the streets), we must transform the material conditions that authorize certain individuals to speak, act, or write in socially legible ways.

Materialism is not synonymous with the primacy of economics. Nor does Marxism require an economic formalism that inevitably relapses into an epistemological foundationalism or intellectual orthodoxy. In the third volume of *Capital*, Marx defines capital as a specific relationship between human beings, the "immediate coalescence of the material relations of production with their historical and social specificity" that created a "bewitched, distorted and upside-down world haunted by Monsieur le Capital and Madame la Terre, who are at the same time social characters and mere things."[19] Instead of reducing human consciousness to a secondary effect of the development of historically variable modes of producing and reproducing the material requirements of everyday life, Marx describes materialism as the historical moment that constitutes the identity between object and thought, between the material relations of production and their "social specificity." This material moment is what allows capital and labor power to assume a "ghostly presence" as both social characters and mere things "at the same time." This spectral presence of capital endows the commodity form with a dual character as both use value (mere things) and exchange value (congealed social relations).

In Marx's analysis materialism does not presuppose the existence of a given set of economic facts that can lend themselves to quantitative analysis; nor does materialism suggest that economic facts possess any kind of moral preponderance over cultural issues such as gender and sexuality. Marx clearly does not see value exclusively in economic terms; rather, Marx describes capital as an "enchantment" that renders our material and social worlds indistinguishable from each other. Capital, in other words, is not simply an economic order but a kind of haunting, a structure of social relations that is legible only through its traces.[20] Precisely because capital has coalesced the material conditions of production and their "historical and social" elements into a single enchanted world, the interpretation of material life requires an account of the discursive framework of intelligibility ("historical and social specificity") that constitutes human subjects. This framework determines in advance what configurations of gender and sexuality are permitted to enter the field of politicization while others remain cultural impossibilities. In turn, this framework of intelligibility is materially sustained and reconstituted. The reproduction of our cultural norms requires the support of military, police, legal, and political economic structures that ensure the concentration of power and resources in the hands of the elite within territorially segregated zones of accumulation. To "change the world" in the materialist sense Marx describes in the eleventh thesis requires a recognition of the inseparability of economic and cultural dimensions of the human subject. Instead of economic reductionism, materialism for Marx offers an optic for interpreting—and changing—the mutual entanglements of economic structures and the prose of the enchanted world.

But Marx's seductive and powerful formulation leaves many questions unanswered. Why is capital presumed to be gendered male ("Monsieur le Capital") in this metaphor, with Earth as its female counterpart ("Madame la Terre"), and how is the gendering of human beings related to the reification and personification of capital? Does the former precede the latter? Are these processes fully autonomous or bound up with each other? Or is gender itself a reification of social relations, an illusion of substance retroactively assigned to a person's interior core through a nominalizing grammar? Is the proprietary view of gender as something that belongs to the modern possessive individual derived from capitalism and its fracturing of the social world?

In this passage Marx suggests that capital personifies in performing a form of ghost-walking as dialectically paired social characters—capitalists and laborers, revolutionaries and dictators, women and men. At the same time, a deeply exploitative relationship between the sellers of labor power and the capitalist owners of the means of production takes on the appearance of a free, transparent, and equitable relationship between things. As Marx's own enigmatic metaphors of Madame la Terre and Monsieur le Capital suggest, capitalism cannot be comprehended as a set of mathematical problems without a human subject who is gendered, racialized, and otherwise produced through discursive norms. Conversely, the conception of the human as a social relation in Marx's labor theory of value highlights the need to understand the role of material institutions and inequalities in the social production of human differences. But Marx's explanation of how human beings become things and how things become human beings is not a tautology. Rather, it is a historicist argument. From Marx's point of view, capital's simultaneous appearance as (gendered) social characters and mere things is the consequence of a historical development of primitive accumulation, which resulted in the "immediate coalescence of the material relations of production with their historical and social specificity." Though this coalescence is "immediate," its phenomenological appearance is "mediated" (bewitched, distorted, and upside down).

This paradox we have seen in the passage quoted from the third volume of *Capital* has far-reaching implications for how we read the contradiction between formal and real subsumption that Marx discusses in the so-called unpublished sixth chapter of the first volume of *Capital*, "Results of the Immediate Process of Production" (hereafter "Results").[21] Formal subsumption (*formale Subsumption*) is Marx's theory of the materiality of the encounter between capital's self-expansion and precapitalist relations. By contrast, real subsumption (*reale Subsumption*) is the full socialization of labor powers into the technological system of increased productivity and scientific management. In the *Economic Manuscripts of 1861–63*, where the concepts were first introduced, Marx writes, "Historically, in fact, at the start of its formation, we see capital take under its control (subsume under itself) not only the labour process in general but the specific actual labour processes as it finds them available in the existing technology, and in the form in which they have developed on the basis of non-capitalist relations of production. . . . [A]t the beginning it only subsumes it *formally*, without making any changes in its specific technological character."[22] Formal subsumption of labor under capital occurs when a preexisting labor process—such as handicraft labor or small-scale self-sustaining peasant farming—is brought within capital's valorization process but the labor process is not actually transformed by it. For contemporary queer theory, the power of Marx's reading lies in the insight that the capitalist mode of production does not create its own conditions of reproduction ex nihilo. Instead, capital meets, subsumes, and reconfigures preexisting temporalities—relations of production and property, gendered hierarchies, and kinship—without creating a homogeneous world. This incorporation indirectly changes the quality, intensity, and purpose of the labor process without changing its underlying personal relations of domination and dependence.

Subsumption is not the same as incorporation or integration. It also means being made disposable, appearing irrelevant to the development of capitalism. Earlier interpretations of the Marxian distinction between formal and real subsumption tended to cast it as referring to a historical transition brought about by technical innovations and corresponding to the distinction between absolute and relative surplus.[23] In "Results," however, Marx makes clear that real and formal subsumption should be understood as two aspects of the same process because capitalist incorporation requires the homogenization of infinitely varied human subjects and, conversely, the transformation of labor power into a social hieroglyphic. Marx begins this section by noting that what appears to be the "immediate" process of capitalist production is in fact a delayed temporality and a form of "mediation," "always an indissoluble union of labor process and valorization process."[24] The labor process is the moment when labor power produces additional value over and above its own value. Although this surplus value is created during the process of production, first it has to be realized through the valorization process, the sale of commodities, before capital can appropriate it for its self-expansion and reconstitution.

In both the labor process and the valorization process, mediated social relations—gendered, racialized, or geopolitical differences—are reified as objective or "immediate" conditions. Though the labor process involves the transformation of material goods, it is also the objectification of a specific quantum of what Marx calls "socially necessary labor" and the expression of a specific social relationship. While emphasizing the social, irreducibly human, character of the labor process, Marx also reminds us that the valorization process takes place outside the immediate site of production—in the market. "The valorization process . . . never enters the product materially in the form of its own use-value."[25] As such, the valorization process requires "the capitalist's ability to supervise and enforce discipline" over labor to ensure that its products exceed the value of what reenters the production process as variable capital (objectified living labor) and constant capital (buildings and machinery).[26]

This conception of capitalist production as the formal subsumption of delayed temporalities and the reification of human (subjective) and nonhuman (objective) conditions is essential to Marx's thinking. Marx accuses bourgeois economists of having "made the blunder of confusing the elementary forms of capital, money and commodities, with capital as such" precisely because they see capitalism as an accounting problem that requires only an economic formalism.[27] Indeed, one of capital's effects is that value is made to appear to originate directly from the productive process rather than from the social domain. By contrast, Marx emphasizes the importance of understanding materialism as the unity of the immediate production process and what transpires outside or prior to it: the production of human subjectivity: "On the one hand, we find the material means of production, the *objective* conditions of production, and on the other hand, the active capacities for labour, labour-power expressing itself purposively: the *subjective* condition of labour."[28]

Instead of describing a formal economic problem, Marx in "Results" develops a theory of the human subject. If the production process, as Marx explains it, entails both material labor and the reproduction of the relations of production, it follows that Marx's theory already contains a framework for reading gender and sexual differences in the reconstitution of the human subject in capitalist relations of production. Indeed, this point is the basis of Louis Althusser's concept of interpellation—widely cited by queer theorists— in the essay where he identifies the family, the media, and culture as among the ideological state apparatuses capital requires to reproduce its own conditions of production.[29]

In Michael Hardt and Antonio Negri's rereading of Marx, the notions of formal and real subsumption are understood to refer to a historical transition within postmodern capitalism, when capital evolves from a hegemonic ideology to the full extractive industry of the earth and its ecosystem, immaterial ideas, and social institutions: "In the phase of real subsumption, capital no longer has an outside. . . . All productive processes arise within capital itself and thus the production and reproduction of the entire social world take place within capital."[30] As early as the 1930s, Chinese Marxist theorists already refuted this interpretation of the distinction between real and formal subsumption as referring to chronologically conceived stages. Wang Yanan, a non-Communist Marxist economist, argued that 1930s China instantiated a particular historical moment of capitalism in its semicolonial form. Instead of employing a stable definition of what capitalism ought to be, Wang insisted that China's semicolonial situation demanded a revision of the definition of capitalism itself. In other words, Wang understood China's semicolonialism as a regime of formal (as opposed to real) subsumption, a necessity in the history of capital's primitive accumulation on a global scale rather than capitalism's distorted path of nondevelopment.[31]

Building on the work of Wang and other Asian Marxists including Yamada Moritarō and Uno Kōzō, Harry Harootunian has recently argued that capitalism has never achieved the real subsumption of social totality across the globe. Rejecting the conception of the commodity form as an all-encompassing structuring force of thought, Harootunian warns against the conception of the notions of formal and real subsumption as historical stages created by technical progress. In particular, Harootunian rejects theories of a time lag that identify unevenness as a sign of backwardness and collective underdevelopment.[32] Instead of stagism, Harootunian finds it more useful to read Marx's notions of formal and real subsumption as the coexistence of production relations and reciprocal exploitation. As Rosa Luxemburg did before him, Harootunian emphasizes that capital accumulation always requires an outside. For Harootunian, Marx's concept of formal subsumption provides a framework for comprehending capitalism as the copresence of different temporalities instead of seeing it as a completed totality, "a way to reinvest the historical text with the figure of contingency and the unanticipated appearance of conjunctural or aleatory moments" in order to understand "the coexistence of different economic practices in certain moments and the continuing persistence of historical temporal forms, rather than merely 'remnants,' from earlier modes in new historical environments."[33] My work explores the implications of this thesis for materialist queer theory. Instead of situating China as capitalism's premodern form or its historical negation, this rich scholarship on formal subsumption in East Asian Marxist theory from Wang Yanan to his contemporary interpreters demonstrates the value of rethinking the motions of global capitalism from its margins.[34]

Arc of This Book's Arguments

The Specter of Materialism contributes to this debate through a consideration of the subsumption of various social formations that are both geographically racialized and gender/sexuality based. While Marxism, far from being a thoughtless universalism inattentive to local histories, has already developed a compelling case for why the analysis of capitalism needs East Asia, the theories of capital's constitutive outside need to be augmented by a fuller consideration of gender and sexuality. To that end, in this study I offer an analysis of three different forms of subsumption in China's capitalist transformations: those of literature, the Cold War, and gender.

The first two chapters of this book outline the theoretical stakes. Chapter 1, "Alterity in Queer Theory and the Political Economy of the Beijing Consensus," offers a contrastive reading of early 1990s queer theory's concept of the constitutive outside and contemporary Marxist analyses of postsocialist China's constitutive outside (in the forms of gender and sexual minorities and the rural-urban divide). My aim is to establish, in the clearest terms possible, the crucial difference between liberal queer theory's and international Marxism's approaches to materialism and the ethics of otherness. While queer theory utilizes hypotheses of gender variance in the noncapitalist world to reveal the constructedness of "homosexuality as we understand it today," I turn to Marxism to develop an account of capitalism as a moving totality that, in the context of the restructuring of US-Asian labor relations, led to the financialization of China's agrarian hinterlands, the creation of a novel hegemony and South-South Cooperation programs, and the privatization of socialist institutions. Under these conditions, new classes of gender and sexuality—such as *dagongmei* (female migrant laborers in China's export-oriented sunbelt), money boys (rural-to-urban sex workers), and high-*suzhi* (quality) transnational queers—emerged as part of the new politics of human value.

This analysis lays the groundwork for the discussion of the intellectual trajectories of queer theory's own encounters with materialisms in the next chapter, "The Specter of Materialism." Here I consider various historical attempts to synthesize queer theory and Marxism since the 1990s and their limits. While some critics seek to update the concept of production through Michel Foucault's biopolitics, others focus on intersectional analysis of overlapping and convergent fields of power and conditions of vulnerability. Collectively, and despite their intellectual differences, these projects reveal contemporary queer theory's desire to develop a materialist perspective after many years of being associated with the so-called linguistic turn in the humanities. The specter of materialism is an enabling kind of haunting, one that keeps us on our toes, worrying productively about the best way to stay true to the radically anticipatory and anti-identitarian orientation of early queer theory. Through a close reading of an emblematic example, the trajectory of Judith Butler's thought from *Gender Trouble* (1990) and *Bodies That Matter* (1993) to *The Force of Nonviolence* (2020), I argue that queer theory, even in those moments when it has emphatically disavowed materialism, remains ineluctably in materialism.

The second part of the book examines three historical cases of capital's subsumption of social differences to develop a perspective on queer theory's future materialization and dialogues with Marxism. Chapter 3, "The Subsumption of Literature: Lu Xun's Queer Modernism in the Chinese Revolutions," focuses on Lu Xun as a historical example of how forms of queer subjectivity have been erased in the accumulation of capital. Both inside and outside China, Lu Xun's life and work have been equated with the birth of Chinese Marxism. In the contemporary period, scholars in debates about the Beijing Consensus continuously turn to Lu Xun for a renewed understanding of China's revolutionary spirit and its socialist past (or future). My analysis intervenes in these debates, recasting Lu Xun's literary project as a queer modernism that was forgotten and repressed in the historiography of China's transition from socialism to the age of the Beijing Consensus. The subsumption of literature entails the selective remembering of Lu Xun's queer subjects despite their central role in his critical realist representation of China's violent incorporation into the capitalist world system and the creation of an ever-growing disposable population.

While chapter 3 uncovers the queer roots of a Marxist icon, chapter 4 restores to view the material contexts of a queer icon. These two chapters form a chiasmic pair of readings of the mutual embeddedness of queer struggles and the material conditions of history. "The Subsumption of the Cold War: The Material Unconscious of Queer Asia" explains why the Cold War was a crucial phase of capital accumulation in Asia and hence a Marxist question. The chapter's central argument is that ethnic tensions were created by the Cold War in Asia, and this regime of social apartheid is what keeps China's manufacturing workforce immobilized and the influx of capital from Taiwan and Hong Kong afloat. Grounded in a Marxist reading of political economy, this chapter examines the making of *Swordsman II*, the first mainstream Chinese-language film featuring a transgender character, as an example of how the economic and political contradictions of the Cold War are transformed into narratives of sexual autonomy and postcolonial liberation. Consequently, I argue that the Cold War in Asia is not over—rather, it has been transformed and subsumed. Following the arguments put forth by Asian Marxist critics including Kuan-Hsing Chen, Wang Hui, and Dai Jinhua, I redefine the Cold War as an enduring "problematic of the present," an emotional structure that continues to shape the contours of popular culture, academic discourse, and queer identity formations in ways of which we are not always fully conscious. With this reading I propose a reconceptualization of the Cold War as a materialist methodology for the study of sinophone gender and sexual cultures.

The third and final case study of the book, chapter 5, "The Subsumption of Sexuality: Translating Gender from the Beijing Fourth World Conference on Women to the Beijing Consensus," explores how sexuality has been erased from view in China's public discourse. This is certainly true at the level of the Chinese state, which is invested in gender-mainstreaming policies in part because such policies provide legitimacy for Chinese leadership in South-South Cooperation programs and capitalist ventures overseas. But my analysis shows that this erasure also comes from civil society–based feminists who understand their work to be antithetical to the aims of the state. I argue that these efforts are inflected by the contradictions of China's uneven incorporation into world capitalism. I trace this erasure or subsumption through an examination of how Chinese feminists and policy makers translated the analytic *distinction* between sex and gender. Through an account of these concepts' travel across boundaries of culture and economic formations, I also make a case for the importance of Chinese theories of sex/gender for anglophone and transnational feminisms.

The Specter of Materialism grew out of my second book, *Queer Marxism in Two Chinas* (2015), and it was written in response to the valuable criticisms and suggestions of its many readers, in particular those requesting a clearer exposition of the theoretical framework that I began to develop there. While my previous monograph focused on queer Marxism as an intellectual practice, the present study foregrounds the history of labor struggles and the contradictions between capital's self-expansion and forms of social life. With particular attention to the concept of the constitutive outside, I develop a new perspective on the subsumption of sexual difference under capital's self-reproduction in the service of an augmented materialist queer theory.

This book was written in dialogue with the exciting and rapidly growing body of literature on queer anticapitalism, which includes the works of Kevin Floyd, Alan Sears, Jules Joanne Gleeson, Holly Lewis, and Peter Drucker. But two objectives distinguish my approach from the existing scholarship. The first is to expand our archive of intellectual references and historical examples for a more global conversation about queer Marxism. In so doing, I aim to show that the United States—the site to which queer theory imagines itself to have been indigenous—is not the globalizer but part of the globalized world. My second objective is to offer a new kind of materialist queer theory grounded in a historical understanding of capital. Put differently, this book is an endeavor to rework the methodologies of queer theory through a decentered perspective on the history of global capitalism. Analyzing capital as a dispossessive logic on a global scale rather than as a matter of wealth inequalities or class identities, I offer an alternative to the critiques of pinkwashing or homonationalism in currently available forms of queer anticapitalist analysis. With this theoretical framework, my hope is that *The Specter of Materialism* will contribute to the collective labor of reimagining new modes of political solidarity and transformation beyond what progressive liberalism has taught us.

PART
I

Theory

Alterity in Queer Theory and the Political Economy of the Beijing Consensus

Haunted by Materialism

We live in a queer time when being queer is no longer queer enough. Academic conferences and publications clustering around topics of "What is queer about queer studies now?" "what is left of queer," "after queer theory," or "after sex—on writing since queer theory" suggest either the demise of the field or a conviction in the usefulness of its remains. In the case of the latter, the consensus seems to be that what is left (in the double sense of what is left-wing and what remains) of queer theory must be radicalized through reengagement with materialist questions such as racial oppression and distributive justice. Instead of single-themed approaches to lesbian and gay history or cultures, we now find an increasing number of intersectional studies situating queerness in contexts as diverse as anti-Black racism, assisted reproductive technologies in the global South, the rise of humanitarian security regimes, crip resistance to austerity politics, and the neoliberal logic of homonationalism. By adopting a host of materialist concepts—including the neoliberal state, the maldistribution of life chances, and the global precariat—contemporary queer theory is calling for a new political optic for understanding the intersectionality of gender antinormativity and material stratification.

Though 1990s queer theory was generally perceived as the reflection of a linguistic turn in the humanities, in fact the study of gender and sexuality has always been ineluctably haunted by materialism. Contemporary queer theory is imbued with an ever greater sense of urgency that this antinormative project must evolve from the linguistic deconstruction of gender norms to a collective transformation of the existing systems that produce these constructions, or make certain constructions count more than others, in the first place. The crisis-ridden post-2008 era supplied palpable evidence that progressive queer theory wants to be more materialist. Increasingly, new scholarly projects are bringing questions of political economy and the state back into a conversation that was once dominated by a hermeneutics of suspicion crafted in the post-structuralist idioms of deconstruction and psychoanalysis. Yet queer critiques of neoliberal capitalism rarely address key Marxist concepts such as abstract labor, expanded reproduction, the organic composition of capital, the falling rate of profit, the transformation problem, or primitive accumulation. To the extent that queer theory glances worriedly at class, it conducts its anti-capitalist critique mostly through a moralizing language against privilege or discrimination. In other words, though new queer theory declares itself to be materialist, it has more in common with mainstream progressive liberalism than Marxism. Consequently, the focus of contemporary queer anticapital-ist analysis remains more centered on denouncing US corporate greed and reified desire than on understanding capitalism as the subsumption of labor in the global South. If Marxism has remained an underutilized resource in the current critical scene of queer anticapitalist thought, the revolutionary experience and Marxist theories of China's "actually existing socialism"—as well as the way the formerly socialist country became the world's second-largest capitalist economy today—are simply forgotten. *Neoliberal capital-ism* is a phrase that trips easily off the tongue. But without a theory of the geographic process of capital accumulation and dispossession, it has served more polemical than analytic purposes in queer theory.

The difference between a liberal critique of capitalism (understood as wealth inequalities) and a Marxist critique of capitalism (understood as pro-cess) could not have been clearer. Consider, for example, the 2017 special issue of *TSQ* (*Transgender Studies Quarterly*) on what the guest editors, Dan Irving and Vek Lewis, refer to as "Trans- Political Economy."[1] In the "General Editors' Introduction," Paisley Currah and Susan Stryker describe the special issue as demonstrating that "the production of vulnerability in racialized and colonized gender-nonconforming populations is not accidental but *integral* to capitalism . . . from the commodification of a legible minoritizing trans identity in asylum claims . . . to the affective yet marginalized labor demanded of some trans people in the Global South."[2] But how, exactly, does the production of vulnerability (in the social sense) relate to the production of value (in the capitalist sense)? How does the expansion of capital into the global South require a working-class consciousness that posits itself as white, heterosexual, and cisgender? How does the capitalist class respond to declining profitability by developing new financial instruments that shackle the working class in the global North with debt and induce the displacement of agrarian populations in the global South? How does the incorporation of gendered subjects in the global South impact the fragility of small-scale village livelihoods through the melding of financial arrangements such as pensions, insurance, credit, and debt?[3] While the concept of "trans political economy" implicitly raises these questions, the special issue does not answer them. None of the contributors explain how capitalism (or trans political economy) works as a *system* through the valorization of value-forming labor. Instead, what is meant by *capitalism* in these essays seems to be consumerism, namely, the problem that corporations and the entertainment industries are bombarding us with subliminal messages to trick us into buying things we do not need while disseminating normalized images of gay, lesbian, trans, and disabled people to recruit an expanding range of populations into the productive flow of the national economy.

In the special issue on trans political economy, for example, Emmanuel David, in "Capital T," offers a compelling analysis of the cultural commodification of transgender. David observes several related developments: the recent rise of transgender-specific products and consumer markets; the emergence of trans-specific workforces, including those that promote trans employees as a brandable form of value; and social enterprise companies that target trans entrepreneurs. In another piece, "Drag Race to the Bottom?," Cory G. Collins examines the profitability of the popular American reality television show *RuPaul's Drag Race* to delineate the political economy of the drag industry. In "The Afterlife of Data," Lars Z. Mackenzie discusses the experience of trans people who changed their names on credit reports and rental housing applications as a way of illustrating the complex logics of neoliberal capitalism. While these analyses yield valuable insights, the phenomena described here—the assimilation of a previously devalued population into the mainstream media, the workforce, and the consumer and housing markets—could very well have taken place in any society, capitalist or not.

As we know from the first volume of Karl Marx's *Capital*, although generalized commodity exchange (defined by the formula commodity-money-commodity) is a precondition for capitalism, it is not itself capitalism (defined by the formula money-commodity-money). Marx contends that while capitalism requires the commodification of labor, the latter does not imply the former: "[The subsumption of labor under capital] is the general form of every capitalist process of production; at the same time, however, it can be found as a *particular* form alongside the specifically capitalist mode of production in its developed form, because although the latter entails the former, the converse does not necessarily obtain [i.e., the formal subsumption can be found in the absence of the specifically capitalist mode of production]."[4] But for new progressive theorists of trans political economy, an understanding of capital as a geographically determinate cycle of accumulation and dispossession is not needed because wage labor, gender, and sexuality are treated as analogous themes in a multiculturalist force field of struggles. A focus on the interpellation and co-optation of trans subjects displaces the analysis of capital, creating a thematic approach to class that results in a missed opportunity to dialogue more fully with Marxist value-form theory.

New materialist queer theory's lack of attention to Marxist theories of value is not a simple result of intellectual siloization. A recurring trope in 1990s queer theory is that Marxism has treated race, gender, and sexuality as "merely cultural" questions of secondary importance to class struggles; in so doing, it is claimed, Marxism has installed a deterministic, totalizing view of history at the expense of unmeasurable particularities. Moreover, there is no scholarly consensus that Marxism is or should be a materialism.[5] With queer theory's materialist turn, however, a parallel development has occurred in Marxist approaches to literature and cultural criticism. In the wake of resurgent crises of unemployment, permanent war, racialized violence, disinvestment in the humanities, and ecological disasters, Marxist literary criticism in the years between the Gulf War and the 2008 financial crisis made a distinctive shift from the critique of capitalism as reified desire to a materialist analysis of capitalism as a translocal mode of value production.[6]

Renewed interest in value-form theory makes it possible to reorient Marxist criticism from moral outcries against the unequal distribution of capital's surpluses in the global North to the analysis of capitalism as a relentless drive to subsume the labor process in the global South. This key insight into how capital requires noncapitalist and noneconomic relations for its expanded reproduction, as my analysis of the subsumption of gender and sexuality in the age of the Beijing Consensus shows throughout this book, allows us to understand the restructuring of gendered dispositions, worldviews, and subjectivities as the basis of the contemporary capitalist order. This understanding provides a materialist form of queer Marxism that can serve as an alternative to analytic models that are more focused on surface inequalities, as seen in certain versions of critiques of pink-dollar (and purple-dollar) capitalism, neoliberal pinkwashing, or queerbaiting.

To bring into sharper focus the distinction between liberal and Marxist approaches, I offer a contrastive reading of two different concepts of alterity in the following sections of this chapter. The first type of alterity, the concept of the constitutive outside, forms the basis of a mode of analysis that I term *allochronic queer criticism*. Allochronism, as Johannes Fabian defines it, is the denial of coevalness, the insistent reading of coexisting human cultures as belonging to or embodying different temporalities.[7] Allochronic arguments in queer theory cast the Other in terms of what appears to be missing in comparison to the speaker's own culture and place that subject in another time—prequeer or protoqueer, precapitalist or Asiatic. In the 1990s, queer theorists habitually turned to the non-Western world in search of examples of gender variance in order to reveal the constructedness of what Eve Kosofsky Sedgwick called "homosexuality as we understand it today."[8]

Over the years this concept of the constitutive outside has lost its allure, and queer theory has become a transnational dialogue between languages and knowledge paradigms. Whereas 1990s allochronic criticism turned to the global South for *examples*, transnational queer theory in the age of the Beijing Consensus turns to the global South for *epistemologies*. Unlike earlier efforts to historicize the invention of homosexuality through speculations about its absence in non-Western cultures, transnational queer theory has come to question the terms that constitute the first-person plural in "homosexuality as we understand it today," asking why earlier writers have simply accepted that the "we" must unproblematically refer to the white Euro-American male, and how the construction of the West as a coherent and knowable category is accomplished through the exclusion of other languages and locations. Abandoning the vexing question of queer theory's or homosexuality's cross-cultural applicability, transnational scholars ask what queer studies can learn from the perspectives of those working and living in the global South. Though some scholars think of queer theory as a Euro-American project and describe the work of queer scholars in nonanglophone languages as translation, appropriation, or resistance, in fact the conceptual boundaries of queer theory are constantly expanded and revised by the historical experiences and cultural institutions of the global South.[9]

The second type of alterity considered here derives from recent Marxist arguments that the political economy of postsocialist China emerged through the reconstitution of social relations that are not, strictly speaking, capitalist. I argue that the history of labor struggles in China reveals that capital cannot accumulate without a constitutive outside, and that "outside" is both socially differentiated (marked by gender and sexuality) and geographically segregated (China's agrarian hinterland and its investment in extractive industries in Africa and other parts of the global South). The case of China provides a perspective that is largely absent in queer-materialist critiques of homonationalism and neoliberal capitalism. Because value production is geographically dispersed and temporally delayed, it is not always identical to what one can "see" as visible inequalities. The Beijing Consensus calls for an examination of global capitalism as a form of interstate competitive accumulation based on the coercive synchronization of different forms of wage and unwaged labor. The accumulation of capital by dispossession does not take place across undifferentiated spaces, bodies, and genders. Rather, it does so by grounding immobilized, racialized, and gendered subjects in territorially segregated and splintered spaces. The political doctrine of the Beijing Consensus emerges in this conjuncture of China's capitalist transformation, providing an ideological basis to support the geographic segregation of multiple capitals for competitive purposes while creating nationalist sentiments to bind each nation's working class to the specific needs of its capital.

While 1990s queer theory conceived of the sexual organizations of non-Western, "tribal" societies as an alterity to the Western invention of homosexuality, I turn to Marxism to develop an account of capitalism as a moving totality. As my analysis in the following pages shows, the restructuring of US-Asian labor relations led to the financialization of China's agrarian hinterlands, the creation of a novel hegemony and South-South Cooperation programs, and the privatization of socialist institutions. These new conditions created new classes of gender and sexuality, including female migrant laborers, rural-to-urban sex workers, and high-*suzhi* (quality) transnational queers as part of a new politics of human value, while China's economic expansion in Africa through resource-backed loans reconfigured notions of race, masculinity, and cultural membership.

With attention to the imbrication of gender and political economy in these examples, I demonstrate how a Marxist analysis of the Beijing Consensus provides useful tools for new materialist queer theory and a less cannibalistic ethics of otherness. By adopting a more historical understanding of capitalism's reproduction on a global scale, queer theory can immunize itself against the logic of liberal inclusion that frames cultural productions in the noncapitalist world as counterexamples to Western notions of gender, sex, and sexuality.[10] Conversely, my approach shows why Marxism cannot be limited to the analysis of relations of production and property. As queer theory of materialism shows, bodies become matter (including the object of capital) only through the mediation of gendered and sexual regimes of power. Never simply an economic structure or policy, capitalism produces a form of compulsion that mediates gendered and racialized life.

Queer Theory's Constitutive Outside

Queer theory is broadly understood as a critical project that denaturalizes heteronormative and cisnormative assumptions in the workings of culture. Despite the enormous growth of nonbinary identities such as genderqueer in recent years, *queer* in queer theory is neither an umbrella term for all forms of nonconforming gender and sexual expressions nor yet another mode of self-identification.[11] Rather, queer is a material reminder of one's relation to an unequal structure of power and a sign of linguistic humility, a way of taking stock of the necessary gap between the horizons of human cognition and the actual diversity of bodies, identities, and sexual practices in human cultures. The term *queer* allows us to acknowledge that the world is a much more complex and mysterious place than we ever thought possible. This conception of queer as a placeholder for a collective historical subject-in-process highlights the problems of cultural comparison, linguistic translation, and political community. Geopolitics is not merely implied here. It is constitutive of this understanding of *queer*, destabilizing the sovereignty of the knowing subject in the global North and placing it instead within a material structure of coexisting but asymmetrical worlds.

Queer does not describe something that already exists; instead, it inaugurates a certain kind of future of intelligibility for beings who are not yet available for description and political mobilization.[12] On the basis of this insight, queer theory argues that all identity categories are necessarily partial and incomplete. Identities are constituted by that which cannot be known or defined in advance—what queer theorists refer to as the subject's "constitutive outside."[13] Queer theory, unlike positivist forms of gay and lesbian studies, begins with the acknowledgment that one cannot define the terms of a political project in advance.[14] For Lauren Berlant and Michael Warner, the political efficacy of queer is derived from precisely the term's resistance to definition: "Because almost everything that can be called queer theory has been radically anticipatory, trying to bring a world into being, any attempt to summarize it now will be violently partial."[15] Rather than suggesting that gender is fluid or freely chosen, queer theory begins with the recognition that all social beings are constituted differentially through exclusions that return to haunt those subjects through democratic contestations.

The emergence of transgender discourse in queer theory, unanticipated by those writing in the 1990s, serves as a clear example of how arguments and analytics that once belonged to a different discursive context are themselves subject to resignification and part of a field of incessant political struggles and transformation. As I show further in chapter 5, the analytic distinction between sex and gender, originally formulated to dispute biologically deterministic explanations of women's subordination, has taken on an entirely different meaning in transgender theory and social movements seeking to decouple a person's sex assignment at birth from their future gender identity. At the same time, theories of intersectionality, women-of-color feminisms, and transnational feminisms have all developed their own theses of gender variability to contest the myth of the universal woman. The ways in which women-of-color, lesbian, transgender, nonbinary, and gender-nonconforming subjects have all come to trouble the notion of gender bear witness to both the limitations and the achievements of queer as an anti-identitarian category.

These developments in contemporary theory, which I trace back to Marx's analysis of the contradiction between the formal and real subsumptions of the useful body, arise from early queer theory's understanding that human subjects become legible only through a relation of alterity to their constitutive outside. This recognition requires a form of definitional incoherence and semantic openness that transforms into a productive failure. Queer theory's poststructuralist orientation produces a conviction that, contrary to certain structuralist and psychoanalytic views of the subject as necessarily emerging through a dyadic structure of sexual differentiation, it is always possible and even necessary to change the subject.[16] Queer is hence not a preexisting identity or set of identities but a futurity that furnishes possibilities for acts of resistance and resignification.[17] As a political imagination that orients one to a future that is yet to be crafted, queer has much in common with the global explosion of antisystemic struggles in the 1960s socialist world, from the Cultural Revolution to the Prague Spring—what Christopher Connery once described as "the foregrounding of new time, a time toward futurity."[18] For some, queer provides an alternative method for archiving the past; for others, queer offers an invitation to a futurity that reworks and contests our present paradigms.[19] For the theorists of futurity, queer articulates a form of collective refusal and "poetry from the future" against the "unequal calculus of visibility distribution" grounded in the logics of racial capitalism.[20] "We are not yet queer," José Esteban Muñoz told us in *Cruising Utopia*, "but we can feel it as the warm illumination of a horizon imbued with potentiality."[21] For Muñoz, whose thinking on this matter was informed by the Marxist philosopher Ernst Bloch, the historical accumulation of queer deaths translates into a composite that is both an unspeakable loss and a utopian desire for imagining a different future. And like Bloch before him, Muñoz insisted that the creation of concrete utopias requires a historical consciousness of capitalism's contradictions. This insight led Muñoz to define cruising utopia as "a backward glance that enacts a future vision."[22]

The notion of the constitutive outside has proved to be indispensable for queer critiques of the mutual implications of marked and unmarked categories of gender. This theory shows that abjection is produced by violent exclusions that secure normative identities. Monique Wittig, for example, has argued that lesbians are not women because they are outside the political economy of heterosexuality.[23] For Wittig, lesbianism functions as the constitutive outside of heterosexuality, creating an instability inherent within any monolithic understanding of gender. Hence, Wittig concluded that there is only one sex: the feminine, because the masculine is not a gender but the general.

Judith Butler's *Gender Trouble* offers the authoritative parsing of Wittig's thought and other French poststructuralist feminist theories on this point. Butler contrasts Wittig's position (there is only one sex—the feminine) with that of Luce Irigaray, who argued that there is only one sex (the male sex) because women are the "sex which is not one."[24] Within a phallogocentric language, women are the sex that cannot be thought, a linguistic absence. Both women and men are always already marked as masculine, and the symmetry between Same and Other is only an optical illusion of the masculine economy of univocal signification.[25] These are powerful claims. But what happens when we turn this analysis of the marked and the unmarked on queer theory's own relation to the non-West? Can we say that liberal queer theory's efforts to include, represent, and explain non-Western sexualities as alterities to "homosexuality as we understand it" produce an optical illusion of diversity within an economy of univocal signification?[26] Is it possible that, within a Foucauldian taxonomy of sexualities, both Western homosexuality and non-Western gender variance are projections of the same concept, while the actual history of the non-West remains an aporia that cannot be thought, a linguistic absence? What happens when we consider how queer theory itself is constituted through the exclusions of non-Western histories and cultures that return to haunt a global history of sexuality as demanded by developments in contemporary capitalism?

For all its exposure of heterosexuality's passing as the natural order of things, queer theory has not critically reflected on the construction of the West as a disembodied location. While queer theory has developed a compelling account of the failure of all linguistic efforts to capture the definitional and experiential complexities of the gendered subject, critics fail to acknowledge that queer theory itself is constituted through a relation of alterity to a world created by the uneven accumulation of capital. Queer theory's critique of the invisibly naturalized asymmetry of value assignment between hetero- and homosexual lives has not been extended to a critique of the asymmetry of knowledge systems between anglophone and nonanglophone cultures. This lack of reflection has resulted in a problematic view of Western organizations of gender and sexuality as the default basis of queer theory, from which viewpoint one then seeks to extend visibility and recognition to an imagined "gender pluralism" of noncapitalist societies. Searching for "great paradigm shifts" in a global history of sexuality risks assimilating the Other as an anthropological specimen in the speaker's own frame of reference, which is enriched and expanded but not altered in the process.

While queer theory addresses how certain bodies fail to materialize as a consequence of their exclusion from culturally available ideals of embodiment, the cultural variability thesis equivocates between anthropological incommensurability and gender heterogeneity. It is not always clear whether the notion of the constitutive outside refers to the internal contradictions within heteronormative understandings of gender or to the view that gender categories are context dependent and therefore perpetually haunted by definitions that are literally—that is, geographically and linguistically—outside the speaker's own horizons of cognizance. Indeed, non-Western sexualities (the constitutive outside in the second sense) are too often projected as the "unimagined communities" of prequeer populations in order to deconstruct unitary and heteronormative notions of gender (the constitutive outside in the first sense).

Allochronic queer theory of the 1990s relied on accounts of premodern sexual practices (pederasty) as well as modern non-Western subjects of sexuality (*hijra*, *travesti*, berdache, *tongzhi*, *muxes*, and *kathoey*) for demonstrating the constructedness of Western understandings of homosexuality. Thus conflated with the prehistory of Euro-American notions of homosexuality, non-Western subjects of desire have served as the constitutive outside of US-based queer theory. As David M. Halperin acknowledges, "Constructionist discourse about the modernity of sexuality and the historicity of pre-modern sexual formations often has the effect of aligning marginal or non-standard sexual practices in post-industrial liberal societies with dominant sexual practices in developing nations, thereby perpetuating the hoary colonialist notion that non-European cultures represent the cultural childhood of modern Europe."[27] To avoid viewing sex as a transhistorical category, queer theorists strive to historicize sex; this historicization inevitably adopts an evolutionary narrative akin to Marxist stagism.[28] Indeed, much of early queer theory was founded on the social constructionist thesis that heterosexuality was not natural but invented. As Michel Foucault puts it in *The History of Sexuality*, "The sodomite had been a temporary aberration; the homosexual was now a species."[29] The importance of Foucault's speciation argument cannot be overstated, as it has provided the basis of constructionist histories of sexuality developed by Arnold Davidson, Ian Hacking, George Chauncey, Halperin, and many others.[30] Toward the end of *The History of Sexuality*, Foucault further characterizes sex as a "fictitious unity" and a "causal principle" that makes it "possible to group together, in an artificial unity, anatomical elements, biological functions, conducts, sensations, and pleasures."[31] Foucault bases his argument about the arbitrary nature of sex as a category on the distinction between the West and the non-West, which he refers to as the culture of *scientia sexualis* and the culture of *ars erotica*, respectively: "On the one hand, . . . China, Japan, India, Rome, and Arabo-Moslem societies . . . endowed themselves with an *ars erotica*. . . . Our civilization possesses no *ars erotica*. In return, it is undoubtedly the only civilization to practice a *scientia sexualis*."[32]

Two broad implications of Foucault's speciation argument dominated queer theory in the 1990s. First, Foucault believes that homosexuality was invented in and by the West and implies that Christianity (described through concepts such as the incitement to discourse, the hermeneutics of the self, pastoral power, and the confessing animal) was historically necessary for this development. Indeed, what Foucault means by the societies of *ars erotica* (China, Japan, India, Rome, and Arabo-Moslem groups) is simply code for non-Christian societies.[33] Second, since the homo-/heterosexual definition was arbitrary rather than universal, there must be other cultures in the world that do not conform to this taxonomy. The social constructionist thesis thus requires an alterity, which takes the form of the discovery and racialization of other sexual cultures. As Evren Savci has judiciously observed in the case of the construction of neoliberalism and Islam as diametrically opposed entities in Western queer theory, a reading of "nonnormatively gendered and sexualized subjects elsewhere through the paradigm of anthropological difference . . . results in positioning queers in the non-West either as authentic local subjects or as modernized, globalized, and therefore inauthentic."[34] A project that began as an effort to denaturalize gender and sexual categories in the West quickly turns into an argument for the incommensurability between the West and the rest. The thesis of gender variability (between, for example, lesbians and heterosexual women in the modern West) becomes a thesis of cultural variability (between Western and non-Western worlds). An unexpected consequence of this logical conflation is that cultures outside the West come to be seen as definitionally outside and beyond queer theory. In the work of certain queer theorists, this view becomes a paradoxical ethical injunction *against* the application of queer theory to non-Western contexts. Those critics caution us to limit the purview of queer theory to Western examples only, seeing any effort to explore areas outside the United States through a queer methodology as a self-aggrandizing colonial epistemology. This injunction against non-Western research in queer theory, offered in the name of a critique of Western cultural hegemony and universalism, paradoxically silences and excludes non-Western languages and paradigms in gender/sexuality studies.

An example of this conceptual double bind can be seen in one of the founding texts of US queer theory, Sedgwick's *Epistemology of the Closet*. Sedgwick begins her magistral work with a sweeping claim: "An understanding of virtually any aspect of modern Western culture must be, not merely incomplete, but damaged in its central substance to the degree that it does not incorporate a critical analysis of modern homo/heterosexual definition."[35] A few pages later, Sedgwick adds a disclaimer: "It is very difficult for [this book's choice of the Euro-American male as its subject matter] to be interpreted in any other light than that of the categorical imperative: the fact that they are made in a certain way here seems a priori to assert that they would be best made *in the same way everywhere*. I would ask that, *however sweeping* the claims made by this book may seem to be, it not be read as making that particular claim [of applying the analysis to non-Euro-American cultures]."[36] But contemporary transnational queer theory contests precisely this point about the self-obviousness of the Euro-American male as the proper subject of queer studies. While 1990s queer theorists cautioned us not to apply queer theory to non-Western cultures, for today's queer theorists there is no more urgent task.

Allochronic queer theory's search for examples of gender pluralism in the global South was central to the advancement of social constructionist theory, sometimes over and against the dominance of Marxist thought on the left. In "The Traffic in Women," Gayle S. Rubin proposes the concept of the sex/gender system as a corrective to the gender blindness of Marxist historical materialism. A sex/gender system is a mode of sexual reproduction that converts women as raw materials into domesticated wives. Toward the end of the essay, Rubin considers several examples from New Guinea and other non-Western societies—the Nuer, the Kachin, the Trobriands, traditional Tonga, and Samoa—to demonstrate that kinship, bridewealth, and marriage customs are culturally specific arrangements that result from different sex/gender systems. Although Rubin's arguments are compelling and illuminating, the forms of human sociality that constitute gender and sex clearly exceed the exchange of women in heterosexual marriage and patrilineal reproduction, and the explanatory force of "The Traffic in Women" is undercut by Rubin's own research on sexual diversity, which includes sadomasochism, leather, pornography, and sex work.

In "Thinking Sex," an essay written several years later with a significantly different argument and an autocritique on precisely this point, Rubin again turns to the distinction between modern Western homosexuality and non-Western configurations of same-sex desire: "The New Guinea bachelor and the sodomite nobleman are only tangentially related to a modern gay man, who may migrate from rural Colorado to San Francisco in order to live in a gay neighborhood, work in a gay business, and participate in an elaborate experience that includes a self-conscious identity, group solidarity, a literature, a press, and a high level of political activity. In modern, Western industrial societies, homosexuality has acquired much of the institutional structure of an ethnic group."[37]

Rubin's own views on these questions have evolved significantly over time.[38] However, the anthropological thesis of sexual pluralism has proved to be quite central to the development of queer/LGBTQIA+ studies, finding further elaboration in works such as Will Roscoe's research on two-spirit males (*berdache*) in Indigenous North American societies and *māhū* in Native Hawaii, Tomás Almaguer's thesis that Mexican/Latin American sexual systems (which do not stigmatize the penetrating partner) have no cultural equivalent to "homosexuality" in the Euro-American sense, and Joseph Massad's critique of the imposition of Western notions of sexual development in the Arab world.[39] In Southeast Asian studies, a rich body of scholarship has documented a plurality of locally grounded understandings of gender, sex, and sexuality and their articulations in Buddhist, Islamic, Christian, or Confucian cosmologies.[40] In addition, scholars of this region have emphasized the importance of displacing the question of queer's cross-cultural applicability with more historical work on the contexts of sexual formations in the global South.[41] Similarly, historians of Chinese gender/sexuality have proposed different reasons that *tongzhi* (same-sex desire) is distinct from *gay* or *queer* in the Western context.[42]

It is not my intention to question the progressive value of anthropological research on non-Western sexual subjects.[43] Rather, my goal is to highlight— through an immanent critique—early queer theory's dependency on a liberal logic of multicultural inclusion. My work proposes a thorough displacement of the terms of the cultural appropriation–versus–gender pluralism debate. Turning instead to the contradictions of a globalizing capitalism, one that erodes national boundaries (formal subsumption) without creating a homogenized culture (real subsumption), I suggest that a Marxist analysis can help establish an alternative conception of US queer theory as a minority participant in a global conversation sustained by the labor of scholars and activists working in other languages. Instead of demanding more representation of non-Western examples in US anthologies, Marxist-inspired transnational scholars reverse this power relationship, provincializing US queer theory itself as a limited form of knowledge that has yet to earn its membership in a global, mostly nonanglophone queer conversation.

The changing conditions of global capitalism, in which China has been at the center, provide important reasons for queer theory to move from the history of sexuality to the location of sexuality. Indeed, contemporary queer critics are thinking more rigorously about the geopolitical contexts for the production of sexual expression, identity, and communities.[44] The turn to locations and geopolitics, in lieu of a Foucauldian taxonomy-based evolutionary narrative, makes it possible for non-Western subjects to be the protagonists of queer theory rather than its cultural resistance. An example of this turn can be seen in the 2016 special issue of *GLQ* "Area Impossible: The Geopolitics of Queer Studies." Cautioning against the "anthropological voyeurism of [queer theory's] early forays into sexuality" in a spirit similar to my intervention here, the coeditors, Anjali Arondekar and Geeta Patel, point out that "queer geographies have undoubtedly stretched to include hitherto untapped regions of the world (read: specifically spaces in the global south), albeit with the local/vernacular reappearing (once again) primarily through ethnographic salaciousness, if it is at all, as incident, exemplar, or evidence, as spatial fodder for the queer mill."[45] While concurring with many aspects of Arondekar and Patel's analysis, my work emphasizes more explicitly that the impulse for mining non-Western examples to expand queer theory's multiculturalist claims (or what Arondekar and Patel refer to as "the queer mill" and "US mappings of queer," 46) stems from the material inequalities induced by global capitalism.

The emergence of China as a new center of capitalist accumulation and exploitation in the twenty-first century confronts the limits of monolingual queer theory. However one identifies or disidentifies with the category of "homosexuality as we understand it," it has become apparent that the "we" in this phrase is a subject that cohabits a conflict-ridden world with others and that the persistence of this "we" is made materially possible by the labor of those beyond the borders of law and shared culture. This recognition has forced queer theory to revise many of the categories and assumptions that went relatively unchallenged in the 1990s. A clear problem arising from Foucault's speciation thesis is the postulation of the West as a unified, natural, and self-evident category. In Sedgwick's *Epistemology of the Closet*, the coherence of the category of the West is simply "axiomatic": "Most moderately to well-educated Western people in this century seem to share a similar understanding of homosexual definition, independent of whether they themselves are gay or straight, homophobic or antihomophobic."[47] Not fully attentive to the formative role of class in her own example ("most moderately to well-educated Western people"), Sedgwick continues to develop her most powerful and enduring claim: the figure of the closet is not just a matter of sexuality; rather, it is the defining epistemology of the modern Western world as a whole. Sedgwick argues that, because the homo/heterosexual definitional crisis is constitutive of other binarisms (knowledge/ignorance, secrecy/disclosure, private/

public, same/different, etc.), the study of sexuality is the foundation of all social inquiry rather than its afterthought. On the basis of this argument, Sedgwick proposes that the figure of the closet is an organizational principle for "twentieth-century Western culture as a whole."[48]

But one must wonder how a project that is so skilled at denaturalizing sexuality, and so exemplary in the insights, care, and nuanced readings it brings to particular texts, would uncritically accept the concept of "twentieth-century Western culture as a whole" despite the diversity of authors she considers in her work. A well-intended critique of the universalizing pretensions of Western knowledge ends up precluding consideration of non-Western examples in queer theory and alleviating scholars of the burden to learn about languages and cultures that are not their own. The disclaimer "in the modern West" was ubiquitous in 1990s queer theory, providing a convenient way to bracket one's project with more modest and local conclusions. Though the disclaimer was intended to be a sign of respect for non-Western peoples and cultures, it also obviated the need to know the Other and to critique the global capitalist system that created such a division in the first place.

Allochronic queer criticism of the 1990s thus created an impression that writing about nonanglophone subjects under the rubric of queer theory would automatically constitute a form of cultural imperialism. This impression, in turn, reinforced the disciplinary divide between anthropological research on gender pluralism in non-Western societies and queer theory-based literary criticism. Though the labor of describing the Other always carries the risk of unconsciously reproducing the hegemonic value of the speaker's own culture, the non-West, in my view, is something we cannot not theorize in queer theory—to paraphrase Gayatri Chakravorty Spivak's definition of deconstruction as "a persistent critique of what one cannot not want."[49] I consider this paradox to be foundational to the development of US queer theory and symptomatic of its incomplete and unresolved encounters with a world capitalist system fraught with contradictions between formal and real subsumption. While the scope of queer theory has extended to worlds beyond US borders (the disclaimer "in the modern West" implicitly recognizes the existence of a non-West), the intellectual labor of those reading and writing in languages other than English has not been incorporated into the regime of generalized commodity exchange in the same ways as the material production of food, services, and raw materials. In an effort to historicize the invented-ness of our own categories, we end up racializing subjects and experiences outside the West as the unspeaking and the unspeakable. The fact that early queer theory was animated by this equivocation between these two different senses of the constitutive outside indicates that, even before its materialist turn, queer theory was already indissociably linked to the historical transformations of global capitalism that have facilitated and have been facilitated by the rise of China.

The Political Economy of the Beijing Consensus

Though in the development policy cycle it is more common to see descriptions of China's economic ascendancy as the result of an internal policy change, namely, its market liberalization, Marxist analysis supplies an alternative explanation of this development as the result of a dialectical relation between China and its constitutive outside—the shifting conditions created by global capitalism's real and formal subsumption of labor. Long before we entered the age of the Beijing Consensus, Ernest Mandel had already pointed out that the nature of late capitalism necessitates a rethinking and expansion of Marx's reproduction scheme, which was traditionally understood to operate across two sectors: Department I, the production of the means of production; and Department II, the production of consumer goods. Mandel proposed a theory of formal subsumption by adding a third department, the production of the means of destruction. Unlike the production of raw materials, energy, buildings, and machinery (used to replace and extend the means of production) and the production of consumer goods (used to reconstitute the labor force), the production of weapons renews neither constant nor variable capital. In other words, it does not reenter the process of capitalist reproduction. However, it constitutes a moment of capital's formal subsumption because the interstate arms race is required for the valorization of capital.[50] Mandel argues that the expanded production of the means of destruction is a key feature of late capitalism. Financed out of the surplus value of productive workers, the production of arms provides a significant source of primitive accumulation and plays a considerable role in the acceleration of industrialization.

Following Mandel's analysis, we can see that capital's formal subsumption resulted in both the production and destruction of value. The fact that, in order to survive, peripheralized nations such as China had to modernize their industrial bases as well as their war machines reflects an interstate capitalist structure of compulsion, which Moishe Postone has famously described as the "treadmill effect" of late capitalism. Because of militarized interstate competition, "increased productivity results neither in a corresponding increase in social wealth nor in a corresponding decrease in labour time, but in the constitution of a new base level of productivity."[51] Sometimes simply understood as development, the treadmill effect indirectly alters the purpose of production and the nature of the labor process in both capitalist and non-capitalist regions of the world.

From Mandel to Postone, Marxist scholars have theorized capital's formal subsumption as a mode of abstract compulsions and constraints that continues to exist in the absence of bourgeois relations of distribution. In this sense, capital accumulation functions as the constitutive outside of formally socialist nations. For this reason, some Marxist and Communist scholars have rejected China's claim to ever have formulated a socialist alternative to capitalism. As described by the collective of the Chuǎng project, China is neither an ahistorical exception to the laws of capitalism nor a carbon copy of the Soviet Union but a socialist developmental regime forged out of the global imperatives of capital accumulation:[52]

> [The success of the Chinese Communist movement left] the region stuck in an inconsistent stasis understood at the time to be "socialism." The socialist system, which we refer to as a "developmental regime," was neither a mode of production nor a "transitional stage" between capitalism and communism, nor even between the tributary mode of production and capitalism. Since it was not a mode of production, it was also not a form of "state capitalism," in which capitalist imperatives were pursued under the guise of the state, with the capitalist class simply replaced in form but not function by the hierarchy of government bureaucrats. Instead, the socialist developmental regime designates the breakdown of any mode of production and the disappearance of the abstract mechanisms (whether tributary, filial, or marketized) that govern modes of production as such. . . . But the construction of an industrial system is not the same as the successful transition to a new mode of production. . . . Meanwhile, there was no evidence of any transition toward communism, which remained a merely ideological horizon.[53]

The Chuǎng project distinguishes itself from two dominant approaches: the nationalist project of uncovering a secret lineage of culture that explains China's unique postsocialist development, and the utopian leftist project of uncovering where the socialist project "went wrong" and what could have been done to achieve Communism in some alternate universe. Breaking with both, the Chuǎng project employs economic history "to compose a coherent communist perspective on China not muddied by the romance of dead revolutions or the hysteria of rapid growth rates."[54] The different phases of this history—from the development of the first modern industrial infrastructure on the East Asian mainland in the formally socialist period, to the destruction of the "iron rice bowl" during the deindustrialization wave of the 1990s, and finally to the capitalist transformation of agriculture and the creation of China's contemporary proletariat—correspond to key shifts in the degree of China's incorporation into global accumulation imperatives.

The analysis of capitalist modernity as the constitutive outside of socialist China is not the same as the theory of state capitalism, which exists in many forms but tends to deny the difference between today's and yesterday's China. As a taxonomic problem, the state capitalist thesis was more useful to factionalized leftist circles who wanted to deny or support the Soviet system—and across the Sino-Soviet divide—than for providing clarity for Marxist theory and politics.[55] Rather than dismissing the revolutionary transformations of the state's relation to the accumulation of surplus under Mao Zedong, my interest lies in conceptualizing the Beijing Consensus as a dialectical consequence of China's incorporation into a compulsive system that governs radically different economic policies.

In turn, a historical understanding of capitalism's combined and uneven development provides a more useful form of materialism than the inclusion-and-diversity logic of allochronic criticism. Among variants of Marxist accounts of China's postsocialist political economy, world-systems analysis has provided the most useful tools for developing a *longue durée* perspective on China's rise and its constitutive outside. For Giovanni Arrighi, the question has less to do with how China "rose" than with how it returned to its original path of development after the devastations of European imperialism, civil war, the Cold War embargo, and the colonial division of labor.[56] Like Kenneth Pomeranz in *The Great Divergence* (2000), R. Bin Wong in *China Transformed* (1997), and Andre Gunder Frank in *ReOrient* (1998), Arrighi sees the Yangtze River Delta region of eighteenth-century China as a leader of world development that had surpassed Europe's wealthiest countries in levels of commercialization, agricultural productivity, and sophistication of manufacture.[57] For Arrighi, the Chinese model, which focused on internal growth, was the norm, while the extroverted and capitalist character of the European model was the "unusual arrangement" that required an explanation. Until the advent of Western imperialism, the priority of East Asian statecraft was the cultivation of internal stability and progress. The East Asian system exhibited a near absence of intrasystemic military competition and a lack of interest in building overseas empires. By contrast, the European system was driven by the synergy of an incessant armament race, capital accumulation, and territorial expansion that culminated in the industrialization of war. After Great Britain used force to open the Chinese market to opium trade, China became incorporated into the global capitalist system as a peripheralized member. This reorganization of the East Asian system made accelerated military modernization a universal priority and drew China into the kind of armament race that is now a key feature of the global capitalist system. In response to intense economic and military encroachment, the priorities of China since the Opium Wars have shifted from maintaining internal stability to erecting a strong developmentalist state to induce capitalist-industrial modernization. In Arrighi's view, the emergence of China as a major military and financial powerhouse in the age of the Beijing Consensus results from the cumulative efforts it has made within a dynamically evolving capitalist system over the past two centuries, not from its market reforms. Specifically, Arrighi argues that China's economic renaissance was made possible by its inheritance of two legacies of the old Sinocentric system—the ability of the overseas Chinese diaspora to serve as an instrument of economic reintegration and the high quality and low cost of the Chinese rural laboring masses.[58]

Whereas Arrighi emphasizes the legacies of indigenous systems and the comparative asymmetry between European and East Asian models, his advisee Ho-fung Hung makes a different argument about China's constitutive outside by drawing more attention to the global conditions of possibility for China's ascent. Hung argues that the China boom has been made possible by the threefold structural transformations of the global capitalist system since the 1970s: the creation of a new international division of labor, the twin decline of US hegemony and the Cold War order, and the waning of working-class-based, state-power-oriented mass politics. In the 1970s, economic crises and falling rates of profit in the core countries induced corporations to shift from a Fordist, vertically integrated mode of organization to a more flexible form of organization based on multilayered and transnational subcontracting, which outsourced more labor-intensive segments of production to peripheral, low-wage countries in Asia. Replacing the old core-periphery division of labor based on the periphery's export of raw materials in exchange for manufactured products from the core, the new international division of labor turned part of the periphery into new manufacturing bases of the global system. While this role was first taken up by the original four

Tigers (Taiwan, Hong Kong, South Korea, and Singapore), the opening of China to foreign direct investment—initially restricted to its southern coastal provinces—integrated China into the "flying geese formation" of the East Asian multilayered subcontracting system, turning "the rise of East Asia into the rise of China."[59]

Hung's thesis is that the so-called Chinese model or the Beijing Consensus is in fact the snowball effect and intensification of an East Asian Tiger economy that was already in place before its market reforms and that must be explained internationally in relation to the restructuring of the US–East Asian division of labor in the wake of the dismantling of the Keynesian welfare state. At the same time, the collapse of socialist institutions within China was historically connected to the global defeats of working-class movements, the rise of neoliberalism in the era of Margaret Thatcher and Ronald Reagan, and the realignment of geostrategic interests in response to the disappearance of the Communist threat as an ideological bond among the Western core powers. Hung's theory situates the economic foundation of the Beijing Consensus in relation to an alterity, namely, the transformations in the conditions of possibility within capitalism itself.

We can begin to note the sharp differences between a Marxist account of capital as the subsumption of transnational labor and liberal critiques of capitalism as wealth inequalities, as well as the ramifications of this perspectival difference for culturalist questions such as gender and sexuality. None of these factors contributing to the history of labor struggles in China identified by Arrighi, Hung, or other Marxist and neo-Marxist world-systems analysts could be explained in culturalist terms; indeed, this analysis of capitalism stands in stark contrast to variants of the "capitalism and gay identity" thesis that homosexual associations and identities were created by urban industrialism in a hermetically sealed society. At the same time, world-systems analysis suffers from its insufficient attention to gender and sexuality. An emphasis on the macroanalysis of systemic changes reduces human subjectivity to statistics, and the nuances of gendered life—which are not to be confused with women's participation in public labor—are overlooked. Therefore, the argument that capital cannot accumulate without an outside must be augmented to include an analysis of the differentiation of bodies as another form of subsumption.

Before we can turn to the analysis of gender and sexuality in the subsumption or rearrangement of social relationships in China, we must first examine the Beijing Consensus as the creation of new inequalities between geographically bound populations and the concentration of wealth and power into monopoly power across class and gender lines. While mainstream economists enthusiastically praise China's transformation from a third-world country into a global powerhouse, what we have witnessed in the past few decades is the "creation of one of the most unequal societies in the contemporary world out of one of the most equal only three decades ago."[60] China's much-touted growth is in reality the mounting social inequality between an emergent capitalist class and a dispossessed rural class, fueled by a reckless developmentalism justifying human rights abuses, onslaughts against the environment, suppression of freedoms of speech and assembly, and belligerence toward Taiwan, Hong Kong, and Xinjiang in the name of national sovereignty.[61] China's neoliberal transformations in the age of the Beijing Consensus exemplify the ways considerations of economic growth have trumped demands for broad-based democracy, created inequalities in rent-seeking behaviors, polarized the urban population's income levels, diminished economic benefits for so-called individual households (*geti hu*), and kept an outmoded welfare system that simply cannot keep up with rising inflation and a general sense of social insecurity.[62]

By the Chinese government's own account, mass labor protests increased from ten thousand incidents in 1993 (the year after Deng Xiaoping's Southern Tours) to sixty thousand incidents involving more than three million protesters in 2003 (two years after China's entry into the World Trade Organization).[63] Marxist value theory provides a way to understand that what appears to be progress and growth for urban elites results from the same process that brings about the underdevelopment and expropriation of China's hinterlands. Chinese-language social scientists describe this convergence as *sannong wenti*—a term coined by the rural analyst and activist Wen Tiejun for the nexus of the peasantry, the rural areas, and agriculture in China's capital accumulation by dispossession.[64] In this new era marked by "the end of the peasant," the agrarian economy is simultaneously seen as a cheap source of capitalist modernization and a dumping site (literally and figuratively) for China's urban problems and environmental waste.[65]

The present dilemmas of the Beijing Consensus have their origins in the land reforms of the 1950s. The peasantry—one of the "souths" and constitutive outsides examined in this book and the focal point of Lu Xun's fiction, discussed in chapter 3—has been the historical bedrock of Chinese Communism. In Mao's theories of voluntarism and the mass line, the peasant was seen as the historical agent of a revolution that was coming from within "with Chinese characteristics" and as the Chinese experience's primary distinction from

Soviet-style central planning. Between 1946 and 1952, the Chinese Communist Party launched a series of land-reform (*tugai*) campaigns that redistributed forty-seven million hectares of farmland (46.5 percent of China's total), together with draft animals, agricultural implements, and grains, from landlords to peasants.[66] Having thus created a peasant economy in which households became landowner-cultivators, the Chinese Communist Party from 1953 onward began to assume collective ownership of expropriated land through the creation of agricultural production cooperatives that transferred property rights from the landlord class to the Chinese state.

During the Great Leap Forward, launched in 1958 to counter America's Cold War strategy of containment, the agricultural production cooperatives were reorganized into people's communes in an effort to accelerate China's industrial revolution.[67] This shift created a regime of capitalist primitive accumulation that allowed the developmental state to transfer the surplus of both rural and urban production into the heavy-industry sector. Abandoning the culture of socialist democracy and voluntary cooperation that characterized its origins, mid-1950s China introduced a mobilizational collectivism that became an extractive mechanism subordinating the interests of rural producers to those of industry and the state.[68] With the introduction of the household responsibility system under the market reform of 1978, the peasants retained use rights to the land, but its ownership was nominally transferred to the rural collective. This unique land-tenure system continues to be the key to China's identity as a socialist country today despite its "agrarian capitalism," namely, the financialization of rural land through paid lease and transfer of use rights.[69] China's agrarian capitalism embodies the contradiction between Mao's promise of the land-tenure system and the current effort by the People's Republic of China to modernize the rural economy by injecting capital into the agricultural sector as a solution to the problems caused by China's overall transformation into an export-oriented economy. Driven by the imperatives of capital accumulation, new rural land-reform policies created large business conglomerates and a linked banking system to channel rural savings to the urban centers.[70]

As financial capital began to be infused into the agricultural hinterlands, state migration policies based on a two-tier *hukou* (household registration) system became more relaxed in 1984. After losing land rights to large agribusiness companies in the "new socialist countryside," dispossessed peasants became China's "floating populations" (*liumin*), migrant workers streaming into large cities seeking employment in precarious conditions.[71] Indeed, the China boom is financed by two mechanisms of capital accumulation: the commodification of rural labor and the financialization of rural land. Scholars estimate that China's economic success in the past four decades has been powered by the labor of 287 million rural migrant workers who travel seasonally because the *hukou* system prevents them from settling in the urban centers, effectively creating a form of social apartheid.[72] This system of precarious and contingent employment gives China a low-cost competitive advantage in the global capitalist economy, while allowing rural lands to be expropriated at low cost and auctioned to urban real estate developers.[73]

The signification of the peasant has transformed from the actor of revolutionary force in the Maoist era to a symbol of feudal backwardness and an impediment to postsocialist modernization.[74] Paradoxically, rural-to-urban migrant workers also constitute the "indispensably disposable" workforce in China's postsocialist modernization, providing an inexhaustible reserve army of labor that accelerates capitalist development by contributing to an overall depression of wages and keeping labor costs in China internationally competitive. China's postsocialist development is a clear demonstration that capital accumulation requires and produces differentiated populations. In this process, gender becomes a particularly pronounced form of difference. Primitive accumulation involved the separation of the spheres of production and reproduction, the devaluation of women's knowledge, and gendered enclosures.

Women's work—whether unwaged or remunerated—created the infusion of expropriated value that perpetuated capitalism.[75] The vulnerability of women as a group is amplified by China's neoliberal transformations, which brought about deeply unequal relations to capital accumulation and wage labor in a new gendered class, *dagongmei* (female migrant laborers in sweatshops). Concentrated in China's export-oriented regions such as Guangdong, *dagongmei* experience a particular form of precarity in that they are at once relegated to feminized labor and considered radically substitutable and expendable. Despite their structural position as second-class citizens in the global workplace, *dagongmei* are routinely deprived of the capacity to articulate class consciousness—a condition that Pun Ngai describes as their "discursive dyslexia."[76] The emergence of *dagongmei* as a gendered class is part of a broader transformation of preexisting livelihoods and social ties that were once based on China's unique kin-based networks, culture of lineage consciousness, and gender-based hierarchies.[77]

In addition to *dagongmei*, another particularly instructive example of how the financialization of rural land transformed gender relations is the population known as *money boys* in China. Money boys are rural-to-urban migrant workers who entered the sex industry in search of a new means of subsistence after the collapse of socialist institutions. Dispossessed, displaced, and having literally nothing to sell except their bodies—which are often seen as lean, naturally fit, and thus desirable by white-collar gay men holding office jobs in the information economy—rural sex workers perform a new form of proletarianized labor. Money boys are not necessarily oppressed or exploited, and they are certainly not trafficked. Rather, it is more accurate to say that they embody the contradictions of China's agrarian capitalism without surrendering their agency. Travis S. K. Kong's ethnographic research shows that money boys typically go to cities to escape their peasant backgrounds and have the same goals and cosmopolitan aspirations as other rural-to-urban migrants: personal freedom, romantic encounters, entrepreneurship, and upward social mobility. Kong describes money boys as exemplifying the "autonomization and responsiblization of the self," a new form of self-fashioning under the conditions of China's neoliberalism.[78] The rise of commodified male same-sex sexual labor forms an important aspect of China's "pink capitalism," which has created a significant expansion of queer public spaces, including parks, bars, clubs, community centers, and, most important, social-networking mobile applications that make these encounters possible.[79]

But as is the case with other instances of formal subsumption, the economic incorporation of money boys' labor does not entail their social integration, and new hierarchies ensued. Rooted in the contradiction between differentially valued rural and urban labor, the discourse of "quality" (*suzhi*) has gained prominence in Chinese debates about class respectability in the postreform era. *Suzhi* discourse is an important technology of neoliberal governmentality, whose real aim is to rationalize the postsocialist state's expropriation of rural land in the name of the government's effort to improve the cultural upbringing of peasants.[80] The influx of sex workers into urban centers changed the parlance of middle-class gay men, who are now using the term *money boys* to differentiate themselves anxiously and emphatically from those deemed incapable of the proper embodiment of desire.[81] Money boys' queer labor constitutes an undertheorized dimension of the new politics of human value in China today, one that transforms the material struggles of minoritized subjects of gender and sexuality into the production of higher-quality selves for global capitalism.[82]

China's capitalist transformations produced far-reaching consequences for gendered life and queer kinship.[83] Money boys who move from rural areas to urban cities to improve their "quality" articulate a new ethics of the self. Similarly, transnational queers—development-induced migrants and returnees who receive their education in English-speaking countries—participate in the new discourse of *suzhi*. Media studies scholar John Wei proposes that *suzhi* discourse has created a distinct form of "gated communities" and "stretched kinship" in China's queer culture. As it becomes increasingly common for Chinese gay men and lesbians to seek higher education abroad in order to escape compulsory heterosexuality and procreative familialism, migration produces a social hierarchy between "high-*suzhi*" queers (transnationally educated, urbane, properly employed) and "low-*suzhi*" queers (rural born, culturally unkempt, and accented).[84] Produced by the mutual entanglements of economic and sexual transformations, new forms of gendered classes, from *dagongmei* to money boys, exemplify capital's dispossessive power.

China Going Out

While world-systems theorists identify the decline of US hegemony, among other factors, as a constitutive outside of China's ascendance and labor struggles, we can extend this analysis to China's expansion into Africa and other geographic spaces for a renewed understanding of capital as transnational value production, before returning to a reconsideration of how this form of Marxist analysis can assist us in revising and expanding queer theory's materialist claims. In the twenty-first century, China has become the largest bilateral lender for public-sector loans across the African continent. Though met with mixed feelings, China as a donor and development partner appeared particularly credible to African leaders because of China's own recent history as a late-industrializing country, its success in poverty-reduction programs, and its own experience as a recipient of foreign aid.[85] From 2009 to 2012, China provided $10 billion to Africa in the form of concessional loans. During President Xi Jinping's first overseas trip to Africa in March 2013, he doubled this commitment to $20 billion over the next two years.[86] A particularly controversial practice, which came to be known as the Angola model because it began with a 2004 low-interest $2 billion loan to Angola, allowed African nations to use their commodities, oil reserves, or other natural resources as collateral for Chinese loans.[87] After financing Angola's postwar reconstruction projects, including a $3.5 billion Kilamba Kiaxi satellite town in the outskirts of Luanda, the resource-backed lending model for financing infrastructure projects became the standard practice between China and the Democratic

Republic of Congo, Ghana, and Guinea. Thanks to these deals, China surpassed the United States as Africa's largest trade partner in 2009, and by 2016 it had established itself as the continent's largest single investor. Though cooperation between China and countries in the global South has existed since the 1955 Bandung Conference, South-South Cooperation, estimated to exceed $20 billion, has become the signature element of contemporary China's economic growth and global influence.[88]

With the creation of South-South Cooperation as an alternative to traditional development-assistance programs, China entered a new era that Xi Jinping officially anointed as China's "Going Out" policy (Zhongguo zou chuqu). If, during the Bandung era, the relationship among China, Africa, and Latin America was primarily imagined as a form of anti-imperialist solidarity (tricontinentalism), China in the age of the Beijing Consensus is using the rhetoric of South-South Cooperation to construct a very different geopolitical order.[89] To many commentators outside the People's Republic, China's current interest in the global South is largely driven by neocolonial ventures, representing a new scramble for Africa to make it "Beijing's second continent."[90] The global South is no longer the former third world of which China once imagined itself to be a part but a new frontier to explore, conquer, and assimilate. Under this regime of surplus extraction, new forms of South-South racialization come into being.[91] Unsurprisingly, China's investment in extractive industries in the global South has garnered much criticism from international human rights activists, who now see China's economic expansion, rather than the World Bank and the International Monetary Fund, as the main problem in the developing world.[92]

From the Chinese state's own viewpoint, however, these economic activities fulfill two main goals: first, to counteract the legacy of China's isolation and "delinking" from the world economy during the Maoist era; and, second, to create a multipolar world order with a focus on South-South Cooperation as an alternative to the Washington Consensus rooted in the neoliberal doctrine championed by Margaret Thatcher and Ronald Reagan. Introduced in 2013, the Belt and Road Initiative (originally named One Belt One Road) is perhaps the most ambitious element of China's Going Out policy, a form of "state-mobilized globalization" that involves infrastructure development in over seventy countries in Europe, Asia, the Middle East, and Africa.[93] This project aims at a fundamental geopolitical reconstitution of the global system of capitalist trade into a Sinocentric one—through the creation of overland routes (Silk Road economic belt) and Indo-Pacific sea routes (maritime Silk

Roads) with China at the center.[94] Though often perceived as a novel effort to establish China's global hegemony, the Belt and Road Initiative has its origins in a long history of declared principles of political noninterference, global third-world struggle against imperialism, and cultural ties.[95]

The concept of the Beijing Consensus names the complex debates about China's relations to the global South—whether China offers an alternative model of development to the Washington Consensus or is actually a neocolonial power in disguise that uses "debt-trap diplomacy" to expand its soft power and secure mining rights in the global South.[96] The characterization of China's economic activities in the global South as neocolonial remains controversial. Ching Kwan Lee, for example, offers an important critique of the moralizing framework of anticolonial critique and proposes in its place an empirical analysis of what Chinese state capital does in the copper and construction industries in Africa. Distinguishing between private and state capital, as well as their logics of accumulation, regimes of labor, and ethos of management in Zambia, Lee argues that China's political culture since the Going Out policy does not represent a new form of colonialism because it is not accompanied by religious proselytizing or military occupation. Instead, Lee recommends that we analyze Chinese foreign investment in Africa through a renewed understanding of capital as process, relation, and embeddedness instead of as quantifiable economic units.[97] T. Tu Huynh provides another caveat against the uncritical conflation of Chinese migrants and state actions. Extending Cedric Robinson's concept of Black Marxism to Chinese labor in South Africa, Huynh argues that the framing of China-Africa relations within the experiences of the West—using terms such as *neocolonialism*, *scramble*, or *takeover* to describe the activities of China's state-owned enterprises and private capitalist entrepreneurs—disregards the long history of engagement between African and Chinese peoples. It represents a selective amnesia about the indentured Chinese labor introduced to the gold-mining industry at the Witwatersrand after the Anglo-Boer War. Indeed, Chinese laborers played a significant role in South Africa's incorporation into the British Empire and in its organization of white labor—in other words, Chinese labor in Africa has always been part of the continual expansion of European racial capitalism rather than its epiphenomena.[98]

Fact or fiction, the Beijing Consensus is embraced by thinkers from a wide spectrum of political positions. A central argument among China's left intelligentsia, especially those supporting the nonprivatization of agricultural land, the preservation of state-owned enterprises, and participatory social democracy, is that China has been the site of a countermodernity whose problems and solutions are both distinct from those of the capitalist West.[99] Rural analysts such as Wen Tiejun argue that postreform China is still home to the world's largest rural population and is defined by unique issues that require the reconstruction of rural cooperatives and associations on the model of Mao-era communes. As Wen sees it, the Beijing Consensus is a unique product of China's history as a late-industrializing country in a semicolonial context; it is therefore analytically distinct from the problems of deregulation and austerity brought about by neoliberalism in the United States and the United Kingdom. Without the possibility of transferring the institutional and social costs of capitalist development abroad through colonial expansion like its Western predecessors, China achieved the age of the Beijing Consensus— through the three stages of primitive accumulation, industrialization, and financial capitalism—with the infusion of Soviet capital and a structure of "government corporatism with Chinese characteristics."[100] Under this government corporatism, rural landownership was transferred to village collectives, private capital was banned in 1956, and the crises of urban China were resolved by transferring the cost to the rural communities. Despite the emergence of "reform and opening" as an export-oriented alternative to such crises, the economic structure of contemporary China remains mired in the monetary and social problems of the "development trap." In short, what sets the Beijing Consensus apart from Western neoliberalism is the internal structure of the cost transfer that created the rural-urban divide during the socialist (or, as Wen calls it, state capitalist) period.

Minqi Li, a prominent Chinese Marxist economist associated with the New Left, contends that China's economic ascent does not indicate its integration into global capitalism. Rather, China destabilizes that system through its revolutionary dynamics and working-class militancy in a way that hastens the demise of the world capitalist system.[101] Despite having developed an exploitative relationship with Africa, China, Li argues, remains a semiperipheral country that transfers surplus value produced by tens of millions of workers to the United States and other imperialist countries.[102] Other scholars argue that the Communist Revolution helped to create the conditions for post-1978 China to achieve a regime of "accumulation without dispossession" and a "non-capitalist market society" that successfully protected town and village enterprises against monopolistic interests in the rural sector and forestalled the rise of an independent capitalist class in urban cities.[103] While many writers explain China's prodigious growth rates in the age of the Beijing

Consensus as a consequence of its socialist-revolutionary culture, others go back even further in time to the Ming dynasty, before the "great divergence," to emphasize the singularity of the Chinese model.

By contrast, international commentators tend to be much more suspicious of such claims to distinction and exceptionalism. In the opinion of the Argentine critic Luciano Damián Bolinaga, far from discarding the logic of the Washington Consensus, Beijing has in fact extended it as an instrument to compete with Western powers in the periphery: "The Beijing Consensus appears to substantiate an asymmetrical link scheme, based on the comparative advantage and commercial complementation logic, which implies the large-scale exploitation of natural resources by means of Chinese financial capital."[104] The exploitative character of these economic activities has a gendered dimension as well. Africa-based critics of the Beijing Consensus have pointed out that these deals were sealed behind closed doors without democratic planning and independent oversight, and most of the impacted populations are women and young populations. Land grabbing violates their rights and shows a thorough disregard for social, economic, environmental, and gendered consequences.[105]

Conversely, gender has functioned as a new kind of conceptual border between China and its racialized Other. With China's economic expansion into Africa, it is becoming increasingly common for African men to seek citizenship or asylum through heterosexual marriage to Chinese women. This phenomenon represents a process of forced displacement where racialized identity and norms of gender—masculinized ideals of self-reliance and respectability, hypersexualized masculinity, and reproductive prospects—become entangled.[106] At the same time, the subsumption of gender and sexuality in China's new capitalist ventures need not always be coded as exploitative. It can also become an occasion for mutual learning and coalition building. An example is Queer University (Ku'er Daxue), a participatory community video-production program organized by the Beijing Gender Health Education Institute. As the queer media scholar Hongwei Bao has examined, from 2017 to 2019, Queer University collaborated with groups such as GALZ (Gays and Lesbians of Zimbabwe) and Drama Queens (a feminist and pan-Africanist theater organization based in Accra) to conduct transnational queer video-making workshops in Zimbabwe and Ghana, bringing together filmmakers from China and Africa to discuss how to use film to conduct queer activism. Grassroots queer activists in Africa used the platform to exchange knowledge, skills, and ideas with their Chinese counterparts in a joint battle against heteronormativity and homophobia (homosexuality is illegal in both Zimbabwe and Ghana).[107] These conversations led to renewed understandings of queer struggles' embeddedness in the unequal power structures of global capitalism, while allowing the participants to formulate an alternative epistemology that takes queerness as a starting point for reimagining the transnational connections and engagement between China and Africa in the age of the Beijing Consensus.

Conclusion

The Beijing Consensus represents several kinds of mutations of global capitalism: the expansion of fictitious capital and debt into Africa and Latin America, the financialization of rural land, and the commodification of gendered labor. In those instances, gender and sexual differences are subsumed to suit the needs of capital, making queerness yet another form of constitutive outside that remains undertheorized in the Marxist literature on China's political economy. This differentiation between rural and urban classes in China gave rise to the discourse of human quality that is mapped onto proper and illicit forms of desire, while women in the care economy and feminized forms of labor face new conditions of precarity. As such, China's postsocialist experiments entail both socioeconomic transformations and the rearrangement of desire through the production of cosmopolitan aspirations, gendered subjectivities, normative ideals, horizons of possibility, and appropriate and inappropriate longings.[108]

In what way is this analysis of the subsumption of sexuality under China's postsocialist political economy useful for queer theory's materialist turn? As I explore more fully in the next chapter, the development of queer theory as a field has been critically shaped—haunted, even—by a discourse of the material derived from Marxism, but a limited understanding of materialism has led critics to consistently frame queer politics and anticapitalist organizing as oppositional projects. As a result, though contemporary queer theory strives to be more materialist, a focus on multiculturalist inclusivity keeps displacing the critique of capital and blocking materialist queer theory from forming a transformative politics. A Marxist analysis of the kind I offer in this chapter provides an understanding of capital as a dispossessive logic for queer subjects. This perspectival shift can inaugurate a global queer Marxism that does not quite exist yet.

The Specter of Materialism   2

The development of queer theory as a field of academic studies in the United States is indissociable from the so-called linguistic turn, a paradigm shift in the humanities in the 1980s and 1990s that contributed to a decline of general interest in Marxism and materialist approaches to race, gender, and sexuality. Historically coincident with the collapse of the Soviet Union, China's market reforms, and a new vogue for neoliberal economics, the institutionalization of queer theory in the early 1990s, along with women's studies, ethnic studies, postcolonial theory, and ecocriticism, created a post-Marxist academic idiom of new social movements to challenge the priority of Marxian class analysis. The polarity between the old class politics and the new identity politics produced a common conception of Marxism and queer theory as analytically distinct and historically successive projects. Since the onset of neoliberal crises across the globe, however, queer theory has been imbued with a renewed sense of the urgency to understand the material connections between nonconforming genders and precarity. A renaissance of Marxist political and economic thought has equipped queer theory with a rich vocabulary for theorizing gender and sexual minorities as precarious subjects who are increasingly abandoned by systems that consider them to be replaceable and exhaustible. The question of the material has returned to haunt queer theory in its confrontations with financial crises, chronic unemployment, and the criminalization and racialization of illness.

This materialist haunting brought about an expansion of themes and concerns in queer analysis and new ways for scholars of gender and sexuality to reimagine their alliance with Marxism. We can detect traces of this haunting in numerous works in recent queer theory. Dean Spade's *Normal Life* stands out as a particularly compelling and sophisticated example of this resurgence of queer interest in materialist analysis. Spade argues for a "critical trans politics" distinct from the neoliberal demands for normalization and inclusion. One of Spade's key examples is the subtraction and exclusion model on which the American legal system operates. While harm comes in many different forms, American law recognizes only individualized and intentional actions that cause demonstrable harm to others (for example, hate crimes and overt discrimination). As a result, this legal system cannot redress materialist inequalities such as the maldistribution of life chances for trans people. Even in contexts where no overt discrimination is present, trans people may face significant barriers and structural inequalities. For example, discrepancies between documents issued by different state agencies (departments of motor vehicles, the Social Security Administration, or the Internal Revenue Service) can prevent a trans person from accessing health care, receiving family-based social welfare benefits, passing through airport security without harassment, or utilizing sex-segregated facilities and essential services such as women-only domestic violence programs.[1] Spade draws on Michel Foucault's understanding that power does not operate exclusively through prohibition or permission but also through the production of norms and through a differential distribution of security. With this Foucauldian concept of power, Spade argues that trans and queer people should not limit their political goal to the acquisition of formal equality in the eyes of the law. Instead, a critical trans politics must combat the administration of gender—the deployment of a binary notion of gender in US security culture, militarization, racialized criminalization and incarceration, neoliberal onslaughts on welfare programs, and immigration enforcement.

Writing in a related but different vein, Jasbir K. Puar critiques the "trans hailing by the US state"—a new trans-homonationalism that threatens to assimilate and reorient trans people into the productive flow of the nation and nationalized aspirations for possessions, property, and wealth.[2] A discourse of civil rights becomes a process of value extraction. Resisting the temptation to normalize noncompliant populations in accordance with neoliberal mandates regarding capacitated bodies, Puar makes the provocative claim that it is in the best interest of trans people to see their conditions as continuous with disabilities. While the collective battle against pathologization, medi-calization, and stigmatization is clearly urgent and understandable, Puar's work makes us wonder if our desire to decouple trans identities from legally recognized disabilities is itself motivated by an unexamined and internalized phobia about the disabled body, a phobia that stems from capitalism's struc-tural need to rehabilitate and recruit all bodies into the national economy to maximize productivity. Recognizing that demedicalization or depatholo-gization has been a common goal for trans politics, Puar argues that such strategies produce a conundrum for trans bodies that are reliant on medical care, costly pharmacological innovations, legal protection, and public ac-commodations from the very institutions and apparatuses that functionalize gender normativities and create systemic exclusions. As Puar's work shows, queer issues are never just about personal identities and expressions. Rather, the analysis of queer and trans bodies requires a materialist critique of the neoliberal mandate governing the medical industrial complex.

Spade's and Puar's works are examples showing that if *queer* was once trumpeted as a synonym for *freedom, indeterminacy, fluidity, portability,* and *mobility* in contrast to the constrictive definitions of "gay and lesbian," queer theory in the age of the Beijing Consensus is animated by a scholarly desire to understand neoliberal capitalism's material constraints on sexuality. While neither Spade nor Puar writes in an explicitly Marxist idiom, the mate-rialist turn in queer theory was possible only because Marxism had provided the conceptual tools for the systemic analysis of the mutually entwined pro-cesses of sexual and nonsexual regulation. A queer-materialist critique opens up a field of inquiry into the production and reproduction of subjectivities, rendering visible the underlying socioeconomic nexus between seemingly unconnected experiences and events. This revival of materialist analysis pro-vides an opportunity for a rapprochement between queer theory and Marx-ism. As we formulate new leftist strategies for combating contemporary capitalist crises, we also need to relearn tools we have discarded as obsolete, insights we have jettisoned as merely of interest to the mechanistic analysis of economic matters. In turn, the materialist turn in queer theory also neces-sitates a rethinking of what is meant by the material in traditional Marxism, disrupting the dogmatic doctrine of the primacy of economics.

Materialism is not a new idiom in queer theory. It has always served as a lacuna against which queer theory defined itself. Before the postmillennial re-surgence of queer interest in anticapitalist critique, discussion of the concept of the material was already routine in queer theoretical writings that sought to establish an autonomous field of gender and sexuality studies. Indeed, queer theory in the 1990s developed many of its most powerful claims by positioning itself as a corrective to materialism, although what was meant by "the material" could vary wildly from context to context. The concept of the material in queer theory has evolved in an oblique relation to other discourses, including "thing theory," the material unconscious, new materialism, racial mattering, and object ontology. Among these discourses, three different critiques of the material have been the most prominent: the material as the economic, the material as the empirical (as opposed to the linguistic or the socially constructed), and the material as corporeal existence. All three notions of the material have significantly shaped the trajectory of queer theory by providing different kinds of negative space against which influential critics proposed new conceptualizations of gender and sexuality.

Fearing that the project would turn into a subsidiary movement in Marxism, numerous writers in the early days of queer theory used the term *material* to describe the pitfalls of economic reductionism to be avoided in building an autonomous field of sexuality studies. In the years following the publication of key interventionist texts, such as Joan W. Scott's "The Evidence of Experience," queer critics became increasingly suspicious of the claim that identities reflect transparent, objective, and unmediated categories of social existence. In this context the concept of the material acquired a newfound importance in queer critiques of empiricism. Antiempiricist queer critiques rejected impermeable categories, dualisms, and interest-group politics to "embrace the mess" of our social worlds instead of searching for generalizable, positivist, and measurable patterns of behavior and visible acts.[3] The material became a critical idiom in the constructivist-versus-essentialist debate about whether the analytic distinction between sex and gender is useful or even possible to maintain.[4] Certain poststructuralist feminist theorists argue that sex is already a gendered category: our anatomy, chromosomes, hormones, and reproductive capacities may be "material" facts, but our perceptions and understandings of such facts—how and why they matter, how they relate to each other, and what they say about a person's identity—are always produced and organized by language. It is culture, rather than biology, that construes certain material facts as fundamental and others as irrelevant. For feminist and queer scholars who maintain such views, materialism is often tantamount to a naive empiricism.

Nonetheless, in more recent years "the materiality of the body" has resurfaced as a rallying point for scholars of critical race studies, trans studies, and crip theory engaging with the social facticity of power and agency.[5] The matter of the body is not exterior to the matter of capital; rather, the body is the textualization of capital's catastrophic effects.[6] In these accounts the body has an irreducibly material existence that anchors it in the world in ways that are too important, often too violent, to be explained away as a linguistic construction. The body is racially marked and marred, differently capacitated and utilized, critically dependent on institutional protection and social recognition, and vulnerable to violence and brutality. Racial domination configures bodily states and somatic processes, generating unruly conceptions of materiality and dislocated calculations of humanity.[7] Though we might understand gender as a work of fabulation, as antifoundationalist queer theory claims, we cannot ignore the material role that race plays in the prehistory of the subject.[8] As Zairong Xiang's work on transgender materialism reveals, early queer theory's focus on language and representation was limited in its explanatory power because "embodiment . . . cannot and should not be explained only by ways of discursive formation, linguistic construction, and representational citationality."[9] New scholarship in transgender Marxism has brought to our attention that Karl Marx's definition of labor begins with what counts as an acceptable or a useful body. Because gender transition requires an eruption in the alignment of property regimes, working patterns, family structures, domestic life, and liberal optimism that capitalism requires, the twinning of value-form theory and transgender experience yields a powerful perspective on how we might overturn class divisions and develop new forms of nurture beyond the family.[10]

If the body is irreducibly material, it is also bounded in time and space. This important insight has led Indigenous queer scholars to argue for a critical understanding of the dispossessed material ground on which the body stands.[11] In a related fashion, queer ecologists have investigated the ways in which sexual relations organize both the material world of nature and our perceptions, exploitation, and debasement of that world, while tropes of nature—masculine, rural, and virile qualities—serve as disciplinary tools in the criminalization of nonconforming genders and sexualities as degenerate and unnatural.[12] Jordy Rosenberg reminds us that *Stoffwechsel*, Marx's term for commodity exchange or "exchange of material," is grounded in a concept of social metabolism derived from Justus von Liebig's work on soil science; moreover, recent studies in transgender histories have revealed that this conception of nature as the metabolic ground of human life was tied intimately to sexology. Hence, we cannot separate Marx's critique of capitalism from the emergence of a binary concept of sex as a "concrete abstraction."[13]

These three concepts of the material—as economics, empiricism, and corporeality—are by no means mutually exclusive. In fact, some of queer theory's most powerful insights come from proposals to reconsider the connections between seemingly unrelated notions of the material. Judith Butler's *Bodies That Matter*, for example, offers precisely this kind of intervention. Butler engages two senses of matter in this work: the materiality of the body (physical matter) and what "matters" in the political field. In the first sense, the materiality of the body refers to the constructivist/essentialist debate over whether the body, or some part of the body, is discursively constructed.[14] The problem of the materiality of the body is clearly related to the *sex/gender system*, which since Gayle S. Rubin's conceptualization of the phrase has been used to differentiate between the biological or chromosomal makeup of a person (sex) and its cultural meanings (gender). But as Butler argues in *Gender Trouble*, it is conceptually problematic and politically counterproductive to imagine a prediscursive material sex on which gender is culturally inscribed. If gender predetermines what one can "see" as sex, there is no way to epistemologically access sex without gender. While the analytic distinction between sex and gender disputes the biology-is-destiny formulation, it ends up reinstating culture as destiny. In Butler's view, it is simply impossible to retrieve a pristine notion of sex that is not in some way already gendered.[15] Indeed, the very idea that sex must be either female or male (as opposed to other possibilities) is produced by a binary concept of gender. *Bodies That Matter* further extends this argument by connecting the materiality of the body to the grid of intelligibility through which certain bodies come to matter, while others remain cultural impossibilities. Though those two senses of matter are clearly different, Butler's strongest argument is, in fact, that they are one and the same insofar as we can only see and hear what matters to us. What defines matter, then, is not the empirical existence of an object but the matter of concern. Bodies become matter when they exemplify injuries that we recognize as morally and politically urgent; bodies acquire a material existence only when we create a collective vocabulary to describe their pain.[16] Here Butler's account of the materiality of the body deliberately (and usefully) conflates the problem of value (what matters) with epistemology (what we know), and epistemology with ontology (what is). In this version of the problem, the second and third senses of the material—the empirical and the corporeal—are fully merged.

My purpose in rehearsing these arguments is to show that, historically, the relation between queer theory and materialism has not been a polar opposition. Rather, it was a tortuous conversation that is best comprehended dialectically. It is crucial to underscore this dialectical relationality because most critics today characterize queer theory and materialism as incommensurable traditions and treat the latter as a synonym for Marxism. Owing partially to the immense influence of Ernesto Laclau and Chantal Mouffe's *Hegemony and Socialist Strategy*, scholars commonly believe that the emergence of queer theory signifies the displacement of Marxism by poststructuralist thought, multiculturalist politics, and new social movements.[17] But the global history of capital accumulation and Marxist revolutionary thought, as I trace it in this book under the concept of the Beijing Consensus, cannot be conflated with the logic of class in American liberal pluralism, which has reduced the intellectual dialogue between queer theory and Marxism to a description of the combined effects of economic inequalities and sexual discrimination. We do not always sufficiently acknowledge that the most commonly taught canon of queer theory represents a particular form of US area studies that takes American history, politics, and popular culture as its natural and unspoken context. Having a global perspective makes it possible to rewrite the material history of queer theory's encounters with Marxism without relapsing into the multiculturalist conception of race, gender, class, and sexuality as commensurable identities.

If we accept the multiculturalist view that regards queer theory as the intellectualization of nonnormative sexualities, and Marxism as the politicization of class interests, the dialogue between them is closed except through an intersectional study of multiply disadvantaged populations. In this chapter I offer a reconsideration of the status of the material in queer theory and Marxism in order to recast them as subjectless critiques grounded in the problem of social structuration.[18] Reconceived as subjectless critiques, queer theory and Marxism would relinquish their proprietary claims to existing categories of identity and resist the discourse of rights and representation that drives liberal politics of recognition. Distinguishing Marxism's and queer theory's methodologies from their presumed objects (class and sexual identities), I propose the concept of queer Marxism to uncover their common preoccupations with the material grounds of subject formation. In my view, this conceptual move is necessitated by the subsumption of gendered and sexual life under the new conditions of global capitalism I describe as the age of the Beijing Consensus. Conversely, the political economy of the Beijing Consensus also creates the condition of possibility for a rethinking of the premises of queer theory and Marxism in the service of new modes of solidarity and activism.

The Unhappy Marriage of Queer Theory and Materialism

The prevalent perception that queer theory emerged out of the demise of Marxism is strongly rooted in a reductive understanding of Marxism as a historical materialism committed to the doctrine of the primacy of the economic. Gayle S. Rubin's classic essay "The Traffic in Women" offers a succinct formulation of this problem: "The failure of classical Marxism . . . results from the fact that Marxism, as a theory of social life, is relatively unconcerned with sex. In Marx's map of the social world, human beings are workers, peasants, or capitalists; that they are also men and women is not seen as very significant."[19] Rubin understands the field of sexuality studies to be in an agonistic relation to a leftist cultural politics dominated by Marxist concerns. From this perspective, the future of sexuality studies very much depends on our ability to overcome some of the explicitly materialist baggage of traditional Marxism. It is important to remember, however, that the "classical Marxism" to which Rubin was reacting at the time of her writing was not the intellectual practices of global Marxism but a distinctively American reception and use of Marxism mediated by 1970s socialist feminism. By this point, Marxism had acquired a reputation in the Anglo-American world as a dogmatic and monolithic system that threatened to subordinate all other social concerns to the imperatives of class struggle. As Heidi Hartmann wrote, "The 'marriage' of marxism and feminism has been like the marriage of husband and wife depicted in English common law: marxism and feminism are one, and that one is marxism. Recent attempts to integrate marxism and feminism are unsatisfactory to us as feminists because they subsume the feminist struggle into the 'larger' struggle against capital."[20] Following Rubin and Hartmann, scholars accepted the characterization of Marxism as a closed, gender-blind system that is constitutionally incapable of handling questions of sexual difference. As Johanna Brenner put it wryly, despite the vast body of Marxist writings on the woman question in the works of Friedrich Engels, V. I. Lenin, Emma Goldman, and Alexandra Kollontai—and we can certainly add to this list the newly discovered early twentieth-century Chinese anarcho-feminist writer He Yin-Zhen—"it has generally been accepted without much proof that classical marxist theory had little to say about women's oppression and the little it had to say was wrong."[21]

In "'Gender' for a Marxist Dictionary," Donna J. Haraway proposes that Marxism never developed a concept of gender for two reasons:

> First, "women," as well as "tribal" peoples, existed unstably at the boundary of the natural and social in the seminal writings of Marx and Engels, such that their efforts to account for the subordinate position of women were undercut by the category of the natural sexual division of labour, with its ground in an unexaminable natural heterosexuality; and second, Marx and Engels theorized the economic property relation as the ground of the oppression of women in marriage, such that women's subordination could be examined in terms of the capitalist relations of class, but not in terms of a specific sexual politics between men and women.[22]

It appears that Marxism suffers from this theoretical weakness because it is based on a monocausal explanation of social phenomena that treats all cultural issues and identities as derivative of economic inequalities. Indeed, many Marxist feminists, especially in the 1980s and 1990s, have insisted on the priority of economic analysis in understanding gender and sexual relations. Marxist feminism typically takes as its point of departure Engels's influential formulation of the materialist conception of history, which claims that "the determining factor in history is, in the final instance, the production and reproduction of immediate life."[23] What Engels calls the production and reproduction of immediate life corresponds to a binary concept of gender: "This, again, is of a twofold character: on the one side, the production of the means of existence, of food, clothing and shelter and the tools necessary for that production; on the other side, the production of human beings themselves, the propagation of the species."[24] While Engels considers production (men's wage labor) and reproduction (women's domestic work and child care) to be both central to the motions of history, this theory ultimately presents women's oppression as a secondary effect of capitalist oppression.

Engels's definition of the materialist conception of history received a feminist update in Rosemary Hennessy's contention that all social theory must begin with an explanation of a historically variable division of gendered labor that determines how human beings produce what is needed to survive. For Hennessy, heterosexism and patriarchy are culture-ideologies that legitimize capitalism's extraction of surplus value from workers, though they do so in an overdetermined and diffuse manner.[25] Another version of this thesis is found in Nancy Hartsock's work, which seeks to establish a feminist materialist standpoint from which to explain how women's subsistence labor (nurturing, childbearing, and domestic work) is both distinct from men's labor and required for the capitalist reproduction of a phallocratic world.[26] In Sandra Harding's theory, feminist scholarship "must begin from the politically activated perspective of women in the division of labor by sex/gender," a perspective that is "analytically impartial and epistemically non-relativist" and "able to understand sex/gender as an organic social variable which has become visible to us only because of changes in historical social relations."[27] While the feminist materialism of Hennessy, Hartsock, and Harding has focused on historical changes in lieu of geopolitical differences, the scholarship of critics in the global South, such as Neferti Tadiar's theorizations of the capitalist logic of the "sexual economies" of migrant domestic workers, has significantly expanded the international scope of this discussion.[28]

Building on feminist standpoint theories and feminist historical materialism in the 1980s and 1990s, social reproduction theory in the twenty-first century foregrounds the complex interactions among the reproduction of the conditions of production, the reproduction of the labor force, and biological reproduction to develop a more historical understanding of how unwaged feminized labor operates within and perpetuates capitalism.[29] Orthodox Marxist theories of the causal linkages between economic and sexual modes of (re)production, however, are empirically unconvincing, not least because of the paucity of Marxist literature on the historical experiences and structures of non-European societies. Even on a rhetorical level, it is all too easy for queer theorists to refute theories of economic determinism by pointing out that the distinction between the cultural and the economic is unstable, at best, and that there is no way to comprehend what counts as economic without recourse to a cultural frame.

In turn, Marxists and neo-Marxists have objected that queer theory has not only ignored the critique of capitalism but actually rendered it impossible by convincing the public that a ludic postmodernism of irony and parody is the same as radical politics and action. This objection, first strongly formulated by Teresa Ebert against poststructuralist feminism and more recently rehearsed by James Penny against queer theory, has become a recurring trope in numerous scholarly writings, solidifying the perception of the incommensurability of queer theory and Marxism.[30] But the more sophisticated version of this critique comes from Fredric Jameson, who characterizes queer politics as a single-theme struggle created by the atomizing, fragmentizing effects of capitalism. For Jameson, queer theory's focus on sexuality presupposes a form of possessive individualism that is itself a consequence of the division of labor created by the historical rise of industrial capitalism, which dissolved the organic reproduction of agrarian life, unseated the family as the primary economic unit of self-reproduction, and created social space for sexual and emotional intimacy outside the familial system. Instead of challenging the systemic reproduction of inequality, of which the oppression of sexual minorities is part, queer theory and other poststructuralist projects represent an intellectual retreat from the radical politics of the 1960s into a paralyzing quietism. In Jameson's view, psychoanalysis (from which queer theory is derived) stands as an important example of this culturalist retreat. Jameson argues that while psychoanalysis and queer theory resist the totalizing claims of Marxism, such discourses actually participate in and embody the transformations of capitalism, which provided their historical conditions of possibility: "The conditions of possibility of psychoanalysis become visible . . . only when you begin to appreciate the extent of psychic fragmentation since the beginnings of capitalism, with its systemic quantification and rationalization of experience, its instrumental reorganization of the subject just as much as the outside world."[31] The debate quickly became an argument over the priorities of one's object: Why should we care about pleasure, desire, sexuality, and "lifestyle choices" when vast numbers of human beings on this planet are still denied access to clean water, sanitation, personal safety, health care, food, and shelter? Formulated by influential critics such as Slavoj Žižek, this question challenges both the logic and the ethical commitment of queer theory, further hardening the impression that queer theory and Marxism are ultimately incompatible projects.[32]

Queer Anticapitalist Analyses Today

The works of Rosemary Hennessy, Teresa Ebert, James Penny, Fredric Jameson, and Slavoj Žižek represent different conceptual knots in the historical polarization of queer theory and Marxism, whereas queer scholars of a younger generation tend not to bother with Marxism at all. But despite the prevailing narrative that queer theory once found itself at odds with Marxism and has now left it behind, queer theory has never fully worked out the problem of the material. Instead, queer theory remains eminently troubled by a sense that something important lies beyond its limits. If the concept of the material once provided the negative space against which queer theory developed its most influential arguments, this dialectical relation also means that materialism has functioned as queer theory's constitutive outside, a sign of its incompletion that preserves its radically anticipatory and anti-identitarian nature.

The idea that queer theory somehow comes after Marxism to supplement it with sexuality is thus an illusion. In fact, queer theory has always thought about materiality, and sex has been in Marxism all along. In what follows, I offer a brief consideration of five different approaches to synthesizing Marxism and queer analysis, and the reasons such approaches need to be augmented by a more global reading of capitalist political economy in the age of the Beijing Consensus. I discuss the richness and limitations of this body of literature before proposing an alternative framework for mining the confluence of queer and Marxist insights. In my mind, all five approaches sketched here symptomatize the logic of US multiculturalism in that they start with the assigned objects of Marxism and queer theory—class and sexual identities— before arguing for their mutual embeddedness. It is necessary to develop a perspective that dissociates both queer theory and Marxism from their objects in order to arrive at the most powerful insight unifying these two intellectual currents: the conception of the self in a sociality of unknowable Others and material circumstances beyond one's control. This constitutive haunting of the self by unknowable Others is central to both queer theory and Marxist analysis. Recognizing it is essential for dislodging both theories from their unexamined basis in US area studies toward a more transnational dialogue in the age of the Beijing Consensus.

The first approach seeks to "queer" Marx by revealing sexuality or homosociality as the disavowed and deflected origins of a tradition that was too quickly dismissed as economistic. In "Unthinking Sex," Andrew Parker argues that the letters between Marx and Engels (which, as we know, provided Marxism's intellectual as well as material foundation) could be seen as love letters of sorts that embody an unacknowledged, disavowed queer relationship.[33] Clearly influenced by Eve Kosofsky Sedgwick's queer reading of deflected homosociality in heterosexual arrangements in *Between Men*, Parker's analysis shows that the perceived absence of queerness in the Marxist canon is actually a result of our own inability to attend to the unconscious of the text, our failure to read "the scene of writing": "Dramatizing links between core elements of Marxist theory, moments from nineteenth-century political history, and scenes from Marx's and Engels's 'private' lives," Parker's essay "suggests that Western Marxism's constitutive dependence on the category of production derives in part from an antitheatricalism, an aversion to certain forms of parody that prevents sexuality from attaining the political significance that class has long monopolized."[34] Through a rhetorical analysis, Parker recuperates a queer potentiality in Marx and Marxism that usefully complicates conventional interpretations of the tradition as having emerged independently of gender and sexual questions.

The past decade has seen an expansion of literary studies of the queerness of Marx's rhetoric. Sianne Ngai's recent work represents yet another innovative method for queering Marx. Through a close reading of key passages in the first and second volumes of *Capital*, Ngai uncovers a rhetorical shift in Marx's concept of abstract labor from capitalist abstractions (the transformation of independently produced commodities into money in exchange) to physiological abstractions (value as the congealed mass of human labor). This rhetorical ambiguity forms the basis of Ngai's insight that Marx's theory of capitalist reproduction is critically dependent on a conflation between the analytic and the phenomenological senses of the body that she terms "visceral abstractions." Marx's concept of abstract labor, firmly grounded in visceral abstractions, lends itself to rewriting as erotic encounters and queer affections. As Ngai shows in her reading of contemporary war poetry, visceral abstraction "stages the interpenetration of queer and Marxist thought."[35]

The second approach is the opposite of the first: it attempts to rematerialize queer theory by developing a comprehensive vision of the interrelatedness of sexual and nonsexual issues in a way that reveals queer's material unconscious as well as its radical potential. Cathy J. Cohen, for example, offers compelling arguments for why, and how, the queer movement must also consider the process of economic exploitation and issues that do not appear to directly affect LGBTQIA+ people: "Organizations and groupings within LGBTTSQ communities have to figure out a praxis concerning issues of economic exploitation. Fundamentally, we have to reach beyond those class or worker issues that are clearly bound to gay and lesbian identities, such as domestic partnership, to other class issues that structure the daily lived condition of 'queer' people more generally."[36] Emphasizing queer theory's opposition to "the category-based identity politics of traditional lesbian and gay activism," Cohen proposes that queer "symbolizes an acknowledgment that through our existence and everyday survival we embody sustained and multisited resistance to systems (based on dominant constructions of race and gender) that seek to normalize our sexuality, exploit our labor, and constrain our visibility."[37] In making these arguments, Cohen develops a materialist theory of the subject as social structuration.

Attention to how capitalism produces a mass-mediated LGBTQ consumer culture is a key feature of contemporary queer theory.[38] Lisa Duggan's influential theorization of homonormativity as the "sexual politics of neoliberalism" shows the complicity between neoliberal privatization—"the transfer of wealth and decision making from public, more-or-less accountable decision bodies to individual or corporate, unaccounted hands"—and the rise of "a politics that does not contest dominant heteronormative assumptions and institutions but upholds and sustains them, while promising the possibility of a demobilized gay constituency and a privatized, depoliticized gay culture anchored in domesticity and consumption."[39] For Clare Hemmings, the continued fantasy of lesbian and gay identities as the "repeated celebration of overcoming oppression" is precisely what allows queer people to knowingly participate as consumers in a globalized service industry.[40] Aren Z. Aizura develops a persuasive account of the paradox of trans necropolitics, showing that gender-variant bodies are both incorporated into the circuits of capital and rendered disposable by capital: "Thus, considering value and racialization alongside necropolitics illuminates our understanding of transphobic hate speech and violence, but also the modes of subjectivation that stage exclusion from the social as merely another way to *include* bodies in the structural grind of capital."[41] Collectively, these works uncover the material conditions for emergent sexual identities that, at first glance, appear unconcerned with questions of political economy.

The third approach utilizes queer theory to update the definition of labor in Marxism. The starting point of this form of queer Marxism is that twentieth- and twenty-first-century conditions of production under multinational digital capitalism have become so complex that they have rendered traditional Marxism's focus on the industrial worker obsolete.[42] Instead of the production of commodities, contemporary Marxist critics turn to the production of affect. While most writers in this school make use of Foucault's theory of biopolitical production, others draw on György Lukács's concept of reification or Herbert Marcuse's analysis of surplus repression to formulate innovative readings of desire in capitalism.[43] Kevin Floyd's *The Reification of Desire* is perhaps the most influential example of this type of scholarship.[44] Floyd's central thesis is that the twentieth century witnessed a dissociation of sexuality from gender because of the dynamic of social reification produced by capitalism. In Floyd's view, under contemporary capitalism, what is reified, or transformed into commodities, is human desire. Although Floyd draws mainly from Foucault and Lukács to develop this framework, his analysis resonates with Michael

Hardt and Antonio Negri's reading of the present moment as the biopolitical reproduction of immaterial labor and information commodities.[45] In a move parallel to Hardt and Negri's conceptualization of "the multitude" as the new subject of collective struggles in the age of immaterial labor, Floyd substitutes the queer for the proletariat in an updated cultural Marxism for the twentieth and twenty-first centuries.

In what ways is compulsory heterosexuality contingent on a system of compulsory able-bodiedness produced by neoliberal capitalism? The crip queer theorist Robert McRuer argues that the current century has witnessed a proliferation of "flexible" heterosexual and able-bodied subjects whose sense of subjective wholeness—often projected as heteronormative epiphanies in the media—corresponds to the "flexible and innovative" corporate strategies required by contemporary capitalism.[46] The emergence of a flexible hetero-sexual and able-bodied subject, spectacularly celebrated by corporate capital, facilitates the fragmentation of the labor pools into increasingly smaller and more expendable groups around the globe. For McRuer, post-Fordist regimes of flexible accumulation and affective labor are critically dependent on a culture of tolerance and diversity (working with people with disabilities and alternative sexualities) and on the projection of modern workers as sufficiently flexible and innovative to make it through moments of subjective or economic crisis.

Floyd's and McRuer's analyses of the transformations of labor under neo-liberal capitalism can be profitably compared to Holly Lewis's *The Politics of Everybody*, which argues that Marxism must depart from the "old, unfashion-able approach of Marx's materialism" that has identified the working class—as Lukács did—as the historical agent for a revolutionary transformation. Unlike Floyd and McRuer, who are more invested in modernizing Lukács and making his theory of the proletariat compatible with the conditions of the precariat of the twenty-first century, Lewis proposes a "politics of everybody" that incorporates queer, poststructuralist feminist, and trans perspectives into an analysis of race, class, and gender in capitalism as "mutually conditioning components of an ideology produced by material social relations."[47]

The fourth approach is intersectional analysis, which considers the formation of social subjects by overlapping and convergent identities and fields of politicization. Theories of intersectionality hold that identities such as "gay and lesbian" are necessarily partial and incomplete. Insofar as identity is possible only in relation to its constitutive outside, intersectional work seeks to move past the opacity of the self by grounding its analysis in the locations and experiences of multiply constituted identities and hybrid subjects. Intersectional analysis asks, for example, how queer people of color in the urban ghetto are more vulnerable to the threat of AIDS and HIV, how the expansion of gay commercial scenes contributed to race-based divisions in America, or how capitalist development and gentrification affect trans sex workers differently from middle-class white gay men seeking marriage equality.[48] The importance of this kind of work cannot be overstated, since even within LGBTQIA+ communities there is a growing perception that *queer* simply means affluent white gay men; many people do not recognize themselves in representations of queer culture in the media. This conundrum led José Esteban Muñoz to propose "disidentification" as a critical concept and survival strategy for those who do not fit the normative scripts of the white, middle-class, cisgender subject of queer theory.[49] Calling for a shift away from queer theory's traditional focus on the Euro-American male, Anjali Arondekar, David L. Eng, Roderick A. Ferguson, Gayatri Gopinath, E. Patrick Johnson, Eng-Beng Lim, Scott Lauria Morgensen, José Esteban Muñoz, Jennifer C. Nash, Hoang Tan Nguyen, Chandan Reddy, Juana María Rodríguez, Andrea L. Smith, C. Riley Snorton, Salvador Vidal-Ortiz, and many others have constructed the framework of queer-of-color critique. For Ferguson, who is often credited with coining the phrase *queer-of-color critique*, this line of inquiry necessitates a reconfiguration of Marxist understandings of historical materialism.[50] Queer-of-color critique recenters the materiality of race and class by interrogating the normativity of the white middle-class subject in queer theory. Inspired by queer-of-color critiques, scholars of social justice have developed cross-class and antiracist projects committed to redirecting queer studies away from elite institutions to serve poor and minority students.[51]

Finally, the fifth approach rewrites the narrative of the transition from feudalism to capitalism in terms of the emergence, consolidation, and proliferation of sexual identities. Though many seminal works have developed materialist and dialectical perspectives on the history of sexuality, the earliest and perhaps best-known exploration of the connection between the development of capitalism and the invention of homosexuality is John D'Emilio's classic essay "Capitalism and Gay Identity."[52] D'Emilio argues that "gay men and lesbians have not always existed. Instead, they are a product of history, and their emergence is associated with the relations of capitalism; it has been the historical development of capitalism—more specifically, its free labor system—that has allowed large numbers of men and women in the late twentieth century to call themselves gay, to see themselves as part of a community of similar men and women, and to organize politically on the basis of that identity."[53]

"Capitalism and Gay Identity" gained significant currency and popularized what I describe as the Stonewall-centered liberation story. As D'Emilio sees it, the invention of modern gay identity resulted from a particular development of modern capitalism in the United States. D'Emilio's theory locates the origins of gay communities in the segregation of men and women in the armed forces during World War II, the postwar resettlement of GIs in coastal urban centers like San Francisco and New York, and the disruption of traditional patterns of gender relations and procreative sexuality owing to the developments of free labor capitalism.[54] The mass migration to coastal urban centers, in turn, created the preconditions for the Stonewall riots in 1969, which supposedly led to the gay liberation movements in the United States and everywhere else.

We can identify several problems with the Stonewall-centered liberation story's claims to precedence and singularity. To begin with, the Americanist explanation of the invention of homosexuality as a social identity overlooks the interpenetration of global and local forces in the making of communities. Clearly, not everybody who self-identifies as queer would see themselves as a descendant of American GIs or as a participant in the culture or community they created. This explanation also falsely homogenizes the racially diverse histories of San Francisco and New York. As several important studies have demonstrated, the sexual culture of these urban centers was shaped by the influx of southern and eastern European Catholics, Jews, Arabs, Latinxs, and Asians.[55] Conversely, the experience of each subcommunity may be radically different, calling for more critical analysis of the intersections of race and sexuality in the form of queer diasporic studies and queer-of-color critiques. D'Emilio's theory ignores the fact that many of the participants in the Stonewall riots were trans people of color and that the events occurred in conjunction with the civil rights movement, the anti–Vietnam War movement, and other intellectual currents of the global counterculture of the 1960s. The Stonewall riots were themselves created by transnational flows in a global context shaped by political economic asymmetries. The projection of the Stonewall riots as the origin of modern gay identity is an act of appropriation that erases the racial, class, and gender complexities of the movement in the service of a homogeneous tale of middle-class, cisgender, able-bodied, and white homosexuals' cultural and legal victories.

"Capitalism and Gay Identity" fails to address the emergence of sexual cultures and movements outside the United States, which cannot be attributed to the dissemination of a US model of sexual politics with the Stonewall story as its blueprint.[56] Changes brought about by transnational capitalism—the ease of travel, new technologies, and accelerated flows of migrants, commodities, and information across national borders—have produced neither a viable strategy for legislating gay rights on a global scale nor a universal consensus on what these should be. Against the Stonewall-centered narrative, critics in the global South have pursued transnational analysis to demonstrate the diversity and coagency of global sexual cultures. Josephine Chung-rui Ho, for example, has demonstrated how the emergence of a global civil society composed of nongovernmental organizations, human rights watchers, LGBT cultural events, and internet communities assimilates local movements into a moralistic surveillance network with oppressive and antisex effects.[57] If globalization has produced ambivalent effects on local queer struggles, it may be because the distinction between global and local is never a simple matter.[58] For Jonathan Symons and Dennis Altman, a central irony is that while opposition to gay rights is often justified in the name of culture and tradition and "framed as a defense of sovereignty that resists imposition of western cultural values and identity categories," such anticolonial efforts are often in reality defending laws that were introduced under colonial rule.[59]

D'Emilio's model, which defines capitalism narrowly as free wage labor or urbanization and conflates identity with public association, has lost its persuasiveness. With the post-2008 academic revival of Marxist literary criticism, more nuanced and more globally oriented works have emerged to retheorize the relationship between capitalism and homosexuality, including Benjamin Kahan's "Conjectures on the Sexual World-System" and Christopher Chitty's *Sexual Hegemony*. Both Kahan and Chitty argue that the formations of sexual knowledge and communities are central to the history of capitalism. Reworking Marxist theories of world systems into theories of sexual systems, Kahan reads the archives of print culture in the core of Japan, legal codes in the semiperiphery of Russia, and religious documents in the periphery of Buganda to understand "the encounter between the diachronic force of object choice as the organizing dimensions of sexuality and its collision with a range of other sexual knowledges and organizations."[60] In *Sexual Hegemony*, Chitty links changing attitudes toward sodomy to the chronological succession of the four cycles of capital accumulation (northern Italian, Dutch, British, and American) identified by world-systems theorists. Conversely, Kahan's and Chitty's analyses demonstrate that the history of sexuality cannot be understood independently of the history of property relations and proletarianization. Peter Drucker's *Warped* offers yet another version of the story, arguing that the distinction between heterosexuality and homosexuality was created by capitalism's imperialist expansion. In Drucker's view, European capital accumulation gave rise to various technologies, including pseudoscientific racism, the invention of a working-class family wage, and the medicalization of sexuality. By contrast, as capitalism failed to develop in the feudal societies of Asia—which Drucker defines as those "in whose sexual regimes class and status trumped gender and kinship"—the basic historical conditions for lesbian/gay communities remained absent.[61]

All five approaches have made significant contributions to queer theory and Marxism and have uncovered their surprising affinities. Yet they are primarily concerned with unifying Marxist and queer objects instead of their methods. In my opinion, these theoretical projects have not yet extracted the best insights from the synthesis of queer theory and Marxism and sometimes end up replaying the multiculturalist mantra of race, class, gender, and sexuality only to pit "old class politics" against "new cultural politics." In contrast to these approaches, my interest lies in developing a perspective that dispenses with the multiculturalist language altogether and locates in the concept of the material the possibility for a systemic analysis of the sociality of the self. Instead of combining two standpoints or experiences of victimization, queer Marxism, as I develop the concept, designates a materialist, subjectless critique grounded in queer and Marxist theories of social structuration as demanded by the conditions of capitalist transformation in the age of the Beijing Consensus. The material in both queer theory and Marxism describes how a subject comes into existence by virtue of its constitutive outside—what cannot be known or named in advance, what necessarily escapes categories of identity politics. Insofar as it is queer theory, rather than Marxism, that has developed the most trenchant and complex account of the material, queer theory must turn to its own intellectual origins before we can figure out what it really means to "rematerialize" queer theory.

Materialism, Materiality, and Materialization in Judith Butler

After developing a longitudinal view of queer theory's materialism in broad strokes in the first half of this chapter, I now turn to a close reading of the materialist implications of Judith Butler's work. Here I'm particularly interested in the "accidentally Marxist" strands and "unconsciously materialist" dimensions of Butler's thought, uncanny parallels between theories of performativity and

Marxist labor theory of value, and instances of unwitting and temporary alliances. The primary reason I want to devote the rest of this chapter to Butler's work is the obvious one: Butler's canonical status as a founding figure of queer theory allows them to serve as a synecdoche for that field. But more specifically, I take issue with the widely accepted notion that the structure of Butler's thought furnishes irrefutable proof that queer theory came into being as the result of a linguistic turn that cleaved the notion of gender from Marxist historicism.[62] Indeed, the perception of Butler as a post- if not anti-Marxist thinker seems to have become something of a truism. One need not look past Martha C. Nussbaum's famously vitriolic essay "The Professor of Parody," in which Nussbaum characterizes Butler's work as "hip defeatism," "quietism and retreat," and "the virtually complete turning from the material side of life, toward a type of verbal and symbolic politics that makes only the flimsiest of connections with the real situation of real women."[63]

While Nussbaum's critique may seem utterly predictable given her liberal humanist understanding of what constitutes "the material side of life," characterizations of Butler as an antimaterialist thinker also come from those who are closer to Marxism and queer theory. We might recall that Kevin Floyd begins his account of queer Marxism in *The Reification of Desire* with a critique of Butler's "polemical" and "worrisome" presentation of the lecture that was later published under the title "Merely Cultural," an essay that, in Floyd's view, did much to create "a schism between Marxism and queer theory [that] was impossible not to notice" in the early to mid-1990s.[64] Reading Butler as an iconic figure of post-Marxism, Philip Goldstein tells us that "Butler adopts the Foucauldian notion that, as performative, the norms of gender render agency as the effect of power, not as the subject's independent choice"; however, unlike the structuralists, Butler "fails to consistently accept the 'material existence' of the institutional rituals that, according to Althusser and Foucault, reproduce conventions."[65]

For Goldstein as well as Floyd, Butler's use of Foucault represents a key example of queer theory's antimaterialism. However, as my rereading of Butler's major works in the following demonstrates, the relationship between Butler's theory and materialism cannot be so easily summarized and dismissed. The trajectory of Butler's thought from gender performativity to ethical alterity emblematizes a moment in queer theory that, I contend, has greater affinity to Marxist theories of the impersonal logic of value extraction than is commonly recognized. By returning to the concept of social structuration that subtends Butler's work from *Gender Trouble* to *The Force of Nonviolence*, we can arrive at a more accurate assessment of Butler's (and, by extension, queer theory's) relation to materialism in the service of a more productive dialogue between these traditions. Having reinterpreted the work of one of North America's most prominent queer theorists in this way, in the conclusion I offer some reflections on why this reinterpretation of the material also logically demands a deeper engagement with queer theories produced in languages and cultures in the global South.

Since *Gender Trouble*, Butler's work has gradually yet decisively shifted away from the performative nature of gender to questions of survival and persistence—what makes a life livable, how to preserve the basic conditions and needs of human life, and how to affirm the constitutive role of gender and sexuality in these questions. This shift is not the evolution of one theorist's personal views but, rather, the index of a paradigm shift and a response to increasingly acute global crises and conflicts. We may, in other words, read Butler's work as a continuous attempt to craft a theoretical vocabulary of gender that is capable of handling the most urgent social issues of the age of the Beijing Consensus, an attempt to work out the trauma of the Left and the specter of the material.

The trajectory of Butler's thought from "What is a woman?" to "What makes a life livable?" indicates an implicit response to and an interpenetration of Marxist questions, particularly objections that gender and sexual struggles seem less material, less pressing than food and shelter. On occasion, critics have objected that queer theory merely offers a descriptive account of sexual minorities' experiences of victimization without developing a clear vision of social transformation and agency that is akin to Marxist theory of revolutions. We can detect this critique as the implicit context for Butler's thinking when they write defensively, "How do drag, butch, femme, transgender, transsexual persons enter into the political field? Some people have asked me what is the use of increasing possibilities for gender. I tend to answer: Possibility is not a luxury; it is as crucial as bread."[66] In insisting that the expansion of gender norms is "as crucial as bread," Butler is arguing that gender is a material concern and a matter of survival that demands the same political consideration as food, shelter, and clean water.

While the notion of performativity provided the analytic purchase for the most commonly cited works of Butler's early gender theory, in their later writings Butler has come to focus on dispossession and ethical alterity as the central problems of gender. In *Bodies That Matter*, Butler makes clear that the theory of performativity outlined in *Gender Trouble* does not presuppose a voluntarist subject who chooses its gender at will.[67] Butler's 2004 *Undoing Gender* further develops the argument that gender is not something that a person chooses or authors; rather, it is a citation of social norms and conventions that have no single point of origin.

This critique of voluntarism becomes a fully developed theory of ethics and the basis of Butler's claim for the politicality of queer. Since having a gender necessarily places one in a matrix of social relations, it follows that gender also implicates a person in a social field of responsibilities. Characterizing gender and sexuality as "*modes of being dispossessed*, ways of being for another or, indeed, by virtue of another," Butler argues that having a gendered and sexed body constitutes a primary vulnerability that can become the basis of political communities.[68] Gender disrupts the illusion of bodily autonomy, moving the subject outside and beyond itself with grief, passion, outrage, and dispossession. This relationality necessarily turns "sexual difference" into a "question of ethics."[69] In the social field of gender, a subject is made and unmade, refashioned and dispossessed by unknown Others: "What I call my 'own' gender appears perhaps at times as something that I author or, indeed, own. But the terms that make up one's gender are, from the start, outside oneself, beyond oneself in a sociality that has no single author."[70] For Butler, gender can never be reduced to a volitional act of self-nomination. The critique of the subject as autoconstitution does not equal political nihilism, nor is the account of the gendered self in a field of social structuration the same as a static structuralism. Crucially, the subject's radical dependency on unknown Others is also the source of its agency: "And this means that we are constituted politically in part by virtue of the social vulnerability of our bodies; we are constituted as fields of desire and physical vulnerability, at once publicly assertive and vulnerable."[71] With a nonsovereign account of agency, Butler argues that the gendered implications of one's bodily exposure to the Other reveal the constitutive sociality of the self, which in turn provides the basis for thinking a political community of a complex order.[72]

In arguing that "it is through the body that gender and sexuality become exposed to others, implicated in social processes, inscribed by cultural norms, and apprehended in their social meanings," Butler displaces the voluntarist view of gender and recasts it as an effect of social structuration, forming an unwitting alliance with Marxism.[73] The operative word in Butler's revised theory of gender, *dispossession*, is first and foremost a Marxian category. Dispossession in the Marxist literature describes the process that drives the mechanism of inequality grounded in land, property, and livelihood.[74]

In chapter 27 of the first volume of *Capital*, Marx discusses the creation of a working class through the expropriation of the agricultural population's land, which resulted in the destruction of yeomanry and drove a vast number of forcibly dispossessed peasants and craftspeople into the manufacturing towns. A significant controversy in Marxism, informed by Indigenous studies, revolves around Marx's theorization of the dual processes of dispossession and proletarianization and the weighting of his analytic attention being placed on the latter, as the expropriation of the laborer, rather than the former, as the expropriation of the land.[75] In one of the most influential contemporary formulations of the problem, David Harvey proposes that "accumulation by dispossession" on a global scale has surpassed expanded reproduction as the dominant form of capital accumulation.[76] While Marx understands primitive accumulation to be a set of original events that inaugurated capitalist production, accumulation by dispossession for Harvey has never ceased to exist. And unlike Rosa Luxemburg, who identifies underconsumption as the reason capitalism needs some sort of outside, Harvey argues that overproduction has created enclosure and dispossession across the global economy.

Butler's philosophical reworking of the concept of dispossession represents a move parallel to the efforts of contemporary Marxist thinkers (such as Harvey, Massimo De Angelis, Saskia Sassen, and Michael Levien) to situate Marx's original theorization in a broader context of a global economy splintered by racialized and gendered enclosures. Butler is careful to distinguish between dispossession as an ethical perspective on the limits of the sovereign subject and self-sufficiency (which we must value) and dispossession as "what happens when populations lose their land, their citizenship, their means of livelihood, and become subject to military and legal violence" (which we must oppose).[77] Similarly, Butler highlights the difference between precarity (or precariousness) as an "existential category that is presumed to be equally shared," a form of primary vulnerability to injury and loss that can never be reversed, and "precarity as a condition of induced inequality and destitution" that is characteristic of neoliberal regimes.[78] The fact that both dispossession and precarity carry this double valence is no accident; rather, Butler's recognition of the forms of responsibility and resistance that emerge from a dispossessed subject is critically informed by dispossession in the second, Marxian sense as the suffering of the displaced and disenfranchised under neocolonial, neoliberal, or capitalist conditions. The critique of the sovereign subject in queer theory is hence not a form of linguistic play or postmodern parody, as some Marxists have suggested; rather, it represents a reengagement with the most urgent economic and political questions of the age of the Beijing Consensus.

In "The Inorganic Body in the Early Marx," Butler explicitly draws on Marx's and Marxist works to formulate a new understanding of the body and its persistence. Butler focuses on Marx's *Economic and Philosophic Manuscripts of 1844*, a text often read as reflecting an anthropocentrism that was eventually superseded by the more scientific theory of capitalism developed in *Capital* and the *Grundrisse*. Butler observes that those early manuscripts contain a duality captured by Marx's enigmatic claim that "nature is the inorganic body of humans."[79] The human organism, bound up with inorganic nature for the possibilities of its own subsistence, is living as being both animated in some respects and deanimated in others. Butler interprets Marx's theory as affirming the dialectical interdependency between the living human body and an inorganic ecological and social world to which it is ineluctably tied. In other words, Marx's "nature is the inorganic body of humans" establishes the view that a body is always socially mediated because it belongs with others' lives and finds its means of subsistence only in specific political and economic systems. These systems create conditions that expose certain bodies to precarity, completely abandoned or employable only on a contingent basis. For Butler, Marx provides an indispensable conceptual framework for thinking about the body as a form of social mediation and continuous interchange (not to be confused with exchange or exchangeability), which in turn calls for a decentered, nonsovereign account of the subject to remind us that, "as mediated, as species, we are always more and less than this body, and this body extends to others and to the conditions of life itself."[80]

Though Butler does not invoke the language of "social structuration," their theory of gender as dispossession resonates with Marx's insistence that life is made possible and reconstituted by the fruits of the labor of unknown Others. Marxists argue that the individual is materially reproduced by a chain of social responsibilities and debts and is always part of a matrix of social relations that exceeds the individual's horizons of cognizance. The crucial difference between Butler's concept of dispossession and Marxian labor theory of value, of course, is that Butler has a much more expansive understanding of livability beyond the production of food and shelter. But in *Capital*, Marx already makes clear that a theory of social reproduction cannot be limited to economic activities. In David Ricardo's original formulation of the labor theory of value, the value of a commodity is determined by the amount of human labor expended in the production process.[81] Marx refines Ricardo's theory by locating value at the level of the aggregate production of commodities instead of the production of each particular commodity. Hence, value-producing labor for Marx is necessarily abstract rather than concrete, simple rather than compound, social rather than private, and necessary rather than wasted. By turning Ricardo's accounting problem of individual commodities into a social theory of reproduction and restructuration in the aggregate, Marx developed a new labor theory of value that is resolutely also a theory of ethics premised on the constitutive sociality of the self. The individual producer is no longer considered in relation to the sales of that person's labor power. Each unit of raw materials, equipment, and infrastructure in the production process contains a fraction of congealed human labor from unknown sources; each human life, to the extent that life is renewable and reproducible, contains an inexhaustible list of social and personal histories. In Marx's labor theory of value, society is an infinitely complex fractal formed by a chain of value that allows each human life to be materially sustained by a fraction of the labor of unknown Others in capitalism as a moving totality.

While queer theory argues that, through gender and sexuality, the self is constitutively linked to unknown and unknowable Others, Marxism makes a similar point about the opacity of the self by arguing that the bourgeois subject is merely the reified substance of historical antinomies. Where queer theory and Marxism part company is that the latter maintains that some (but not all) aspects of this interdependence can be systematically analyzed and understood through quantitative "laws" such as the labor theory of value or the falling rate of profit. The Marxist argument that such formalist accounts shed light on crucial aspects of our interdependence does not necessarily amount to a totalizing claim about the all-determining power of the economic. On the contrary, Marxism shares with queer theory the belief that human life is incessantly transformed by norms and forces outside the subject's horizons of cognition. As such, Marx's labor theory of value and Butler's view of gender as the constitutive sociality of the self embody closely related critiques of the voluntarist subject.[82]

Conclusion: Rethinking Queer Marxism in the Age of the Beijing Consensus

Queer theory, even as elaborated by authors closely identified as arguing in favor of a radical linguistic constructivism, turns out to be a materialist theory of social structuration with affinities to Marxism. Queer theory does not argue that gender is fluid, mobile, definitionless, or freely chosen; rather, it shows that identity is produced by political apparatuses, social norms, and other specters of the material beyond one's knowledge and agency. We can—and sometimes must—refuse the established protocols of gender, but none of us can fully escape the complex workings of social power and interconnected forms of subjugation. Insofar as queer theory and Marxism place an equal emphasis on such primary ties to unknown Others as a source of human vulnerability, both are committed to a materialism even when the material remains unnamed, un-identified, or reduced to a spectral presence. Material analysis shows that ques-tions of gender and sexuality are part of a matrix of social interdependence that connects the self to Others beyond all kinds of borders—geopolitical, ethnolinguistic, religious, or otherwise. These Others may speak different languages, inhabit any kind of socioeconomic organization, and subscribe to a variety of cultural beliefs and customs. There is no reason to assume that a queer Marxist project must begin with the intersections of race, gender, class, and sexuality in the United States. Instead, the tools of materialism allow us to look beyond national borders to formulate a more global understanding of capitalism in the age of the Beijing Consensus.

This move is logically demanded by the specter of materialism. Without the concept of the material, Marxism is reduced to an economic doctrine that queer theory has resisted through culturalist themes, but this narrative reflects the provincialism of US multiculturalist politics. In the United States, the liberal-pluralist paradigm continues to be the primary language for progressive social policies, which has produced a deeply entrenched impression that the primary obstacle facing queer people is discrimination, misrecognition, or other forms of mental judgment that impede parity in participation. Instead of demanding distributive justice, queer people in this approach to social change must rely on the goodwill of enlightened individuals for tolerance and acceptance. The liberal-pluralist language of diversity and inclusion presents a reformist strat-egy to assimilate the disenfranchised into the national polity in accordance with mainstream views, instead of a transformative strategy that reconfig-ures relationships of power and expands the field of gender possibilities. A materialist methodology is a timely response to the liberal-pluralist ideology that gender and sexual minorities suffer only from prejudices or invisibility. While being haunted by the material, queer theory has also given us the tools to establish a new ethics that can reorient the subject from liberal possessive individualism to impersonal structures of power and scenes of collective ac-tion in the age of the Beijing Consensus.

PART II

History

The Subsumption of Literature   3

LU XUN'S QUEER MODERNISM

IN THE CHINESE REVOLUTIONS

From the Communist victory in 1949 to the death of Mao Zedong in 1976, Chinese Marxism provided for the non-Western world perhaps the most successful economic alternative to capitalist modernity as well as a theory of literature in the revolutionary process. Mao's chief contributions to the materialist dialectic—his concepts of voluntarism, permanent revolution, and the mass line—explain why a Marxist revolution requires a cultural revolution, in particular the reconstruction of literature, as the material basis of a new society. This conceptualization of literature as encoding a revolutionary subject places human consciousness at the center of history, while refusing to reduce literature to a superstructural instance determined by an economic base. For cultural revolution to serve as a radical means to achieve a classless society and national liberation, a critical literary realism is needed to capture the historical specificities of capitalism's social contradictions.[1] Critical realism opens up an alternative vision of the future by foregrounding the coexistence of antagonistic social formations and temporalities. In so doing, literature furnishes a political optics for articulating the collective subject of history through the aesthetic representation of such contradictions and their social grounds.

Given the Chinese Marxist theoretical understanding of revolution as encompassing and enabling cultural changes, it is no surprise that numerous critics argue that the emergence of China's queer communities was made possible by the achievements of Chinese socialism rather than by its over-coming. Drawing attention to the revolutionary origins of the term *tongzhi* (which means both "gay" and "comrade"), Hongwei Bao situates the pro-gressive potential of queer subjectivities in contemporary China within the socialist ideals of egalitarianism and the revolutionary experiences of mass mobilization. In Bao's reading, the mutually constitutive relationship between China's socialist *tongzhi* and postsocialist queer makes it possible for con-temporary sexual politics to challenge new forms of neoliberal gay identity produced by global capitalism.[2] Huang Yingying and Pan Suiming propose that homosexual identities constitute a key component of an ongoing "sexual revolution" that has emerged since the mid-1980s, which refashioned the socialist idioms of "changing traditions" (*yifeng yisu*) and "class conflict" (*jieji douzheng*) into new social norms decoupling sex from marriage and procreation.[3] But if China's new sexual cultures and its Marxism share an overlapping history, it does not mean that the former simply ensued from the other in a causally linked fashion. Too often, the overdetermined nuances of sexuality were reorganized into a smooth narrative of China's transition from a semifeudal, semicolonial society to postsocialism in canonical Marx-ist historiography. Instead of seeing literature as a repository of capitalism's historical contradictions, mainstream critics expunge modern Chinese liter-ature's queer excesses and subsume it under a unilinear history of socialist revolution and capitalist modernization.

The most important figure in the subsumption of literature is the modernist-realist writer Lu Xun, who has been consistently interpreted by political leaders in the People's Republic of China (PRC) as the embodiment of revolutionary China and its Marxist spirit. This reputation is justifiably linked to Lu Xun's critical realism, which powerfully depicts the encounters between peasants and modern intellectuals at the time of China's violent incorporation into the capitalist world system and the creation of an ever-growing dispos-able population. From Mao's famous 1942 "Talks at the Yan'an Forum of Literature and Art" to Xi Jinping's 2014 "Speech at the Forum on Literature and Art," Chinese leaders have repeatedly emphasized the significance of Lu Xun in the convergence of literature and political leadership as mutually enhancing forms of sovereign creation.[4] But while Chinese intellectual and political leaders applaud Lu Xun for having developed a critical realism that liberated Chinese consciousness from the mental hold of "feudalism," the queer elements of his writing are largely ignored in this accounting of China's revolutionary past and its transition to capitalism.[5] A reinterpretation of Lu

Xun's Marxist realism as a forgotten and subsumed queer modernism thus sheds light on the historical function of an analytic of gender and sexuality in capitalism's global transformations.

The subsumption of this queer modernism poses historical questions about Lu Xun's relations with Marxism that are distinct from contemporary debates about his appropriation or mythologization by the Chinese Communist Party (CCP). Instead of trying to resolve the question of Lu Xun's Marxism by reexamining his political alignment with CCP leaders or the extent and accuracy of his knowledge of Marx, I focus on how Lu Xun's invention of a queer modernist aesthetics expanded the parameters of cultural materialism. Through irony, rhetorical displacement, metafictional excess, and other formal experimentations, Lu Xun calls attention to the limits of human cognition while grounding the speaking subject in the historical conditions of its making. Lu Xun's canvas of "feudal" characters—peasants, illiterate women, servants, laborers, the insane, children—captures the capitalist reification of social relations that are, at first glance, either independent of free wage labor or anterior to primitive accumulation. Lu Xun invests a revolutionary hope, even agency, in capital's disposable populations—queer subjects who are rendered precarious and expendable by the historical motions of capitalism. Focusing on restoring such queer energies in Lu Xun's texts, I explore the political possibilities of thinking about queer literature's relevance for a broader, inter-Asian form of cultural Marxism.

Lu Xun and Chinese Marxism

From the start, the Communist Revolution in China has been a literary affair. As many scholars have observed, a unique feature of Chinese Marxism is that it was led by literary figures who were convinced that China's political revolution must begin with a literary revolution.[6] From the perspectives of its early leaders—Chen Duxiu, Li Dazhao, and Qu Qiubai—Chinese Communism was not merely a revolution in the economic mode of production; it was a revolution of ethics and culture, an iconoclastic rejection of the hegemony of Confucianism that these leaders held responsible for China's failures, from the Qing's military defeats by imperialist powers to the disastrous outcomes of the 1919 Paris Peace Conference. This spiritual revolution, known as the New Culture Movement, provided the context for both the creation of the CCP in 1921 under the leadership of Chen and Li and the emergence of a "plain-speaking" (*baihua*) literature in modern vernacular Chinese, following the pioneering example of Lu Xun. The story of the birth of Chinese Communism has since then become virtually indistinguishable from the story of Chinese literary modernism, though what connects Communist political organizing and Lu Xun's literary project is far from self-evident.

Our lack of clarity on what exactly is Marxist about Lu Xun's modernism no doubt has something to do with the complexity of his writing, which defies clear ideological categorization and as such has fascinated generations of readers both inside and outside of China. Fredric Jameson reads Lu Xun as a paradigmatic third-world writer whose fiction exemplifies why "Third-World texts, even those which are seemingly private and invested with a properly libidinal dynamic—necessarily project a political dimension in the form of national allegory."[7] In Geremie Barmé's view, Lu Xun's writing has "motivated China's voices of conscience," like Liu Xiaobo, Ai Weiwei, and "the recently jailed young Hong Kong democrats," to break the silence and disturb everybody's sleep "in the iron house of Xi Jinping."[8] Gloria Davies calls Lu Xun a Chinese Friedrich Nietzsche who is similarly "trapped in the construction of a modernity which is fundamentally problematic."[9] Qu Qiubai, China's preeminent Marxist literary critic, memorably described Lu Xun as a Chinese Remus, raised on the milk of a wild beast to wield an iron broomstick with which to rid the masses of their slavish nature.[10] The Japanese intellectual Takeuchi Yoshimi in 1948 characterized Lu Xun as a Hegelian dialectician whose writing instantiates Asia's "overcoming modernity" (*kindai no chōkoku*), the moment "when the slave recognizes himself as *slave* [so that] it finally becomes possible for him to free himself from *slavery*."[11]

From being tasked with overcoming modernity to being cast as exemplary of third-world nationalism, Lu Xun has been called into the service of contradictory political projects, but what is most striking is his consistently canonical status in the eyes of the CCP in its long century of ideological transformation from "class struggle" (revolution) in the 1950s and 1960s to "economic reconstruction" (modernization) in the post–Cultural Revolution era.[12] Merle Goldman observes that although Lu Xun's life and work have been "interpreted in different periods to conform to the latest mutation in party policy," the CCP has consistently "depicted him as drawing the blueprint of the communist future."[13] Lu Xun's canonicity was codified by Mao's 1940 speech "Xin minzhu zhuyi lun" (On new democracy), in which the chairman characterized Lu Xun as "the chief commander of China's cultural revolution" and "the bravest and most correct, the firmest, the most loyal and the most ardent national hero, a hero without parallel in our history."[14] By 1966

Lu Xun became an official Maoist icon, turning (as the contemporary fiction writer Yu Hua put it) "from an author to a catchphrase, one that represented eternal correctness and permanent revolution."[15] The Central Cultural Revolution Small Group expended enormous resources to commemorate Lu Xun as a prescient exemplar of Mao Zedong Thought; in July, two months after launching the Cultural Revolution, Mao wrote to his wife Jiang Qing that he and Lu Xun were "of one mind" ("xin shi xiang tong de").[16]

That said, a central problem in PRC scholarship on Lu Xun—Luxunology (*Luxue*)—is how to reconcile Mao's sacralization of Lu Xun as a Communist warrior with the fact that the writer never joined the Communist Party. Despite persistent CCP efforts to reinterpret Lu Xun's writings as expressions of his "boundless esteem and love for Chairman Mao," during Lu Xun's own lifetime (1881–1936) the writer was barely aware of Mao, and the only known direct contact between the two was a congratulatory telegram Lu Xun sent to the survivors of the Long March on their arrival in northern Shaanxi.[17] In fact, Lu Xun frequently parodied his Marxist peers' "revolutionary literature" as an "unfortunate confusion of guns with words"; he also sharply criticized the Communist Party and its politics in his final years.[18] Yet critics who regard Lu Xun as a foundational figure of Chinese Marxism can justify this assessment by citing his so-called Marxist turn after 1927 in Shanghai, where he immersed himself in Marxist theories of revolution, historical materialism, and dialectics while producing translations of Georgi Plekhanov's and Anatoly Lunacharsky's works on Marxist literary theory.[19] Some scholars conclude that by the time of his passing in 1936, Lu Xun had fully embraced the Marxist idea that "inevitable class struggle would result in a proletarian victory."[20]

The relationship between Lu Xun's literary revolution and China's Communist Revolution is not just a question of historical interest but one that critically shapes contemporary debates about the Beijing Consensus and the nature of China's postreform political economy as well.[21] For intellectuals who emphasize that China's modernity is shaped by its socialist legacy, Lu Xun embodies China's historical singularity—its revolutionary tradition and its radical possibilities. We might recall that Wang Hui, the most well-known representative of China's New Left, started his career as a Lu Xun scholar. Wang cites Lu Xun as an "organic intellectual" of a forgotten and suppressed revolutionary tradition that contemporary China needs to reactivate in order to create a form of broad-based social democracy against capitalist imperialism.[22] Using Lu Xun's short piece "Nü diao" (The hanging woman) as an allegory for the past's spectral hold on the present, Wang argues for the continued relevance of revolution at the contemporary juncture when the triumph of economic developmentalism and liberalization seems to have silenced all voices for an alternative social order. Similarly, Wang Xiaoming, Lu Xun's biographer and an influential leftist cultural critic in his own right, identifies the writer as a "spiritual resource and a social legacy" that allows us to believe that the Chinese revolutionary tradition is still traceable in the contemporary capitalist moment and that "its flame has not died out but still burns somewhere in the dark as a 'subterranean fire.'"[23] Another eminent Chinese cultural critic, Qian Liqun, names Sun Yat-sen, Lu Xun, and Mao Zedong as the three revolutionaries responsible for the country's transformation from "a semifeudal, semi-colonial, late-developing society into an independent nation-state, in the course of a long struggle against autocratic rule from within, and oppression and invasion from without."[24] In Qian's view, Sun Yat-sen's 1911 Republican Revolution is the Chinese counterpart to the bourgeois French Revolution, Mao's Communist Revolution is the socialist October Revolution, and Lu Xun's literary revolution is the cultural force that folded the former into the latter. Qian notes that intellectual debates in university circles in the 1980s were filled with calls to "return to May Fourth" and "return to Lu Xun"—which equated China's socialism with Lu Xun's literary project—but after the Tiananmen Square massacre, Lu Xun, like the CCP itself, suddenly fell out of favor and came to be seen as a synonym for despotism.

The easily justified interpretation of Lu Xun as a proletarian writer continues to dominate PRC scholarship in the age of the Beijing Consensus. In a recent essay, Nan Fan draws a parallel between Lu Xun's fiction and György Lukács's theory of socialist realism, which Nan treats as a teleological conception of the inevitability of "the emergence of capitalist society, the awakening of class consciousness, the rise of the proletariat, the maturation of realist literature, and the self-expression of lower-class experiences."[25] Nan commends Lu Xun for inaugurating a literary movement focused on the exploited masses and complex lower-class characters, including Ah Q, Sister Xianglin, Runtun, Mrs. Ninepounder, Aigu, and the unnamed rickshaw driver. However, it is more accurate to say that Lu Xun's interest in the typicality of feudal characters represents a critical realism that is closer to Lukács's sense of the text's aspiration to totality, with "totality" defined as the demand to consider the relationality between disparate phenomena rather than something to be captured by mere description.[26]

In anglophone sinological circles, assessments of Lu Xun as either a realist or a modernist partially depend on the critic's attitude toward the CCP.

From the 1960s to the 1980s, anglophone scholarship has largely adhered to PRC interpretations of Lu Xun as the progenitor of China's socialist realism.[27] However, following Leo Ou-fan Lee's influential 1987 study, *Voices from the Iron House*, anglophone critics began to demystify Lu Xun's contributions to China's socialist culture by recasting him as an accomplished modernist writer instead.[28] Nonetheless, both modernist and realist readings of Lu Xun agree that his writing cannot be separated from the problem of China's *modernity* in the world capitalist system. Shu-mei Shih, for example, considers Lu Xun's modernist narratological experimentation as a meditation on China's status in world history, emphasizing the continuities between Lu Xun's interest in evolutionary science and Darwinism in his pre-Marxist phase and his turn to Marxism as a teleological conception of history: "These vectors are organically connected and are contiguous with each other, and literature is situated within this continuity, not apart from it."[29] For Shih, Lu Xun's literary modernism is itself a form of teleological thinking born out of China's displacement to the world's peripheries. Similarly, Andrew F. Jones characterizes Lu Xun's writings as "developmental fairy tales" informed by the translation of Thomas Henry Huxley's *Evolution and Ethics*, Darwinism, and Lamarckian theories of the inheritability of acquired characteristics: "And perhaps the most important index of this relegation to the disenfranchised fringes of the modern world was the pervasive sense that China's linguistic and cultural heritage was simply unfit for survival in a new global order of racialized competition and predatory imperialism. For Lu Xun and his generation . . . evolutionary thinking had become an axiomatic and necessary prism through which Chinese intellectuals sought to understand their own history, geopolitical position, and developmental prospects."[30]

In this context Lu Xun's modernism does not refer to a literary style opposed to realism; rather, it is a movement to create a new literature in the modern, living, spoken tongue superseding classical Chinese (*wenyan*) in order to modernize China's culture and by extension the country's productive forces in global capitalism. Chen Duxiu's 1917 manifesto, "Wenxue geming lun" (On literary revolution), radicalized this idea and attributed the contradiction between traditional and modern fiction to class conflicts in China. Chen urged Chinese writers to rebel against the "ornate, sycophantic literature of the aristocracy" and replace elite, inaccessible classical writing with "comprehensible, popularized social literature."[31] Calling for a new literature, science, and democracy for China, Chen cofounded the CCP with Li Dazhao in 1921. Organized resistance in the political realm was quickly followed by organized literary activities. Two Marxist literary groups, the Creation Society (founded in 1921) and Sun Society (founded in 1927), began championing a revolutionary literature (see the discussion of Qu Qiubai below) instead of a literary revolution.[32] Despite their internal differences, in 1930 members of Creation and Sun Societies joined others to found the League of Left-Wing Writers under Lu Xun's leadership.

While anglophone critics such as Shih and Jones emphasize the affinity between Lu Xun's thinking and Marxism, Darwinism, and evolutionary science as teleologies, early twentieth-century Chinese Marxist theorists focused on critiquing precisely what they perceived to be the deterministic and teleological aspects of Western Marxism. Li Dazhao's 1919 essay "Wo de Makesi zhuyi guan" (My Marxist views) is credited as the first work that rejected "the necessity for a long period of economic development as a prerequisite for revolutionary political change" and presented "class struggle itself [as] the truly creative force in historical development."[33] As the Marxist scholar Liu Kang puts it, the most innovative aspect of Chinese Marxism was precisely the transformation of the category of the aesthetic "from a bourgeois discourse into a revolutionary tool in struggles for state power."[34] In Chinese Marxism, culture is conceived as having the potential for initiating both action (as a vehicle for historical change) and reflection (as a site of paradox and ambiguity), being "a prism through which to examine the internal contradictions and structural relations" of history.[35] This privileged conception of culture became the defining tenet of a Chinese Marxist theoretical tradition that extends from the early intellectual thinkers (Li Dazhao, Chen Duxiu) and revolutionary commanders (Qu Qiubai, Mao Zedong) to later humanist philosophers (Jin Guangtao, Li Zehou). Qu Qiubai, in particular, offered a well-articulated theory of literature as the motor of China's socialist revolution. On the one hand, Qu considered literature's ability to document the concrete details of a culture's spiritual essence to be the reason China needed to embrace Marxism to reject deterministic and teleological theories of history.[36] On the other hand, Qu believed that literature does not merely reflect reality but, rather, participates in its radical transformation. Taking the investigative realism of Nikolai Gogol, Ivan Turgenev, and Leo Tolstoy as his model, Qu published an impressive number of translations and works of literary criticism with the intent of sparking a literary revolution for China.

Qu was the chief theoretician of the Latinization movement, which sought to abolish Chinese characters to lower the threshold of literacy for the Chinese masses.[37] The masses in question were gendered, as Qu's advocacy for vernacular language reform reflected the transformation of Bolshevik Marxism into a sociological view of women as the reproductive equivalent of men and the subjects of political action.[38] This movement flourished in Lu Xun's final years, and within the short span between 1934 and 1936, he composed at least eight polemical essays supporting Latinization in conjunction with the massification movement to proletarianize the arts and literature. In one particularly famous treatise, Lu Xun compared Chinese characters to a "tubercle on the body of China's poor and laboring masses."[39] In many ways, Lu Xun's project of creating a new literature in modern vernacular Chinese enacts the theories of the revolutionary function of culture in Chen Duxiu's "On Literary Revolution" and Li Dazhao's "My Marxist Views." In the preface to the first collection of his short stories, *Nahan* (Call to arms), Lu Xun recalls the circumstances under which he took up the craft of writing.[40] In 1906, while he was a student of medicine at the Sendai Medical School in Japan, one of his professors showed a slide of a Chinese spy being beheaded by the Japanese. In China studies this particular anecdote has come to be viewed as a sort of primal scene that explains Lu Xun's own development as a writer.[41] The scene of the execution of a fellow Chinese did not elicit a reaction from the other Chinese students in the classroom. Lu Xun observes that "physically, they were as strong and healthy as anyone could ask, but their expressions revealed all too clearly that *spiritually* they were calloused and numb. . . . The other Chinese gathered around . . . to enjoy the spectacle. . . . There was no need to fret about how many of them might die of illness. The most important thing to be done was to transform their spirits . . . [so I decided to give up the study of medicine to] promote a literary movement."[42]

For Lu Xun, language reform and class analysis were intimately related because classical Chinese was inaccessible to the masses and therefore antidemocratic. Though the civil service examination had been abolished in 1905, the mastery of classical Chinese and the Confucian canon remained the cultural capital of the educated literati class. Lu Xun's critique of classical Chinese as an instrument of class domination is inseparable from the incorporation of China into the capitalist world economy, which in turn makes mass mobilization and mass literacy an urgent task for political revolution. Lu Xun's most famous work, "Kuangren riji" (Diary of a madman, 1918)—the first short story published in modern vernacular Chinese—stages the conflict between classical and modern Chinese as an encounter between a medical doctor and a Madman. The story is a framed narrative that consists of two parts. The main text presents itself as the Madman's own diary entries, written in simple, choppy sentences in modern vernacular Chinese such as "Moonlight's really nice tonight."[43] The diary entries are prefaced by the doctor's notes, which are composed in elegant but pedantic classical Chinese. Because the doctor's notes precede the diary entries and frame them as the medical record of a Madman's persecution complex, the reader is initially inducted into the perspective of the doctor's pathologizing gaze and voyeuristically participates in the dissection of a strange mind. William Lyell's English translation uses ornate Latinate expressions to render the stodginess of the doctor's classical Chinese: "There was once a pair of male siblings whose actual names I beg your indulgence to withhold. Suffice it to say that we three were boon companions during our school years. Subsequently, circumstances contrived to render us asunder so that we were gradually bereft of knowledge regarding each other's activities. . . . As to the *lapsus calami* that occur in the course of the diaries, I have altered not a word."[44]

The Madman, however, is not actually mad. The Chinese word translated as "madman" here, *kuangren*, does not mean an insane person; rather, a *kuangren* is closer to Nietzsche's Übermensch, somebody who dares to speak truth to power, a figure whose thoughts appear mad or out of sync with reality because these ideas are ahead of their time. In other words, *kuangren* is Lu Xun's code name for a *revolutionary*. Lu Xun uses the figure to critique the hold that Confucianism continues to have on Chinese thought and practice. In the eyes of the Madman, Confucianism is a form of cannibalism: "I seemed to remember, though not too clearly, that from ancient times on people have often been eaten, and so I started leafing through a history book to look it up. There were no dates in this history, but scrawled this way and that across every page were the words BENEVOLENCE, RIGHTEOUSNESS, and MORAL-ITY. . . . I read that history very carefully for most of the night, and finally I began to make out what was written *between* the lines; the whole volume was filled with a single phrase: EAT PEOPLE!"[45] Readers in China would not miss that "benevolence, righteousness, and morality" (*ren yi dao de*) reference Confucius's teachings and that phrases such as "four thousand years" and "Mr. Antiquity" are allusions to traditional Chinese culture.[46]

"Diary of a Madman" is an exemplary work of modernist fiction. The force of the story hinges on the gap, created by Lu Xun's use of dramatic and verbal irony, among the doctor's perspective, the Madman's consciousness, and the reader's own cultural knowledge of the referents of the Madman's apparently unintelligible ramblings. The reader alone recognizes that the

Madman's diatribe against "benevolence, righteousness, and morality" is an attack on Confucianism, a coincidence that remains incomprehensible to both the doctor and the Madman as literary constructs within the diegetic space of the story. The Madman's madness, as it were, derives from his inability to decipher the truth of his own statements. This modernist use of dramatic irony results in a displacement of narrative authority. The Madman's diary, the meaning of which is opaque to the Madman himself, receives a new contextualization in the hands of the doctor, who pathologizes the Madman and interprets this text as evidence of the latter's paranoia and persecution complex. At the same time, the doctor's preface, written in turgid classical Chinese and embodying its fossilized thinking, is anticipated and ridiculed by the very text it derides. The structure of the story presents a dilemma for the reader. Initially placed in a superior position to both the Madman and the doctor, the reader must decide where their sympathy lies, but that sense of superiority quickly dissipates once the reader realizes that the story is written for no one else but the one reading the story—and the horrifying truth is that the reader, like the Madman, has unknowingly eaten the flesh of others in a cannibalistic society.

In the PRC education system, the story is typically treated as "a call to arms for people to join the [Communist] revolution" and a denunciation of "the time-honored Chinese civilization as a three-thousand-year history of metaphorical cannibalism under the façade of Confucian morality and virtue."[47] The division between the preface's classical Chinese and the diary entries' modern vernacular Chinese is understood to be an argument for the necessity of the Communist Party and its historical mission to instill a revolutionary consciousness in the masses by modernizing the Chinese language. But can this text be reduced to a straightforward ideological message? As Carlos Rojas has argued in a brilliant study, the complexities of Lu Xun's modernist text require a "between-the-lines" approach, "interpreting the story through the overlapping medical frames within which it is implicitly positioned" and underscoring "the degree to which political reform is grounded on a process of recognition that entails the necessary possibility of misrecognition."[48] The Madman's own conviction that he is surrounded by an epidemic of cannibalism and the narrator's suggestion that the Madman may have been suffering from paranoid schizophrenia must be situated in the context of the emergence of immunological and psychoanalytic models for understanding the ills of Chinese society. Hence, "Lu Xun's story functions not only as a clarion call for reforming a cannibalistic sociopolitical structure, as the story is commonly read, but also as a warning about the potentially cannibalistic consequences of reform itself."[49]

Lu Xun was a complex thinker, and his project could not be reduced to a simple call for Communist revolution. Though to some extent the story does seem to embody the modernizing impulse of May Fourth iconoclasm, what escapes most critics' attention is the queerness of Lu Xun's language here. Lu Xun never offers any authorial commentary on the divergence between the doctor's and the Madman's perspectives. He simply presents a narrative situation, foregrounding the ways in which subjectivity is necessarily constructed through the eyes of the Other. Lu Xun seemingly has no moral message to deliver, no doctrine he is codifying—and then he ends the story with a plea: "Save the children!"[50] With this sudden shift in the structure of address, the diary entry is transformed from the private thoughts of an individual into a socially symbolic act that calls on the text's implied reader in posterity to make a difference.

Virtually all of Lu Xun's stories feature a nameless narrator. "Diary of a Madman" is rather unique in this aspect, because it is one of the few texts in which the main character's perspective, that of the Madman, is embedded in another unnamed character's narrative and given an objectified status. In most of Lu Xun's stories, the first-person narrator is not the principal object of narrative interest but rather a framework through which the plights of marginalized social characters are introduced and explored.[51] However, in the course of telling a story about society's outcasts, the nameless first-person narrator typically also acquires an embodied presence and becomes an occasion for a queer form of self-reflexivity and critical thinking.

Lu Xun's Queer Modernism

While most contemporary critics outside the PRC have no problem seeing Lu Xun as a modernist rather than socialist realist writer, few associate this modernism with Marxism, and even fewer would argue that this modernism constitutes a contribution to Marxism because it is gendered in a queer way. Asking whether Lu Xun's modernism is formed through a queer logic of gender is not the same as examining Lu Xun's sexual orientation or his attitude toward women. The latter has been amply explored by Lu Xun scholars, who have been debating for decades whether Lu Xun's treatment of women characters indicates a paternalistic, sympathetic, feminist, misogynist, or instrumental attitude. Images of oppressed women abound in Lu Xun's most celebrated stories. Lu Xun's readers will remember the penetrating insight of "Shangshi" (Regrets for the past, 1925), which depicts the failure of "free love" (*ziyou lian ai*) in a society that remains tethered to the conservative institutions of arranged marriage and heterosexual monogamy. Lu Xun is universally commended for the care he shows in depicting traditional biases and violence faced by women—especially voiceless, rural, and illiterate women—in stories like "Mingtian" (Tomorrow, 1920), "Zhufu" (New year's sacrifice, 1924), and "Regrets for the past."[52]

Lu Xun's lesser-known works, as well as details from his own life, provide an even more complex picture of his gender politics. Critics find evidence of Lu Xun's feminist values in his choice of the goddess Nüwa instead of her male counterpart, Pangu, as the protagonist for the creation story "Butian" (Mending heaven, 1922).[53] His translation of the story of the Spartan woman warrior Selena in "Sibada zhi hun" (The soul of Sparta, 1903) shows admiration for fearless women.[54] Lu Xun's sensitive treatment of women subjects in his fiction echoes significant choices he made in his personal life that seem to indicate a radical view of gender equality. In his letters to Xu Guangping, his partner from 1927 to the end of his life, who was not only seventeen years his junior but also his former student, Lu Xun consistently used the honorific "elder brother" (*xiong*) to address her.[55] Lu Xun's childhood fascination with the hangwoman ("The hanging woman," 1936), his support for the "natural breast movement" (*tian ru yundong*), his various essays on gossip and chastity ("Wo zhi jielie guan" (My views on chastity, 1918)), and his reported distrust of eunuchs and gender-crossing performers ("Lun zhaoxiang zhilei" (On photography and related matters, 1925)), provide rich material for scholars to mine in the reconstruction of his gender politics.[56] Though some critics have faulted Lu Xun for unwittingly perpetuating the assumptions of the gender discourse he critiques, it is clear that his views on gender were too complex to be reduced to a dyadic form of heterosexualism.[57]

But what happens when we examine Lu Xun's feminism as form rather than content? And what happens when we understand this feminism as a queer subversion of the category of women rather than as social advocacy for women as a preexisting sociological group? Lu Xun's modernist redefinition of human subjectivity as form has significant implications for queer theory, Marxism, and social reproduction theories. By treating the human subject as an effect of discourse and cultural norms rather than as their sovereign author, Lu Xun presents a view that is strikingly similar to the understanding of gender as dispossessed alterity in Judith Butler and other queer theorists I discussed in chapter 2. As I argued there, this view of gender also represents an eminently materialist philosophy akin to Marxist understandings of the self as an effect of social structuration. Reading his literary project through these lenses, I suggest that Lu Xun has developed a queer modernism that exceeds the traditional feminist critique of the subordination of women. Instead of focusing on the negative or positive images of women in his fiction, I examine Lu Xun's language itself as an aesthetic apparatus through which the gendered subject emerges. By drawing attention to the subject's dependency on a gendered matrix of social relations, Lu Xun's literary modernism offers a queer strategy for resisting the dyadic structure of thought in language.

Some critics have characterized Lu Xun as a queer writer in a more conventional sense. Ari Larissa Heinrich proposes that Lu Xun's "Gudu zhe" (The loner, 1925) can be read as a source text for queer studies. The principal character's refusal to be married and have children is described by the text itself as "queer" (*guguai, qiguai, yiyang, yilei*, and *yuzhongbutong*).[58] Henrich argues that Lu Xun's text reflects the impact of new political economies on private life and resists the heterosexual imperative of early twentieth-century China's socio-zoological emphasis on husbandry, propagation, and reproduction.[59] Pursuing a different line of inquiry, David Der-wei Wang addresses Lu Xun's interest in female impersonation. As Lu Xun notes in the essay "On Photography and Related Matters," "The greatest, most long-lasting, and most popular art in China is men impersonating women."[60] Wang argues that Lu Xun "shares with contemporary intelligentsia a yearning for a strong, virile Chinese figure, as opposed to China's old emaciated, feminine image"; however, Lu Xun "differs from his contemporaries in that he is capable of looking into the corporeal dimension of the national body politic" and in that sexuality always occupies a prominent place in his investigation of Chinese modernity.[61]

Lu Xun's most enduring contribution to materialist queer theory, however, was his speech "Nala zouhou zenyang" (What happens after Nora walks out). Delivered on December 26, 1923, as a lecture at Peking Women's Normal College, "What Happens after Nora Walks Out" is a penetrating analysis of the differential allocation of vulnerability to gendered populations and a significant contribution to Marxism.[62] As Lu Xun recounts it, in Henrik Ibsen's *A Doll's House*, Nora tells her husband she wishes to leave him for a lover, to which the husband says, "I give you complete freedom. Choose for yourself (whether to leave or not)."[63] Nora does walk out, but in what sense is this a choice? Focusing on this dilemma, Lu Xun interprets *A Doll's House* as a play depicting modern women who "wake from a dream and find there is no way out."[64] Their self-perception as embodied subjects and possessive individuals turns out to be an illusion, because the economic structure of society has not yet been transformed to support women seeking an alternative source of income and means of survival outside heterosexual marriage and childbearing. As Lu Xun puts it, "For Nora, money (or to put it more elegantly, economic means) is crucial."[65] Because Nora's gender prevents her from gaining economic independence, her rejection of heterosexual marriage and childbearing turns out to be a meaningless act; she remains shackled to her duties as wife and mother and to her dependency on such institutions.

Lu Xun makes the important Marxist argument that women like Nora have the freedom to sell their labor power, but this freedom is really comparable to slavery: "Freedom cannot be bought, but it can be sold."[66] For Lu Xun, the slogan of women's emancipation is profoundly empty if we comprehend it as a dematerialized battle against prejudice and discrimination. Lu Xun suggests that Nora is oppressed, not because she is a woman, but because gender is an axis of domination in society, at one end of which are those in control of the economic means of production, mobility, and decision-making, and at the other end of which are disenfranchised subjects who have no choice but to sell their bodies on the marriage market to obtain a lifetime of financial security.[67]

At the same time, Lu Xun is careful to avoid the pitfalls of vulgar Marxism. He writes, "Are you no longer a puppet once you have won economic freedom? No, you are still a puppet. It's just that you are less subject to others' control and more in control of other puppets. In present-day society, it's not only the case that women are men's puppets, but men are other men's puppets, women are other women's puppets, and some men are even women's puppets. This is not something that can be remedied by a few women gaining economic rights."[68] Instead of arguing for the primacy of economics in determining women's subordination, Lu Xun offers a dialectical view of gender and materialism. According to his reading, though Nora proclaims the principle of free love and is granted the freedom to leave ("choose for yourself"), the illusion of choice in free love—like the freedom of free wage labor—is meaningless without the transformation of a society's material conditions. Without these material changes China can have countless Noras rebelling against the family, patriarchy, marriage, and the subordination of women, but gender will not be free. Nora's gender is not something she possesses and reclaims when she walks out—it is part of what dispossesses her, part of what decided her status as a political subject and her positionality in a socioeconomic structure. Nora is, in other words, an instantiation of the contradiction of formal and real subsumption in capitalism.

Lu Xun's reading of the play is brilliant. He points out that the problem Nora faces is not her lack of agency—she has complete freedom to choose whether she wants to stay in a heterosexual marriage or not. Rather, the problem lies with the text's own inability to answer the question posed by its own title—what happens to Nora after she walks out. On this question, "Ibsen gave no answer, and now he's dead."[69] Ibsen's reticence constitutes a lacuna in the text, and it is this lacuna, rather than the story's content, that interests Lu Xun. Lu Xun considers various modern efforts to complete Ibsen's story. In some alternate endings provided by later writers, Nora enters a brothel; in others, she eventually returns home. The fact that the text's original author never tells us what becomes of her is crucial for Lu Xun, whose reading of Ibsen's play can be compared to Louis Althusser's "symptomatic reading" of Karl Marx's reading of bourgeois economists. As Althusser has argued, the problem with bourgeois political economy is not that it contained an oversight (in relation to Marx's sight) but that bourgeois political economy's sight itself is structured through a vision that prevents the figure of labor power from coming into view.[70] Lu Xun similarly performs a symptomatic reading of what is not being said in Ibsen's text—what becomes of Nora after she exercises her freedom to choose. As Lu Xun draws attention to Nora's life beyond the pages of the text as well as our political imagination, he also rejects the conception of gender as the essence of a person or a starting point for a radical epistemology that can ground political action. For Lu Xun, Nora's gender situates her in the material distribution of the economic means of subsistence and survival; consequently, her gender is exposed as an effect of an impersonal structure of domination and resistance.

Lu Xun's "Zhufu" ("New year's sacrifice," 1924) offers a much more explicit treatment of the intersections of gender consciousness, language, and materialism. Linguistically, "New Year's Sacrifice" is of notable historical interest for being the first of Lu Xun's stories to employ the newly invented third-person feminine pronoun *ta*, now written with a *nü* (woman) radical in distinction to the universal third-person pronoun written with a *ren* (human) radical and the ungendered classical Chinese equivalent, *qi*. Invented by Liu Fu (Liu Bannong) in 1917, this neologism was partly an effort to translate distinctions in European languages.[71] The story's protagonist, a raving madwoman called Sister Xianglin, might be seen as the female version of the original Madman and thus the gendering of class consciousness.[72] Sister Xianglin is a village woman who goes to a larger town looking for work after her husband's passing. Now expropriated from agricultural production and transformed into a wage laborer, she encounters various forms of oppression because of Chinese society's feudal, patriarchal, and superstitious nature. Though hardworking and capable, Sister Xianglin is forbidden from touching the utensils during the preparations for the New Year's celebrations because widows are deemed inauspicious. Not long thereafter, her husband's mother appears and collects all of her wages before selling her to a second husband. Now expelled from wage relations, Sister Xianglin returns to the village and gives birth to a son, only to lose him to wolves. She begins to exhibit classic symptoms of Sigmund Freud's repetition compulsion, telling her life story again and again to the villagers to the point that "even in the eyes of the most pious old Buddhist ladies, not so much as the trace of a tear was anymore to be seen."[73] Barely scraping by, she is mistaken by the narrator for a beggar when they meet again; soon after, he learns that she simply "aged away."[74] But while it is easy to describe the story as Lu Xun's indictment of feudal culture and its superstition, patriarchy, and class exploitation, he makes his most potent point through the story's carefully crafted narrative structure rather than its thematic content. The former comes to the fore in an early encounter between Sister Xianglin and the narrator, who is initially sympathetic toward her:

> "So you've come back. Just the man I've been looking for. You know how to read books. Now, tell me . . . is there a soul after a body dies?"
> "Uh . . . I can't say for sure."[75]

Despite his Western education, the narrator, a self-styled modern intellectual, is completely stumped by Sister's Xianglin's question about the soul, which he takes seriously, and experiences an existential crisis. Once that lifts, as a result of his reintegration into society, his initial goodwill toward Sister Xianglin dissipates. As the New Year's celebrations begin, the tragedy of Sister Xianglin, which has given rise to the narrative we have been following, is suddenly declared inconsequential:

> Wrapped in this comforting symphonic embrace, I too was filled with a sharp sense of well-being and felt wholly free of worldly cares. All the worries and concerns that had plagued me from morning till night the day before had been totally swept away by the happy atmosphere of the New Year. I was conscious of nothing except that the various gods of heaven

and earth were enjoying the ritual offerings and all the incense that burned in their honor. Comfortably tipsy by now, they staggered through the sky and prepared to shower the people of Lu Town with infinite blessings.[76]

Here it is important to note that Lu Xun's fiction is not didactic. Instead of creating a narrative voice to instill the correct social (or socialist) values in the people, Lu Xun subjects the narrative perspective itself, and hence the reader's identification, to criticism and reflection. In her reading of this story, Rey Chow points out that Lu Xun presents an ambiguity of feeling toward superfluous and useless existences that leads to an exteriorized fracturing of the narration process:

> If thought patterns are indicative of "subjectivity," no commentary can re-capture sufficiently the ironic, deconstructive quality of the subjectivity in the preceding passage. Evidently troubled by a figure like Xianglin Sao and yet incapable of locating the sources of his feelings, the narrator is beset by a terror that doubles back on the narrative as a constant flight from his own position. . . . While the narrator is a "mind" with which we become acquainted through its contradictions, Xianglin Sao remains someone we observe from without, like an animal: she has "big strong feet and hands" and "would eat anything." She is called not by her own name but "Xianglin's wife." . . . All the representational channels that could have given her a kind of "subjectivity" are carefully blocked. This hardened "object" undermines the lucidity of the narrative from within, fracturing the "subjectivity" of the narrator in the form of elliptic shifts in narrative mood, which is now melancholy, now hopeful.[77]

Hence, rather than treating Lu Xun as a (socialist) realist writer who simplistically portrays the oppression of women, we must understand Lu Xun's investment in the questions of gender as a matter of narrative form and fractured subjectivity. While multiple figures in the story, such as "the most pious old Buddhist ladies," serve as telling examples of the atrophy of the crowd's compassion, the irony of Lu Xun's fiction rests on the fact that ultimately it is the narrator who loses interest in the story he has been sharing with the reader. As it turns out, the story's ending is about not Sister Xianglin—who has already passed away—but the evacuation of the narrator's consciousness.

Significantly, the reader learns of Sister Xianglin's passing through a casual remark by a male servant, "I can't say for sure," which is the same phrase the narrator uses to answer her question about the soul. The narrator then reaches a new realization: "I can't say for sure—what a wonderfully convenient phrase! Even if something does happen, I thought, it will have nothing to do with me."[78] Lu Xun's oeuvre is full of moments like this: "I never saw him again—guess he really did die" (from "Kong Yiji"); "There is not much difference" (from "Dragonboat festival,"); "But . . . but . . . how did she die? Who knows? She's dead, that's all" (from "Mourning the dead.")[79] These recurring phrases indicate Lu Xun's sustained interest in the failure of language, in moments when experiences of dispossession, precarity, and marginality elude representation and defy rational thought. Here Lu Xun's Marxism cannot be reduced to the sympathetic treatment of proletarian subjects. Rather, it is the tonality and design of his fiction that that defines his Marxist approach. Through a queer Marxist framework, Lu Xun connects the disposable populations of gendered subjectivity—the moments of capital that resist rationalization—to the atrophy of revolutionary consciousness.

We can say that Lu Xun is less interested in representing particular identities (the peasant, the wage laborer, women, the mad) than in exploring the genesis of a generalized identity—how the "I" comes into being through an account of the Other. Sister Xianglin's story turns out to be a story of the atrophy of the speaking subject's own compassion. In turn, Lu Xun's critique of the narrator's own consciousness becomes an occasion for reflexivity, a call to examine the historical forces that create our fragmented, reified, and gendered existence. We can detect this historicizing impulse in Lu Xun's persistent return to the discourse of textual objects. In numerous instances the construction of the narrative relies more on the texts within the text than on human characters. The kinds of books each character reads indicate a particular relation to current issues: Lu Xun suggests that a character in "Mourning the Dead" is a rebel against the institution of marriage because she is an avid reader of Ibsen's plays. In "New Year's Sacrifice," the conservative mind of Fourth Uncle is subtly indicated by his study, which is filled with commentaries on the analects of Confucius and the Kang Xi Dictionary.[80] Indeed, Lu Xun's characters are all readers—even illiterate ones. The medical doctor is a reader (of the Madman's diary). The Madman is also a reader (of the "history book" that proclaims the mandate to eat people). Both the narrator of "New Year's Sacrifice" and Sister Xianglin are storytellers who present their own lives as texts for others to read. Sister Xianglin addresses the narrator as "just the man I've been looking for. You know how to read books."

Of course, these stories are nothing but a series of provocations; as indicated by the title Lu Xun gave to his short story collection, *Call to Arms*, the only reader in which Lu Xun is interested is the story's reader in posterity. The final moment of "Diary of a Madman," when the introspective diarist suddenly appears to be directly addressing the story's implied reader with "Save the children!" must be understood in this context. Lu Xun's "Save the children!" is a metafictional structure of address, a deployment of intertextuality, and a modernist experiment in narrative fiction. It is also a call for revolutionary action from the peripheries of the capitalist world economy, a living witness to the incessant contradictions between capital's self-expansion and its disposable populations.

Coda: Debating Lu Xun and Gender in Contemporary Inter-Asian Marxist Dialogues

There is no better example than Lu Xun that illustrates how the life and works of one fiction writer can shape an entire generation's understanding of Marxism and China's role in it. While Lu Xun's sacrosanct aura in PRC history has faded with the discrediting of Maoism, his legacy continues to fuel contemporary Marxist debates around questions of "Asia as method," Sinotheory, and "Asian studies in Asia." For those who understand him to be an indigenous cultural resource, Lu Xun is uniquely positioned to enable a nonessentialist conversation about gender, materialism, and social reproduction grounded in Asia's own history. Because Lu Xun has been central to modern East Asian countries of both Chinese and non-Chinese origins, and inside and outside the socialist bloc, the shift to Lu Xun as a reference point has the potential to disrupt the binary paradigm of Western theory and local reality that has constricted the flow of knowledge to a two-way street between North America and individual countries in Asia. On the other hand, the insistence on finding local bases of theory building, no matter how antiessential, has come under challenge from within cultural studies and Marxism in Asia. For some scholars in gender and sexuality studies, the call to create an inter-Asian referencing model via a critical return to Lu Xun represents an Oedipal crisis of absent father figures, one that risks reducing the creative forces of the region into a mere strategy of anti-imperialism.[81]

It was Lu Xun's modernist thinking on the gendered self that prompted the Japanese intellectual Takeuchi Yoshimi (1910–77) to reflect on the question of "What Is Modernity?" (1948). In this influential essay, Takeuchi argues that Japan's modernity is a superficial kind and predicts that Japanese imperialism will lead only to its own defeat. He locates Japan's problem in its slavish imitation of a Western notion of modernity, which gives rise to "the colonized desire to become a colonizer in order to escape its colonization."[82] For Takeuchi, Lu Xun's rejection of China's literary past is not the devaluation of his own tradition but a kind of negative dialectic that enables China to transcend the enslavement of the West. By contrast, Japan cannot help but reproduce the violence of colonialism (on other parts of Asia as well as itself) precisely because it imagines itself as having overcome the problem of modernity. Lu Xun's literary fiction and the formation of the League of Left-Wing Writers represent both "despair" and "hope" in the context of capitalist modernity, despair at the endless possibilities of (literary, then social) revolutions and hope buoyed by a vision of a utopian future that will overcome the determinism of the present. For Takeuchi, "Diary of a Madman" is the paradigmatic story that spans these polarities by presenting that vision as both "mad" (*kuang*, as in ahead of one's time, not yet accepted by common social standards) and necessary.

Takeuchi conceives of Lu Xun as a source of historical knowledge providing an alternative to the form of modernity that Japan has uncritically reproduced. He makes his arguments through a series of literary observations: to begin with, he repeatedly emphasizes that Lu Xun was well read in Japanese as well as Chinese literature. The type of historical knowledge Lu Xun represents, therefore, is not "Chinese" in the ethnolinguistic sense but an intraregional form of sedimented knowledge, capable of being translated, evaluated, and disseminated. The point, for Takeuchi, is not to promote or dismiss certain literary figures over others or to distinguish between good and bad writers of modernity; rather, he characterizes literature as an access point for comprehending the relation between form and history. Hence, Takeuchi reads Lu Xun's literary criticism and fiction back onto Japanese literature itself. He critiques Japan's famous modernist writers—Kuwabara Takeo, Nakamura Mistuo, Itō Sei, and Natsume Sōseki—as embodiments of a partially obscured understanding of the historicity of the self (one's presence or embeddedness in the historical conditions that make thought possible).[83] Thanks to Takeuchi's influential essay, Lu Xun became a historical legacy for modern Asian thought, critically shaping the works of contemporary writers such as Ōe Kenzaburō and Gao Xingjian and leftist intellectual discourses in different Asian languages.[84]

This trajectory of thought from Lu Xun to Takeuchi provided a historical resource for Marxist social movements in Asia that arose independently of the PRC's Marxism-Leninism.[85] In the 1990s Takeuchi's essay "Asia as Method" and his reading of Lu Xun in "What Is Modernity?" became the foundational pieces for a cross-border East Asian cultural Marxist project, *Inter-Asia Cultural Studies*. Launched in 2000 as a journal, it expanded into a social movement and later a consortium of university programs committed to the activation of alternative intellectual formations, tools, and resources created by Asian thinkers. The project seeks to expand our archive of references for critical analysis. In addition to provincializing the West, the goal is to reconceive Asia as an active agent in the making of knowledge rather than a passive object to be analyzed through research paradigms produced by the West. However, the project is not a nativist or nationalist one that presents Asia as a cultural tradition that perpetually eludes the grasp of Westerners. Takeuchi's concept of "Asia as method" and his reading of Lu Xun are crucial for the project's antiessentialist orientation. Asia is not an empirical region but a *method*, a way of comprehending social and cultural phenomena within the material conditions of their genesis.

In the inaugural issue's mission statement, the founding coeditors—Kuan-Hsing Chen and Beng Huat Chua—describe the project as an intervention in the directions and conditions of knowledge production.[86] Although Asia has been formally decolonized, its consciousness remains colonized by the epistemology of its former masters. Consequently, the production of knowledge continues to be governed by a bilateral dialogue between each individual Asian country and North America, but not with each other. In other words, while it is common for an Asian intellectual to utilize findings and paradigms developed in North America and produce research for the scholarly community in North America, it is much less likely for the same intellectual to learn another Asian language or acquire a basic awareness of current events in a neighboring country's civil society. To counter this tendency, *Inter-Asia Cultural Studies* has an agreement with the leading journals in all the major Asian languages to mutually waive translation rights. The idea is to create a platform for conversations across different Asian languages, which is indispensable for the making of a transnational civil society that can effectively counter the legacy of imperialism and colonialism. Inspired by British cultural studies and the Subaltern Studies Group in South Asia, *Inter-Asia Cultural Studies* is a Marxist project that assumes historical materialism to be the methodology of cultural studies.[87] Compared to those two projects, however, *Inter-Asia Cultural Studies* appears more explicitly informed by queer theory and the dispersal of identities. It recasts Marxism in a broader lexicon that encompasses gender, sexuality, and popular culture. The journal has been the font of many queer projects and intellectual theorizations, some of which explicitly draw on Lu Xun and provide an unanticipated use of the afterlives of the Chinese modernist writer.[88]

Published in 2010, Kuan-Hsing Chen's own monograph *Asia as Method* offers a critical rereading of Lu Xun and other resources provided by Asia's own history to argue that decolonization in this region remains an incomplete project, having been hijacked and derailed by the US installment of a "Cold War structure of feeling" that ensured Asia's division.[89] Though formal colonization has ended, the partition of East Asia into Communist and anti-Communist zones created bipolar subjectivities that persist or even flourish today. Chen proposes the concept of "geocolonial historical materialism" to analyze the relationship between the decolonization of thought and the geopolitical space of the third world.[90] A geocolonial historical materialism radically historicizes cultural formations, situating them in the "immanent complexity of colonialism" beyond nationalism, nativism, and civilizationalism.[91]

Chen's work forms a dialogue with Asia's own leftist thinkers—Lu Xun, Yang Kui, Chen Yingzhen, Takeuchi Yoshimi—in order to formulate an antiessentialist theory of epistemic decolonization, South-South interreferencing, and self-reflexivity. This dialogue is sustained through a series of literary readings, forming a trajectory of thought that we can call an East Asian Marxist reading of literature.[92] Recent scholarship has further expanded on Chen's reading of Lu Xun and Takeuchi as resources for a critical Asian Marxism.[93] Lu Xun, Takeuchi, and Chen represent three radically different historical engagements with Marxism in East Asia. But we can find a common emphasis in the critique of colonized consciousness, the historicity of the self, and reflexivity. All of these concepts have origins in Lu Xun's modernist approach to gender and Marxism. What Lu Xun shows, or enables us to think about, is that a Marxist critique of capitalism is not tantamount to a social realist representation of landlords and peasants. Rather, the object of his representation is the historicity of the self and its gendering, which in turn yields the recognition that the autonomous subject is only an illusion created by capitalism's impersonal structure of exploitation. A Marxist reading of East Asian literature would aim at uncovering this form of radical thinking against the surface of the text for a collective struggle for a more just and democratic world. My next chapter explores the consequences of this critical turn for a revisionist history of queer Asia.

The Subsumption
of the Cold War

THE MATERIAL UNCONSCIOUS

OF QUEER ASIA

Recent human rights abuses in Xinjiang, Hong Kong's Anti-Extradition Law Amendment Bill Movement, and escalating tensions between Taiwan and China once again have the international media's attention centered on the apparent gaps between China's economic liberalization and its political illiberalism. Questions about the status of LGBTQIA+ subjects punctuate these conversations, providing a reminder, as it were, that the Beijing Consensus is anything but a consensus between differently situated populations. Indeed, when compared to either Hong Kong (where mainstream cultural representations of homosexuality, organized queer activist networks, and commercial venues catering to lesbian and gay communities preceded their mainland counterparts by at least a decade) or Taiwan (the first Asian country to legalize same-sex marriage, in 2019), China, despite its rapid economic growth, appears to be significantly behind in the advancement of queer rights.

These developments contributed to a common narrative that nascent forms of queer identities and organizing in many parts of the world stemmed from the worldwide collapse of Communism in 1991 and that the relative weakness of queer civil society in China reflects the country's incomplete transition from socialist authoritarianism. While the narrative of queer liberation, for understandable reasons, paints Hong Kong and Taiwan as more habitable spaces for Chinese people or, indeed, subjects who do not identify as Chinese at all, mainstream commentators typically fail to mention the history of "America's Asia"—the transformation of Taiwan, Hong Kong, South Korea, Japan, and the Philippines into the Pax Americana's military outposts and vehicles of capital accumulation during the Cold War. Regardless of how one stands on Taiwanese independence, Hong Kong democracy, or other pivotal issues in the age of the Beijing Consensus, an uncritical reading of the material effects of the Cold War through the lens of contemporary identity politics runs the risk of dehistoricizing capitalism.

Because the Communist threat played a pivotal role in the endless accumulation of capital during the Cold War, a critique of capitalism must begin with a reckoning of this history. At its founding in 1949, the People's Republic of China (PRC) was an agrarian economy with over one hundred million rural households working in small-scale farming and animal husbandry. Under the doctrine of New Democracy, the Chinese Communist Party sought to advance industrialization under state capitalism.[1] The outbreak of the Korean War in 1950 provided the conditions for China's primitive accumulation and first wave of industrialization. In exchange for getting involved in the war, China was offered aid in the form of technology transfer and a transplant of military heavy industry from the Soviet Union.[2] With the infusion of Soviet capital, the Chinese state was able to accomplish primitive accumulation and proceed into industrial expansion and structural adjustment. During the Cold War, China was encircled by hostile states. Its economic modernization was interrupted until the Sino-American rapprochement of the 1970s brought about a second wave of industrialization. The deterioration of Sino-Soviet relations, which culminated in two bloody border clashes in 1969—with Soviet leaders reportedly considering a preemptive nuclear strike against their former Communist ally—spurred China to improve its relations with the United States.[3]

The geopolitics of the Cold War transformed China from a vanguard state of "world revolution" to a center of capital accumulation. The mending of Sino-American relations marked a turning point in Mao Zedong's thinking from a revolution-driven agenda to development-oriented goals. Mao's successor, Deng Xiaoping, formalized the derevolutionization process with the introduction of the reform and opening policies at the Third Plenary Session of the Chinese Communist Party's Eleventh Central Committee in 1978, replacing the Maoist slogans of "class struggles" and "permanent revolution" with his famous saying, "Black cat or white cat, so long as it catches mice, it is a good cat."[4] Deng understood that cooperation with Washington was necessary for China to gain access to the US-dominated world market. Thus, having repudiated the socialism it had built in the 1950s and 1960s, China entered the international capitalist system.

On the American side, Washington saw China's opening as a golden opportunity to expand the reach of its capitalist market and to contain the expansion of Soviet power, but it would not concede on the issue of arms sales to Taiwan. Because capital accumulates most efficiently through territorially segregated spaces, a divided Asia allowed the United States access to cheap labor and markets without the protection of a strong unified state. Ironically, Washington's geostrategic decision to keep Taiwan as a protectorate ultimately facilitated China's capitalist transformations. Throughout the Cold War era, Washington extended tremendous amounts of financial and military aid to Japan and the Four East Asian Tigers, allies it considered too important to fail in the containment of Communism. With the infusion of US capital and the opening of the Western market, Taiwan and much of the rest of East Asia jump-started the capitalist-industrial takeoff that laid the endogenous foundation for China's own capitalist boom. The story of East Asian capitalism is therefore indissociable from the history of US Cold War efforts to create subordinate and prosperous bulwarks against Communism in East Asia.[5] However, compared to its flourishing lesbian and gay communities, the history of Taiwan's role as a client state in the expansion of America's capitalist interests has not received similar media attention or scholarly treatment. While the United States continues to profit from arms sales to Taiwan and geopolitical tensions created by the Cold War, such divisions have been rewritten as ethnic identities in Taiwan, globally perceived as a democratic, queer-friendly nation struggling to liberate itself from Beijing's imperial ambitions. A crucial phase of capital accumulation in Asia, the Cold War continues to structure the ethnic tensions underlying the "social apartheid" that keeps the manufacturing workforce in China's rural regions immobilized and the influx of capital from Taiwan and Hong Kong afloat.

In this chapter I examine the subsumption of the Cold War under the sinophone world's capitalist fragmentation, which produced a unilinear narrative of queer liberation. I argue that the Cold War has been subsumed and transformed into the material unconscious of this queer narrative, which recent Asian Marxist cultural criticism seeks to restore to view through the concept of Asia as method. Focusing on *Swordsman II: Asia the Invincible* (*Xiao ao jianghu zhi Dongfang Bubai*, directed by Ching Siu-tung and produced by Tsui Hark), a 1992 Hong Kong film hailed as a milestone in Asia's queer liberalization for having introduced the first, and still the most iconic, transgender character in Chinese-language cinema, my analysis proposes a reconceptualization of the Cold War as a materialist method for the study of gender and sexual formations in the age of the Beijing Consensus.

Building on Asian Marxist arguments that the region has never entered a post–Cold War period because of the persistence of American neocolonial capitalism, I redefine the Cold War as a cultural palimpsest where the dialectic of Communism versus anti-Communism is rewritten into a contemporary idiom of colonialism versus self-determination in mainstream narratives of queer freedom and epistemic ruptures. While Communism and anti-Communism are no longer the reigning ideologies that divide China and Taiwan, contemporary cross-strait relations remain overdetermined by a Cold War structure of feeling that continues to shape the contours of literature, art, academic discourse, and political protests in ways that do not always immediately correspond to a legible, binary structure of domination and resistance. Because the Cold War is, in addition to a state of geopolitics, an affective structure, it is capable of polarizing a wide range of discourses and objects beyond the doctrines of Communism and anti-Communism. And because the Cold War is a structure of feeling, it does not always have a material, easily detectable presence. Through a Marxist lens, this chapter examines the transformation of the economic and political contradictions of the Cold War into narratives of sexual autonomy and postcolonial liberation in Asia.

The Cold War in Asia

In an era when we have become accustomed to defining the present against what came before—postsocialism, poststructuralism, postmodernism, postfeminism, postlocalism, postcontemporary interventions—it seems counterintuitive, if not counterproductive, to discuss the Cold War as the material basis for the formation of queer subjectivities in the age of the Beijing Consensus. Instead of returning to something that is almost universally regarded as a closed chapter of twentieth-century history, scholars of queer Asia are more likely to worry that our neologisms cannot catch up with just how fast the world is changing. Why the Cold War? Why now? Is the Cold War not that historical period humanity has already left behind? Is it not an obsolete term—like its conceptual by-product, the so-called third world, which has been replaced by analytic categories such as the global South, the center-periphery divide, and the multitude? How is it useful to think about the Cold War as a relevant context for *contemporary* queer Asia?

Certainly, our field has no shortage of outstanding studies of Chinese-language literature, film, music, radio programs, and newspapers produced between 1946 and 1991 in the PRC, Taiwan, Hong Kong, Malaysia, and Singapore.[6] Very few scholars, however, ever apply the concept of the Cold War to materials produced after 1991. The commonly accepted view is that the Cold War refers to the period of nonhostile belligerence between the capitalist Western bloc and the Communist Eastern bloc from the Truman Doctrine of 1947 to the collapse of the Soviet Union in 1991. East Asia was involved but only as the "hot" battleground for a series of proxy wars between the United States and the USSR. With the fall of the Berlin Wall and the dissolution of the USSR, history has decidedly moved into a post–Cold War, postideological phase.

Accordingly, Asian studies scholars have invented a wide range of periodizing markers to contextualize post-1991 Chinese and sinophone sexual cultures. These include neoliberalism, postmarket reform, the new world order, and New Democracy movements, but the Cold War is certainly not among them. As these periodizing markers gain greater currency in queer studies, the Cold War fades further into the background as an unfashionable topic except among historians and political scientists working in dusty archives. But this bifurcation of Cold War historiography and contemporary queer studies is a consequence of a static conceptualization of the Cold War as a *time frame* rather than a *materialist method*. If we accept the temporal definition of the Cold War as the period of geopolitical tension between the United States and the USSR, surely it has very little bearing on the study of sexualities in contemporary Asia. If, instead, we reconceptualize the Cold War as a materialist method for analyzing post-1991 sinophone cultural formations, we open ourselves to a much broader range of interpretative possibilities and analytic tools, which allows us to ask more nuanced questions about affect, embodiment, belongingness, identity, and dystopia in the Asia of today.

Even if we accept the more empirical, commonsense definition of the Cold War as a time frame rather than a contemporary problematic, we must still ask, Is the Cold War really over from the point of view of Asia, which is still divided into political states and ideological factions derived from the midcentury period? In the midst of frenzied media speculation about whether we are on the brink of Cold War 2.0 because of the deterioration of Sino-American relations, it may be worthwhile to remind ourselves that the Cold War—the original one—is not over in Asia, as many of its Marxist intellectuals have emphasized in different ways.[7] From a Euro-American perspective, the collapse of America's main contender for global supremacy seems to have furnished incontrovertible proof of the end of history. In Asia, however, the "division system" between the two Chinas (the PRC and the Republic of China) and the two Koreas (North and South) remains unchanged, though events since 2018 may have paved the way for a future Korean reunification.[8]

The material history of the Cold War has been eclipsed by a presentist identity politics of queer liberation and nativist consciousness in Asia. As I have been arguing throughout this book, a dematerialized history of sexuality has cast queer communities and identities in Asia as belated copies and beneficiaries of post-Stonewall US sexual politics. This narrative ignores the complex mediation of geopolitics in the constitution of queer subjects and reifies cultural difference as exotic and impenetrable tradition. A rethinking of the Cold War as an instrument of the accumulation of capital in America's Asia—how it shapes contemporary labor struggles and migrancy, how it structures the articulations of gender and sexuality, and how it governs the conditions of knowledge production and the division of intellectual labor between theory and area studies—would be a step toward a different kind of global sexual history, one that utilizes questions and issues that originate from other parts of the world to dislodge the presuppositions and analytic priorities of US-based queer theory.

My analysis proceeds in two parts. The first section develops the theoretical concept of the Cold War as a materialist method for the study of queer history. The second section focuses on *Swordsman II* as a historical example of the subsumption of the Cold War under a liberal cultural logic that facilitates the accumulation of capital.

A Materialist Method

The subsumption of the Cold War is the consequence of three interrelated problems and ossified assumptions: a generalization of imperial history as world history that obscures the agency of Asian subjects and states; a pernicious empiricism that treats the Cold War as a time frame instead of a conceptual problematic; and, finally, the rise of area studies, which reflects a division of *intellectual* labor created by the international division of *manual* labor under Cold War capitalism.

Of these three enduring assumptions, the generalization of imperial history as world history is perhaps the most deeply entrenched. To begin with, the conventional definition of the Cold War as the period from the beginning of the Truman Doctrine to the dissolution of the USSR naturalizes a Western-centered explanatory framework that completely overlooks the experience and agency of East Asia. The assumption that Cold War studies must begin (and end) with the United States and the USSR is part of the imperialist history that organizes all of our temporal-spatial lifeworlds according to the rise and fall of Western empires. As Fredric Jameson observes, the much-touted story about "the end of socialism . . . always seems to exclude China"—and we might add North Korea, Vietnam, Laos, and Cuba to the list.[9] Since political scientists cannot reconcile the rupture thesis with the factual existence of countries that are still officially socialist, the euphoric celebration of the worldwide collapse of Communism simply ignores East Asia.

The partition of East Asia into Communist and anti-Communist zones created nationalities—legal categories, embodied experiences, and subject formations—that persist or even flourish today, despite the dissolution of anti-Communism as a doctrine. But while most critics acknowledge the involvement of American, Soviet, and Chinese interests in the creation of the division system on the Korean Peninsula, the explanation of the origins of Taiwan has become much more complicated. If it was once easy to critique US neocolonialism, the Seventh Fleet, and US arms sales as the material conditions that guaranteed a divided Asia, today it is impossible to make that point in reference to Taiwan without appearing to support Chinese imperialism. Increasingly, the only politically acceptable view of Taiwan is that it is a separate and distinct entity from any concept of China. Those who understand the division of China and Taiwan as a product of the Cold War are quickly branded as prounification Chinese propagandists. While the PRC regards Taiwan as a renegade province and asserts its sovereignty over the island in the name of an anti-imperialist effort to rectify the history of colonial dismemberment, in Taiwan itself an increasing number of citizens see the nation as a victim of multiple colonialisms (Dutch, Spanish, Japanese, and Chinese) currently fighting to liberate itself from the clutches of the Beijing Consensus.[10] Similarly, but for rather different historical reasons, Hong Kong residents are increasingly worried about the "mainlandization" (*daluhua*) of the island and its culture. From the 2014 Umbrella Movement to the 2019–20 Anti-Extradition Law Amendment Bill protests, Hong Kong's autonomy and democracy, and its people's civil liberties, have repeatedly been exposed as precarious. What we are witnessing in the age of the Beijing Consensus is a clash of nationalisms, all of which regard themselves as anti-imperialist movements.

A proper understanding of the Cold War must therefore take seriously the agency of Asian subjects as actors instead of reducing them to objects of foreign influence and manipulation, proxies, or hapless casualties caught in the cross fire between the superpowers. The marginalization of East Asian agency has produced a deindividuation effect—a construction of Asians as faceless and nameless multitudes in Cold War historiography. Conventionally, scholars interpret the Cold War as the rivalry between the two Western superpowers without acknowledging Asian subjects and states as political actors who have also shaped that history. Seen as the mere recipient of foreign ideologies, Asia is given a complex and turbulent twentieth century in US-based Cold War historiography, but this complexity ultimately turns out to be nothing but collateral damage in a history driven by conflicts within the Western world. In an influential study of postwar politics, for example, historian James Cronin argues that the formation of postwar Japanese culture is a reactive, nationalist effort to discover what is putatively unique in its own tradition to compensate for its integration into "military alliances dominated by the United States, and the mass consumption of American goods, with the inevitable Americanization of taste and popular culture."[11] In other instances, studies of contemporary East Asia characterize its culture industry as a response to the traumatic memory of war—especially the "forgotten war" of Korea—but always place more emphasis on the discontinuities than the commonalities between the Cold War and the present. In these accounts, aesthetic objects in East Asia do not appear as the products or expressions of local history; rather, they are described as reactions or resistance to foreign ideologies.[12]

Our inability to understand East Asian subject formation as anything but a reaction to the interimperial rivalry of foreign powers is the result of a scholarly tendency to underplay the agency of nations and histories outside the Atlantic world. In standard US history textbooks, for example, World War II began with Adolf Hitler's invasion of Poland in 1939 and ended in 1945. In reality, this "world" war between the major players began with Japan's invasion of China in 1937 and only later came to involve Europe. Historians typically refuse to recognize that East Asian conflicts were not the ripple effects but rather the beginnings of world history. Nor do they believe that the internal politics of East Asia actually made a difference in the course of the war.

The denial of East Asian agency works hand in hand with the construction of Asian subjects as indistinguishable drones, mobs, hordes, coolies, or other figures without names, histories, or personalities.[13] If asked, "Who did we fight in World War II?" an American of average education would probably respond, "Hitler, Mussolini, and Japan." Unable to attach a name and a face to America's Asian antagonist, the same American might also describe the psychosexual perversions of Hitler in lurid detail. But despite the historical verdicts—Theodor Adorno's among them—that Hitler's Holocaust was the ultimate act of barbarism in the entirety of human history, the United States dropped atomic bombs not on Germany but rather on Japan.[14] The implication is that if Nazi Germany was pure evil incarnate, Japan was beyond good and evil—a mere laboratory for Western experiments. This differential treatment of America's wartime enemies was reflected in the administration's decision to intern more than 110,000 Americans of Japanese ancestry, while the mass exclusion orders did not apply to German Americans and Italian Americans.

Some historians argue that the decision to drop the bomb on Japan was made because Germany had already surrendered (on May 7, 1945) before the bomb was ready. (The first test bomb, called the Gadget, was detonated on July 16 in New Mexico, before the second and the third were dropped on Japan in August.) However, others believe that the decision was racially motivated. Bruce Cumings argues that a prototype was ready to be deployed on Germany, but American leaders decided not to use it for fear that if the bomb failed, the scientifically minded Germans could use it to their own advantage, whereas experimenting on primitive Asians would be strategically safer. In any case, Japan was ready to surrender after the first bomb was dropped on Hiroshima. Since there was absolutely no material explanation for the deployment of the second bomb, Cumings argues that the destruction of Nagasaki reflected a general disregard for Asian lives in comparison to white Europeans: "[Hiroshima] was an atrocity on a large scale and therefore a war crime. . . . Nagasaki is different: If it was gratuitous at best (atomic annihilation as an afterthought), it was therefore genocidal at worst (because it served no clear war purpose)."[15] The trivialization of Asian lives, "subjects without history" who are neither capable of great evil nor deserving of basic human rights, prevents us from seeing East Asia as the true locus of Cold War power struggles.

The second assumption—that the Cold War must be an empirical time frame rather than an internalized mindset that persists in the contemporary world—stems from the rupture thesis popularized by Francis Fukuyama. According to Fukuyama, the fall of the Berlin Wall and the collapse of the Soviet Union marked "the end of history," which signaled the triumph of liberal democracies and hence the end of any power struggles between capitalism and Communism. "At the end of history," he wrote, "there are no serious ideological competitors left to liberal democracy."[16] Defining *ideology* narrowly as the choice among democracy, Communism, and fascism, Fukuyama and his followers proclaim that we now live in a world free of ideologies. Conservative critics regard the collapse of Communism as a powerful vindication of US policy throughout the period. On occasion, the Fukuyama school of thought also appears to reserve the term *ideology* for all alternatives to Western forms of government. In this view, democracy is not an ideology but what humanity has always striven to achieve since the times of Plato—a natural, God-given desire for self-governance that was first articulated by the Greeks, dramatically brought to the fore by the French Revolution, and mythically perfected and put into practice by the Americans. Fascism, Communism, and oriental despotism appear as interchangeable examples of totalitarianism—unfortunate moments when tyrants rise and the people are either unable to make decisions for themselves or ideologically brainwashed to accept them.[17]

Until the 1990s, Cold War studies was fully dominated by the realist paradigm in international relations, which aimed at explaining the behavior of states (conceived of as actors or institutions) within the sphere of power balances and geopolitical considerations. With the sudden collapse of the Soviet Union, historians began to stress the importance of the ideology of culture.[18] The study of ideologies makes it possible to understand the Cold War as the formation of subjectivities, the process whereby power hails individuals into newly available categories of social existence. The creation of new ethnic or racial categories is an example. Under Cold War capitalism, new ethnic identities emerged in ways that cannot be explained through a binary model of domination and resistance. Instead of celebrating the end of British colonialism, Hong Kong residents viewed the 1997 handover as Chinese reannexation and the end of human rights and democracy. The comparison between Taiwanese and Korean responses to Japanese imperialism is another case in point. While the majority of South Koreans regard the period of Japanese occupation as the derailment of their modernization—frequently depicted in Korean literature as *han* (resentment)—Taiwanese leaders characterize the fifty years of Japanese colonialism as a golden age of development that woefully ended with Japan's defeat. With the arrival of mainlanders after the end of the Chinese Civil War, a new regime of racial capitalism was created in Taiwan. Hokkien-speaking populations, mostly descendants of Hoklo emigrants from Fujian, became *benshengren* (people from the local province)— meaning people who are considered authentically Taiwanese. The émigrés who came to Taiwan in 1949 and their children became *waishengren* (people from the outer provinces, namely, outside of Taiwan).

A mutual structure of hostility ensued and created unequal employment opportunities, rural-urban divisions, and rules of class mobility that played a pivotal role in Taiwan's structure of capital accumulation. While the *waishengren* are treated as aliens who cannot be fully assimilated and are marked by their old-fashioned customs and incorrect accents, the *benshengren* were systematically abused and even massacred by the Kuomintang (KMT) government in the initial years of its settler colonialism. After installing an autocratic government, the KMT violently suppressed the uprising of local dissidents in the 228 Incident in 1947. After killing thousands of civilians, the KMT government placed the island under martial law and entered the period that came to be known as the White Terror. The massacre has served as a critical impetus for the Taiwanese independence movement, which is further fueled by the popular sentiment that the KMT regime, unlike the Japanese colonizers, never set Taiwan on the proper path of East Asian capitalist development because it treated the island only as a temporary military base to "take back the mainland and rescue our fellow countrymen" ("fangong dalu jiejiu tongbao," the political slogan of the Chiang Kai-shek administration). In recent years, news reports on almost every earthquake in Taiwan have characteristically included—in addition to compassionate observations of human casualties—asides about Japanese-era construction that is still standing tall and proud next to the ruins of KMT-era buildings.

The concept of *bensheng*, which describes the Hokkien-speaking populations as the indigenous and rightful residents of Taiwan, is falling out of favor because the distinction between *bensheng* and *waisheng* (local and outer provinces) is based on the KMT-era understanding of Taiwan as a province of China, and of the KMT as its sole legitimate government. Since the current mainstream political view is that Taiwan is and has always been a nation of its own, the preference is to refer to the *bensheng* populations as simply Taiwanese. But while some argue that the KMT occupied or colonized Taiwan, it certainly did not do so on its own.[19] Protected by the US Seventh Fleet during the Chinese Civil War and subsequently by the Sino-American Mutual Defense Treaty—an agreement that prevented both Taiwan and China from initiating direct military actions without US intervention—Taiwan from the start has been a product of the Cold War. As Hsiao-ting Lin shows through an examination of recently declassified archives, the creation of two Chinas (the Republic of China and the PRC) was not, as commonly assumed, a simple result of the Chinese Civil War or a reflection of incompatible ideologies and military interests. Rather, it was the cumulative outcome of political compromises, negotiations (between actors who possessed only partial knowledge of the situation), unforeseen circumstances, and ad hoc responses to unexpected turns of events—which is why Lin describes Taiwan as an "accidental state."[20]

Today the majority of the 1949 émigré soldiers, most of whom were "snatched" (*zhuafu*; i.e., illegally conscripted) from the Chinese countryside against their will by the KMT army during the Chinese Civil War, have either passed away or become socially and politically marginalized. As Taiwan's public culture is increasingly defined by Taiwan-born populations with no personal connections to mainland China, more and more citizens support changing the country's name to Taiwan from its current title, the Republic of China. But the PRC's rise as a powerhouse in the new global capitalist order has further isolated Taiwan and rendered its de facto (but not de jure) independent status precarious. Given the PRC's staunch opposition to Taiwanese independence, some "deep-Green" nationalists have gone so far as to argue that Taiwan's only hope is to become the fifty-first state of the United States—a movement known as the Club 51 phenomenon.[21]

The complex politics of China and Taiwan reveals the persistence of the Cold War in the tension-fraught region that China regards as part of the Beijing Consensus. On the other hand, some individuals in both Taiwan and China continue to support the One China principle, which is now more commonly discussed in a modified form as the 1992 Consensus. From the perspective of the PRC, the One China principle is a nonnegotiable principle of national sovereignty in response to a history of Western colonial dismemberment, foreign interference in China's national affairs, and an American strategy of containment that encircled its borders with enemies following the Sino-Soviet split. In other words, China's stance toward Taiwan today is a consequence of its rigidified defense against persistent hostilities from the US-led Cold War in Asia. As Perry Anderson points out, in terms of linguistic, ethnic, or religious differences from the center, in principle both Tibet and Hong Kong have greater claims to independence than Taiwan; therefore, permitting

Taiwanese independence could create a domino effect that China cannot afford.[22] The impasse between China and Taiwan (and that between the two Koreas) cannot be resolved through the romantic nationalism that has historically created settlements in the Americas or reunified Germany. Instead, we need to recognize that Taiwanese, Chinese, and American nationalisms are mutually embedded and interlocked ideologies in the uneven and combined development of capitalism.

Finally, the third difficulty that the Cold War as method seeks to overcome is the division of intellectual labor between the humanities and the social sciences, between discipline and area, and between the study of the West and the study of the rest. As I analyzed in chapter 1, the Cold War period created a new international division of labor that relocated labor-intensive and low-value-added production to East Asia. This international division of labor, as it turned out, was both material and intellectual. In an influential article, Carl Pletsch describes an asymmetrical division of intellectual labor brought about by the Cold War creation of the three-world scheme.[23] Invented by French anthropologists in the 1960s, the three-world scheme divided the planet into three geopolitical categories and created corresponding branches of knowledge that resulted in a chiasmus of area and discipline. Knowledge produced by the first world was institutionally organized by discipline (for example, literature, music, economics, political science, and psychology), but knowledge produced by, for, and about the third world was organized by language and area (for example, China, the Middle East, Africa, and Latin America). This allocation of intellectual labor corresponded to how Westerners felt about the three worlds: whereas the first world was studied in terms of the useful knowledge it produced because it was "technologically advanced, free of ideological impediments to utilitarian thinking, and thus natural," the third world was "marked both by a presumed absence of technology and the presence of a nonscientific mentality, religion, or culture," and the second world was considered "technologically advanced, but burdened with an ideological elite blocking free access to science and utilitarian thinking."[24]

Following the Cold War divide, English became a discipline (literary studies, as opposed to law, economics, or music), but Chinese became an area studies program (the study of China, as opposed to Japan or the Middle East). As Sigmund Diamond has shown in *Compromised Campus* (though he focuses more on Russian research centers than eastern Europe and China), the establishment of area studies programs served the purposes of the intelligence-gathering apparatuses of the US security regime and anti-Communist politics. Even today, academics teaching and writing about Chinese language, literature, and now sexualities cannot dissociate their labor from foundations and institutes that were, explicitly or implicitly, created in cooperation with the Central Intelligence Agency, the Federal Bureau of Investigation, and other intelligence and military agencies. Pletsch's historical investigation sheds light on many of the perplexing phenomena we find in academia today. For example, an Asian studies department might prioritize hiring a scholar of Buddhism over hiring to fill large gaps in course offerings in Chinese, Japanese, and Korean literary history, but a French department is unlikely to appoint a specialist in Catholicism before it can offer courses on topics such as the eighteenth-century French novel. The emergence of queer Asian studies further illustrates this division. While US-based queer theory has been developed and disseminated by scholars in English departments, including Eve Kosofsky Sedgwick, Lee Edelman, Michael Warner, Lauren Berlant, David L. Eng, Elizabeth Freeman, Heather Love, and Jack Halberstam, most scholars working on queer Asia are anthropologists, sociologists, and historians. It appears that when it comes to understanding Asian sexualities, fieldwork, ethnography, and archival research are much preferred to close readings and textual analysis of fiction. As Rey Chow points out, while works that deal exclusively with French examples may be published with generic titles such as *Gender Trouble* or *This Sex Which Is Not One*, authors writing on Asian topics are bound by what she calls the "logic of ethnic supplements" and a "geopolitical realism" that compulsorily requires them to "stabilize and fix their intellectual and theoretical content by way of a national, ethnic, or cultural location."[25]

This division is clearly troublesome, since works produced by first-world thinkers can transcend both national and disciplinary boundaries, while works produced by the global South are perceived to reflect the essences of their societies of origin, which are studied through quantitative and empiricist methodologies. Naoki Sakai traces this division of intellectual labor to a conceptual split between two kinds of subjects of knowledge: *humanitas* and *anthropos*.[26] *Humanitas* refers to humans who are capable of self-reflexivity while embodying particularistic features of a common humanity. By contrast, *anthropos* is reserved for people who participate in the production of knowledge only in the second sense, as particular manifestations of a putatively common human nature. The selection of an area in area studies is not random. Rather, it is a process of enclosure during the historical expansion of capital accumulation on a global scale that has brought about not only expropriation and dispossession but also commensurabilities.[27] The preference for social scientific methodologies in queer Asian studies reflects a positivism historically associated with the Cold War task of identifying and gathering reliable information about the enemy. In other words, the separation of theoretical and empirical inquiry was politically motivated by the Cold War rather than being an organic intellectual development of academic knowledge from within. Queer theory's tendency to mine the global South for examples rather than epistemologies—which I discussed in chapter 1—is a consequence of this Cold War division of intellectual labor in knowledge production that persists today.

Reading Queer Asia's Cold War

To develop a more concrete sense of how the Cold War as the material unconscious of queer Asia might shed light on the persistence of history's hold on the present, I turn to Ching Siu-tung and Tsui Hark's *Swordsman II: Asia the Invincible*. *Swordsman II* is an adaptation of Jin Yong's novel *Xiao ao jianghu* (The smiling, proud wanderer), which was first serialized from 1967 to 1969.[28] The film is considered a milestone in *wuxia* (martial arts) cinema for its allegorical import, emotional drama, use of special effects, fluid camera movement, and cinematography.[29] Before the *Swordsman* series (the first *Swordsman* film was made in 1990, and the third one in 1993), Chinese *wuxia* movies relied on two studio techniques to illustrate superhuman abilities (such as "lightness kung fu"—gravity-defying moves on rooftops, bamboo branches, or lakes). The first technique was based on the trampoline, which combined careful editing and stunt work to create the illusion of flying, gliding, or other highly acrobatic kung fu moves. The second technique, *wire fu* (wirework and kung fu), used wires and pulleys to hold actors in midair during a fight scene. The arrival of Tsui Hark on the scene, however, revolutionized martial arts cinema and made it appear more modern.[30] Tsui's *Swordsman* movies were among the first to employ digital technologies—including computer-aided compositing and computer-generated images—to render superhuman martial arts sequences, which have since become the industry standard. Combining stylized cinematography with intense action scenes and arresting storytelling, the *Swordsman* series has come to be regarded as the beginning of a new chapter in *wuxia* cinema.[31] Thematically, the series is also remarkable for having broken away from the old-fashioned morality tales of revenge, honor, nationalism, and crude kung fu fighting found in earlier martial arts films and shifting to a more complex and visually stunning ecology of human emotions and ethical dilemmas. New martial arts cinema, as works by Tsui and Ching have come to be called, moved the genre past the simplistic hero-villain binary commonly seen in socialist propaganda films and earlier kung fu revenge films.

With its modern visual effects and stylized color composition, the *Swordsman* series offers more than bodily spectacles: it is an invitation to explore the interiority of the human psyche. *Swordsman II* tells the story of Asia the Invincible (Dongfang Bubai), a martial arts master who follows the instructions of a "secret scroll" called *Kuihua baodian* (The sunflower manual) and castrates himself to harness its preternatural martial power. Unexpectedly, Asia metamorphoses into a woman. As I discuss more fully in the next section, the episode in Jin Yong's original novel was conceived as a Cold War political allegory to demonize Mao, employing a homophobic/transphobic perspective to depict how Asia becomes a psychologically damaged and sexually aberrant (*bu nan bu nü*) monstrosity, the price he pays for his political ambition.[32] Jin Yong tells us that Asia's castration causes him to lose all interest in women and become a homosexual who is willing to play the role of a submissive housewife to a low-ranking but masculine member of his clan.[33] The text is not only homophobic/transphobic but also misogynistic, as Jin Yong clearly equates castration with feminization, and feminization with social subordination.

But the 1992 film performed a stunning cultural coup, turning Asia into one of the most celebrated queer characters in the history of Chinese-language cinema. Indeed, since the film's 1992 release, Asia has become a cultural icon among transgender communities in the Sinosphere.[34] Instead of a debased male homosexual, Asia in the film version—portrayed by the talented and scene-stealing actress Brigitte Lin Ching-Hsia (1954–)—is a self-affirming transgender woman who takes much pride in her newfound gender identity as well as her martial powers. Jin Yong reportedly objected to the casting of Lin, as he had meant for Asia to be a source of disgust and revulsion.[35] But as a cultural palimpsest, the story of Asia took on a life of its own, eclipsing and transforming Jin Yong's authorial intentions and the political context of its genesis. Indeed, the story of Asia has undergone numerous adaptations for both cinema and television, creating a diffused form of collective popular memory that has no singular presence.[36]

Using a method she describes as internet ethnography, Egret Lulu Zhou surveys an impressive range of artifacts created by fans of Asia as a transgender icon, including fan fiction, videos (including music videos), photo collages, and webisodes that reimagine the fans' own relationship with Asia's relationship with other male or female characters. Though the character was first created by Jin Yong, Zhou shows that Ching and Tsui's 1992 adaptation transformed Asia the Invincible from an "abnormal monster" into a "cross-dressing goddess"; subsequently, Asia the Invincible became a rallying point for the transgender community and sometimes a synonym for transgender itself through Yu Zheng's 2013 adaptation and online fan-created content.[37] Newer versions of the beloved character continue to appear, most recently in the 2018 television series "Xin xiao ao jianghu" (New smiling, proud wanderer). The making and remaking of Asia the Invincible forms one of the most important episodes in the story of a liberalizing queer Asia.

In Helen Hok-Sze Leung's reading, *Swordsman II* does not merely capture a newly available transgender subjectivity in queer Asia; it is a paradigmatically *queer* film as such:

> In effect, *Swordsman 2* has "queered" three familiar themes in martial arts film. First, it approaches the transformative effect of martial arts on the gendered body as a form of transsexuality. Yet, unlike in the novel, the result from this practice is not portrayed as mutilated monstrosity but instead a perfectly crafted body that is both beautiful and unassailable. Second, the film superimposes two stock relationship types onto its two main characters: the attraction between Dongfang Bubai and the hero Linghu Chong, played by Jet Li, resembles both the free-spirited camaraderie and mutual admiration between men and the heterosexually coded eroticism between the hero and his love interest. Third, when faced with scenes of coy flirtation between the two, the audience is made to see double: their nondiegetic recognition of the stars leads to a sighting of familiar heterosexuality which, within the diegesis, actually signifies the attraction a man feels for a transsexual woman. The film does not allow the audience to "tell the difference" between the two, thus disturbing the boundaries that are supposed to demarcate heterosexuality categorically from queer attraction.[38]

While Zhou's research documents the historical emergence of Asia the Invincible as a queer icon and Leung's nuanced reading sheds much light on the film's queer textuality, I emphasize that such representations cannot be inserted into a unilinear narrative of progress, liberation, visibility, or proliferated identities and identifications. Instead of reading the film or its titular character as a prime example of a queer liberalism, I make a critical return to the geopolitical context of the making and reception of the film. Geopolitical readings of *Swordsman II* are not new—indeed, while most critics have focused on the film's representations of queer sexuality, others have emphasized that Hong Kong's 1997 handover was the "real" referent for this martial arts film set in medieval China.[39] My analysis shows that both queer and geopolitical readings of the film are dependent on a political vocabulary of personal freedom and autonomy derived from Jin Yong's critique of Chinese Communism during the height of the Cold War. The Cold War has become an extremely fungible concept, lending itself to a wide array of rhetorical substitutions and affective displacements. The film is an example of this kind of rhetorical substitution that refashions the contradictions of Cold War East Asian capitalism into a contemporary idiom of mainland Chinese colonialism versus local self-determination as well as a story of gender self-fashioning. Because the film adaptation has transformed its ideological referent from the Cultural Revolution to the specter of the reannexation of Hong Kong, the novel's original historical relation to the Cold War becomes an occluded presence, a disavowed trace in the Derridean senses that requires the methodology outlined in this chapter to be brought into view.

Throughout the 1990s the story of Asia the Invincible has been interpreted by mainstream critics as a film about gender crossing and homoeroticism, in either a positive or negative sense. For some, the film serves as a prime example of homophobia and heterosexism in traditional Chinese culture, in that it conflates castration, femininity, and homosexuality. Chou Wah-shan famously argued that the casting of Brigitte Lin, a cisgender female actress, in the role of Asia (who develops a romantic and sexual relationship with the film's male protagonist, played by Jet Li) is a strategic and homophobic move. According to Chou, the producers cast Lin to heterosexualize a same-sex relationship in order to make it more palatable to the audience.[40] Clearly, the idea that castration can lead to a change in sexual orientation is founded on a cultural perception that homosexuals are somehow comparable to eunuchs, and the conflation of transgender people and eunuchs also perpetuates a phallus-centered understanding of the organization of desires and identifications. For other critics, however, this politically incorrect but aesthetically daring film stands as evidence of an irrepressible queer energy in social undercurrents even in the conservative and homophobic 1990s.[41]

Both sets of critics note the significance of casting Brigitte Lin, whose successful performances in many cross-dressing or androgynous roles before and after this film have earned her a large queer following in Asia, not unlike

Judy Garland, Lady Gaga, and Cher in the United States.[42] Lin's spellbinding performance in this film transformed Jin Yong's Asia the Invincible into a glamorous, diva-like icon in contemporary queer Chinese cultures.[43] Another sign of the film's influence on popular culture is the emergence of jokes about Asia's "sunflower" techniques (sometimes replacing the word *kuihua* [sunflower] with *juhua* [chrysanthemum], the colloquial term for "anus") in queer communities. As a result of the popularity of Lin's character, *Swordsman II* has been exclusively analyzed for its representation of queer sexuality. I contend, however, that it is the contradictions of Cold War East Asian capitalism that explain the emergence of the main character.

There are two separate political subtexts for the film: one is the Cultural Revolution, and the other is the 1997 handover of Hong Kong. As already mentioned, *Swordsman I* and *II* are adaptations of Jin Yong's 1967 martial arts novel, *The Smiling, Proud Wanderer*, which is an allegorical representation of the Cultural Revolution.[44] The question of the Cultural Revolution is inseparable from the ideology of the Cold War. In Cold War historiography, Communism is frequently presented as a distortion of human nature, while capitalism—despite its inequalities and problems—is justified in pragmatic terms as the best of all possible worlds. Following this line of thinking, critics frequently discuss the Cultural Revolution as the most extreme and thus catastrophic outcome of Chinese Communism and a derailed moment in China's primitive accumulation of capital. Representations of the Chinese Cultural Revolution in this light have consistently fueled the politics of global anti-Communism since the beginning of the Cold War. Jin Yong's fictional exploration of the Cultural Revolution and its discontents was embedded in the problems arising from China's uneven incorporation into world capitalism, which provided the conditions of possibility for a historically determinate mode of critiquing Communism.

Written at the height of the Cultural Revolution, *The Smiling, Proud Wanderer* depicts the debasement of political debate into power struggles and machinations for personal gain. Politics is no longer real or meaningful; rather, what is done in the name of ideological causes (unification versus independence) is merely factionalism and the creation of personality cults by power-hungry politicians who have no regard for ordinary people's lives. Jin Yong uses the concept of *jianghu*, a Chinese idiom that refers to both the world of *wuxia* and the world of politics, to describe a scene of perpetual violence. Violence begets violence, and despair follows. There seems to be no exit from the cycle.

As already mentioned, in the novel Asia the Invincible is a villain, not the protagonist's object of romantic interest. The name Dongfang Bubai ("invincible Asia" or "the East that never fails") tacitly alludes to Mao Zedong, whose given name, Zedong, could be translated literally as "bringing prosperity to the East." The film draws attention to this allegorical connection by having Asia always wear a red robe with a symbol of the sun and the moon. In fact, the film has Asia—who is supposed to be living in the sixteenth century—recite two lines from Chairman Mao's most famous poem, "Snow—to the tune of *Qin Yuan Chun*" ("Qin yuan chun, xue"): "This land so rich in beauty / Has made countless heroes bow in homage."[45] This anachronism turns Asia into a political ventriloquist, as if Mao himself were speaking these lines while contemplating the unification of the beautiful and rich land of China. Asia repeatedly describes their own actions, particularly their self-castration, as a sacrifice they have made to "serve the people," in a manner reminiscent of the Maoist slogan.[46] The third installment in the film series, *Swordsman III: East Is Red*, directly references "East Is Red," the Chinese revolutionary song that became the PRC's de facto national anthem during the Cultural Revolution. Before Jin Yong constructed the character of Asia as the master of "sunflower techniques," Mao's personality cult was already symbolically connected to sunflowers. In "East Is Red," the music-and-dance epic version of the revolutionary song that premiered in Beijing's Great Hall of the People in Tiananmen Square on October 2, 1964, seventy dancers appeared in floral costumes performing the prologue of "Sunflower Turning toward the Sun" ("Kuihua xiang yang") to symbolize the masses awakening to Mao's guidance.[47]

In Jin Yong's original novel, Asia the Invincible is the leader of an underground society called the Sun/Moon Sect, which, like the young Chinese Communist Party, seeks to unify China by ousting opposing clans and ideologies. In response to the rising menace of the Sun/Moon Sect, the major martial arts factions—Shaolin Temple, Wudang, and the schools of the five sacred mountains—form an alliance. They refer to themselves as the "orthodox sects" (*zheng jiao*) and refuse to speak of the Sun/Moon Sect by its real name. Instead, all leaders and students of the orthodox sects learn to refer to the Sun/Moon Sect as the demon cult (*mo jiao*), not unlike the way children in the so-called free world (Taiwan and Hong Kong) were taught during the Cold War to speak of the Chinese Communist Party only as *gong-fei* (Communist bandits) instead of *gongchandang* (the Communist Party). While the world of *jianghu* is thus divided between the orthodox sects and the demon cult, the alliance of orthodox sects itself is plagued by a serious disagreement between the prounification camp (those who believe that the only way to stop the advance of the Sun/Moon Sect is to merge into one school) and the proindependence camp (those who believe that the history, culture, and techniques of each school can be preserved only if they remain separate from one another and that the call for a merger is merely one leader's ruse to increase his personal influence and power within the alliance).

While the producers' choice of Asia as their narrative focus allows the film to derive significant allegorical material from the novel's engagement with Chinese Communism under Cold War East Asian capitalism, in the original novel Asia is only a minor character. Asia is a usurper who rose to power and ousted the original leader of the Sun/Moon Sect after acquiring special powers from a foreign book titled *The Sunflower Manual*, which is said to come from the West (*xiyu*). If Karl Marx's *Capital* provided the ideological foundation for the Chinese Communist Party, *The Sunflower Manual* proves to be the literal font of Asia's martial powers and political leadership. Asia's actions in the book replicate the most destructive aspects of the Cultural Revolution. He forces young children to denounce their parents' political mistakes in public—reminiscent of the Red Guards. The same children cheerfully explain to the world the physical and spiritual benefits of studying and reciting the teachings of the holy master every morning, as if they were carrying a copy of Mao's *Little Red Book*. A boy around ten years old says, "If I spend a day without studying the master's sacred instructions, I lose all my appetite and cannot sleep. When I study his sacred instructions, my martial power grows, and I have the energy to defeat our enemies."[48] The novel's protagonist, Linghu Chong, is a student in the Huashan Sect. Like his peers, he is raised to fear and distrust the Sun/Moon Sect, but after a chance meeting with the daughter of the deposed leader, Linghu becomes entangled in the internal affairs of the sect and eventually agrees to help the royalists defeat Asia in order to restore the old master as ruler. But once the old master resumes leadership, he simply becomes another Asia the Invincible, with the same thirst for power, and uses the same kind of ruthlessness to achieve it. In the end Linghu realizes that the problem is systemic rather than personal; in choosing one faction over the other, he is only encouraging the lust for power and wealth and its concomitant violence. As the master in the movie says to him regarding his desire to "retire from the *jianghu*": "Where there are humans, there is *jianghu*. Humanity is *jianghu*." The dream of a peaceful, conflict-free world is not only utopian but naive. Linghu's gradual absorption of this lesson forms the basis of the novel's (and the movie's) sobering political realism.

This thesis is worth careful consideration, for it would be a mistake to simply dismiss *The Smiling, Proud Wanderer* as Maoist or anti-Maoist, Communist or anti-Communist. Rather than launching a predictable critique of Mao's China from a liberal point of view, the novel tells us just the opposite: the ideological choices the Cold War forced on us (between Communism and anti-Communism) reduce the complexity of human struggles to a mere matter of political allegiances and identifications without any awareness of the systemic mechanisms by which social power reproduces itself. While I argue that the Cold War constitutes the political context for the genesis of the iconic queer character, in reality the historical relationship between Jin Yong and Maoist politics was extremely complex. What I am characterizing here is therefore not a one-to-one correspondence between the novel's features and Mao's Cultural Revolution, as if it were simply a roman à clef to be decoded as a piece of anti-Maoist propaganda. Rather, by demonstrating how Jin Yong's critique of the Cultural Revolution in the 1960s transmuted into the social anxiety surrounding the 1997 handover of Hong Kong and then into a narrative of queer liberalization and transgender identities in Asia, I propose a reconceptualization of the Cold War as a cultural palimpsest that is again and again written over from one historical moment to another.

In the initial years of the story's serialization in the newspaper *Ming Pao*, Jin Yong was widely seen as a right-wing journalist in Hong Kong. On May 6, 1967, massive riots broke out on the streets of Hong Kong, leading to an event dubbed the "Great Proletarian Cultural Revolution of Hong Kong." Starting with a labor dispute in a factory in San Po Kong, confrontations between the police and picketing workers quickly escalated into violent crises. After the arrest of several workers, pro-Communist leftists formed the Hong Kong and Kowloon Committee for Anti–Hong Kong British Persecution Struggle. Carrying Mao Zedong's *Little Red Book*, protesters demanded labor rights, equality, the end of British imperialism, and social justice. These large-scale demonstrations against British colonial rule and in support of the Cultural Revolution on the mainland were met with a brutal government crackdown. The leftists then switched to guerrilla tactics and planted bombs around the city. On August 24, Lam Bun (1929–67), a famous radio commentator who had sharply criticized the leftists, was burned alive on his way to work. The leftists then announced that their next target was Jin Yong, who had to go into hiding.[49]

The history of Cold War politics is full of contradictory beliefs and mercurial views. Before Jin Yong came to be seen as a pro-Communist propagandist, a traitor to Hong Kong, and a sellout to Beijing, he had been called an enemy of socialism, a reputation he garnered from the debates between *Ming Pao*, a newspaper he founded, and the pro-Communist leftist newspaper *Ta Kung Pao*. In 1962 Jin Yong published a series of essays criticizing the PRC's response to the crisis of refugees from the regime fleeing to Hong Kong—which, he argued, reflected an increasingly rigid dogmatism within the Communist Party that detached it further from the reality and livelihood of the masses. On October 16, 1964, China successfully detonated its first nuclear bomb, an event its foreign minister, Chen Yi (1901–72), described as the pride and glory of all third-world countries in their common struggles against the Soviet Union and the United States. A few days later, Jin Yong published an essay condemning China's entry into the global arms race. He maintained that by choosing atomic bombs (*hezi*) over pants (*kuzi*), Mao's brand of socialism had shifted its aims from a sustainable livelihood for its citizens to militant nationalism. In response, *Ta Kung Pao* described Jin Yong and his newspaper as "anti-Communist and anti-Chinese, a follower of England and worshipper of America, betrayer of what the people stand for."[50] Although the 1967 Hong Kong leftist riots resulted in threats to Jin Yong's life, they did not turn him into an anti-Communist writer. Instead, he wrote a novel that explores the ways in which political labels—such as leftist and conservative, Communist and anti-Communist—divide our world into normative values and fossilized beliefs, often with violent consequences.

As I have been arguing, the figuration of Asia the Invincible is not an instrument of pro- or anti-Communist ideology but an exploration of the mental hold that such labels have over us within global capitalism. After the fall of Asia the Invincible, Linghu is pursued by the leader of the orthodox alliance, Zuo Lengchan (whose name could be rendered literally as "the chan [Zen] Buddhism of Cold [War] leftist [politics]"). Zuo sees Linghu as all that stands in the way of the unification of China under his rule. Ultimately, Linghu is betrayed by his own teacher, who had raised him as his son. We learn, then, that both the demon cult and its opponents in the orthodox sects have dark sides. The object of the novel's critique is therefore neither Communism nor anti-Communism but dogmatism: the slavish following of inflexible political beliefs. Rather than treating Jin Yong as a leftist, a conservative, a capitalist comprador, or a socialist, it is perhaps more accurate to call him a humanist deeply immersed and invested in China's cultural tradition, something he

believes that the proponents of the Cultural Revolution—and their critics—
have distorted, destroyed, or else forgotten in their ceaseless power struggles
and search for modernity. Linghu is a tragic hero in this sense. He recognizes
that the spectrum of human values and actions cannot be reduced to a Man-
ichaean binary of good and evil but is himself unable, at the end of the day,
to transcend fossilized ideological binaries.

Manichaeism is the telling metaphor here. The idea that the world can be
divided into absolute good and evil, and the various historical religions based
on binary principles, such as Manichaeism and Zoroastrianism, fascinated
Jin Yong and provided rich resources for his creativity. In his 1961 novel *Yi
tian tu long ji* (Heavenly sword, dragon-slaying saber), he uses Manichaeism
(Ming jiao) as the name for an underground society of martial heroes. Set
in the final years of Mongol rule in China, the novel is similarly concerned
with the internecine struggles between an alliance of orthodox schools and a
menacing opponent, the Religion of Light. Like the Sun/Moon Sect, the Religion
of Light is referred to as a demon cult by its enemies. However, the members of
the Religion of Light turn out to be heroes in the 1961 novel; they lead the Han
Chinese to throw off the yoke of Mongol rule. Jin Yong's construction of the
story reveals the influence of a theory proposed in the 1940s by the Chinese
historian Wu Han (1909–69), according to which the founding emperor of the
Ming dynasty, Zhu Yuanzhang (1328–98), chose the name Ming 明 (meaning
"light") to acknowledge the assistance of the Manichees (followers of Ming
jiao) in the revolution against the Mongols. Jin Yong's novel correctly notes
that in medieval China Manichaeism was called the Religion of Light (Ming
jiao), but otherwise his representation is a confused tangle of elements
associated with Persia, Arabs, Nestorianism, Zoroastrianism, and other
Middle Eastern content. For example, the Manichees are said to be fire
worshippers like the Zoroastrians, while in fact they worshipped symbols
of the sun and the moon but not fire.[51] The novel discusses the strange ways of
the Manichees, including nude burial for deceased members, vegetarianism,
and a lineage of virgin female rulers. According to the novel, the word *mani*
was changed into the similar-sounding *mo*, the Chinese word for "demon,"
during the Tang dynasty.[52]

Jin Yong's characteristic blending of fact and fiction adds much flavor to
his stories. It is safe to assume that the Sun/Moon Sect in *The Smiling, Proud
Wanderer* is a code name for the Religion of Light as well, for the Chinese
character *ming* 明 is in fact made up of the characters for "sun" 日 and "moon"
月. That the Sun/Moon Sect is also called the "demon cult" (*mo jiao*) reveals

its affinity to Manichaeism. *Ming* is also clearly an emotionally evocative character for Jin Yong, who once explained that he named his newspaper *Ming Pao* to emphasize its objective, nonpartisan character and his belief in political transparency. But does Jin Yong mean to suggest that the Communist Party is like the Religion of Light and the Sun/Moon Sect in his novels, "demon cults" that are misunderstood and "demonized" for having revolutionary beliefs? To begin with, we should note that the idea of demon cults occupies an ambivalent place in Jin Yong's universe. In *Heavenly Sword, Dragon-Slaying Saber*, the demon cult is unambiguously the victim of a witch hunt, persecuted by self-appointed guardians of tradition and morality. In *The Smiling, Proud Wanderer*, on the other hand, the demon cult is responsible for many atrocities and follows an oppressive and violent doctrine. The shift in Jin Yong's thinking is also discernible in the construction of the two protagonists. Both characters are invited to join the demon cult, but while the protagonist of the earlier novel readily accepts, Linghu rejects the offer and makes an even more radical choice: he becomes the first male head of a convent of Buddhist nuns, to the outrage and consternation of his peers. In crossing the gender line, Linghu challenges a different kind of ideological divide. The earlier novel subverts social conventions by having its villains turn out to be misunderstood heroes and falsely demonized individuals, but its strategy is still predicated on a binary opposition. The later, more sophisticated novel dispenses with the trope of good and evil altogether.

The 1992 film adaptation inherits the binarism of Cold War thinking that Jin Yong introduces and implicitly criticizes, but switches the target from the Cultural Revolution to the 1997 handover of Hong Kong. In addition to the story of Asia, the film significantly expands a minor episode in the original novel that is centered on Blue Phoenix, a Miao woman who rules a subsidiary clan of the Sun/Moon Sect. Curiously, the movie version turns all members of the Sun/Moon Sect into Miao ethnic minorities. The members of the Sun/Moon Sect are introduced as "wo men Miaozu" (literally, "we Miao")—a phrase that is translated as "highlanders" in the English subtitles. The choice of Miao is significant in the context of the contradictory developments of China's capitalism. Consigned to the remote hinterlands, the Miao people have been constructed by the Chinese state as feminized keepers of tradition during its postsocialist reforms.[53] Linghu and other members of the orthodox sects are referred to as Han Chinese (*Han ren*, translated as "mainlanders" in the English subtitles), who are both the oppressors and the modernizers of China. Contemporary labor struggles are thus congealed into ethnic difference,

constructing a binary opposition between feminized, primitive Miao and industrious, cultured Han populations.

Rather than serving as the embodiment of foreign-influenced dogma, Asia
the Invincible becomes the primary object of Linghu's affection and the cause
of his crisis of masculinity. The crux of the movie's emotional narrative rests
on a misunderstanding and an ambiguity: Linghu meets Asia for the first time
when the latter is practicing the forbidden art of *The Sunflower Manual* by a
lake, and Linghu mistakes Asia for an innocent woman with no martial arts
training. Being spoken to as a woman overwhelms Asia with a newfound,
unspeakable feeling. Under normal circumstances, Asia would murder an
intruder without blinking an eye, but Asia decides to spare Linghu's life. This
initial scene of misrecognition is the beginning of Asia's gender transformation, suggesting that it is in and through the eyes of the Other that (gender)
identity becomes possible. Later, Asia acquires a feminine voice from the
powers of the manual, puts on makeup and women's attire, and fully transitions into a woman. She falls in love with Linghu and tricks him into a one-
night stand by convincing him to have sex with her concubine, who serves
as her body double and prosthesis. At the final battle on Black Cliff, where
he is joined by the old master and their allies, Linghu finally realizes the true
identity of the woman he loves. He confronts Asia, but she seems genuinely
puzzled, asking why he wants to interfere in the internal affairs of the Sun/
Moon Sect. Then she turns to the old master and says, "The Han Chinese
have oppressed us Miao for generations, and today you have brought a Han
person to Black Cliff to interfere in our internal affairs. How can you face
our ancestors?"

Asia's response is an apparent non sequitur, which turns Linghu's question of sexuality ("Did I just sleep with a man?") into a question of civil war
and national self-determination ("Why did you bring a mainlander into the
internal dispute within the Miao tribe?"). The latter question is, of course,
at the heart of present political conversations in Taiwan and Hong Kong. As
I have argued in the first part of the chapter, many commentators in Taiwan
do not believe that Taiwan has ever been part of China or ever shared its
culture and identity; hence, they do not describe the current cross-strait relations as the result of a civil war. Instead, mainstream media and academic
discourse treat the presence of *waishengren* in Taiwan as the consequence
of a foreign invasion (Chinese settler colonialism and neocolonialism). This
indeterminacy indicates that the Cold War is very much a problematic of the
present in Asia. The rhetorical sleight of hand in Asia's response registers

this indeterminacy, which provides the real subtext and ideological referent for a question that at first appears to be concerned exclusively with sexuality.

Conclusion

My reading of *Swordsman II: Asia the Invincible* focuses on the cultural logic of substitutions and displacements underlying the rhetorical shift, elision, and slippage between the sexual and the political. The film's ostensible interest in the sexual narrative requires a specific cultural narrative of Cold War East Asian capitalism that has been seared into the national consciousness of Hong Kong, Taiwan, and mainland China. Asia the Invincible is the Janus-faced figure and emotional fulcrum that connects the Cultural Revolution critique and the narrative of Hong Kong's impending doom in 1997—the past and the present of the Cold War in Asia. Through the story of Asia the Invincible, a Cold War framework connects two separate political events—the Cultural Revolution and the 1997 handover of Hong Kong—and imbues them with the same emotional responses and ideological significance. This example shows how the unlikely use of the Cold War as method might yield new insight into an iconic queer film's embeddedness in a partially obscured historical conjuncture. In turn, a textured reading of the film also develops a renewed understanding of the Cold War as a multilayered and sometimes contradictory ideological formation.

Just as we can no longer afford to subscribe to a global queer liberationist narrative that views the emergence of new sexual communities and gender identities in Asia as imitations and derivations of post-Stonewall US sexual politics without the mediation of the region's own geopolitics, we must abandon the view of the Cold War as solely the story of the United States and the USSR. But to properly restore to view the agency of Asia in the making of the Cold War, we need not a conspiracy theory of secret deals behind closed doors but an account of the quotidian lives of families torn apart by the civil war. Building on the concept of Asia as method in recent Asian Marxist cultural criticism, we can begin to understand that the Cold War transcends geopolitics, being a persistent structure of feeling that shapes the discourses, sexuality, and labor struggles of contemporary Chinese cultures. Conversely, because the Cold War is a complex psychological phenomenon diffused in everyday life and sustained by the participation of ordinary people in Asia, the study of the Cold War in Asia requires a textual approach to its subsumption under capital's logic of self-expansion and endless accumulation. It is in cultural products such as *Swordsman II* and its queer discourse that we find the best tools for understanding the subsumption of the Cold War. History is not a collection of transparent facts—it is a social text and a mysterious one at that. The history of the Cold War is a tangle of ideological distortions, literal and figurative displacements, contested emotions, obscured visions, political appropriations, and fragmented memories. Reconceived as a cultural palimpsest, the Cold War demands reimagined interpretive paradigms, theoretical approaches, and analytic tools. For a renewed materialist history of queer Asia, these goals carry distinct promises as well as burdens.

The Subsumption of Sexuality

TRANSLATING GENDER FROM

THE BEIJING FOURTH WORLD CONFERENCE

ON WOMEN TO THE BEIJING CONSENSUS

Organized queer communities in China appeared first in the 1990s. The 1995 United Nations (UN) Fourth World Conference on Women in Beijing was a particularly important milestone that brought together lesbians from all over China and birthed a discourse of lesbian rights as human rights.[1] As China entered the age of the Beijing Consensus, the adoption of neoliberalism and its associated privatizations created public spaces, entertainment venues, and activist networks for LGBTQ communities.[2] In 1997 homosexuality was decriminalized in China, and in 2001 it was removed from the Chinese Classification of Mental Disorders (CCMD-III).[3] The expansion of queer organizing and identities inevitably challenged existing understandings of the concept of gender. Until 1995, gender was, for the most part, understood as a feminist issue and not a queer one. In the 1980s, Chinese scholars translated works of Western feminism and developed their own theories of gender in order to reclaim women's consciousness from the state. During the Maoist period, the Chinese Communist Party (CCP) sought to strengthen national economic development through the incorporation of women's public labor. The Chinese Communist Party encouraged women to understand themselves as equal to men by "holding up half the sky."[4] In this process, the Maoist state also created a desexualized image of women as productive workers. The development of gender theory in China was originally a counter discourse that focused on recovering women's feminine essence from this Maoist legacy.

Since 1995, however, discussions of gender in China have expanded from feminist concerns to queer sexualities. Critics have come to see that *gender* also means *gender identity*, and thus it would be a mistake to equate gender with the sociological category of women. Thinking about gender in the age of the Beijing Consensus means that we are also thinking about the social stigma attached to specific gender presentations, the regulation of queer desires, nonheteronormative families, access to gender-transition or gender-affirmation surgeries, the rise of transnational surrogacy and assisted reproductive technology for same-sex couples, and the fracturing of queer lives owing to the persistence of Chinese familialism. These are questions of gender, but they are not exclusively concerned with women. Indeed, the cisnormative and heteronormative understanding of *gender* as a synonym for women works to preclude these issues from entering the field of politicization. As queer critiques of the restrictive understanding of gender in post-Maoist feminism entered the fray, the analytic distinction between sex and gender emerged as a particularly controversial topic. Instead of conflating gender with women, queer thinkers have proposed a reconceptualization of gender as the very apparatus that naturalizes sex as the binary system of female and male.

In this chapter I examine different Chinese theories of the analytic distinction between sex and gender that emerged since the 1995 Beijing Fourth World Conference on Women. I argue that gender is always a materialist concept because, as these debates reveal, the discourse of gender is persistently imbricated in China's capitalist transformations. While the 1995 Beijing Fourth World Conference on Women introduced new queer interpretations of gender, it also codified gender mainstreaming [*xingbie zhuliu hua*] as a state goal. The rise of the Beijing Consensus discourse has further promoted a conception of women as both instrument and object of China's reintegration with the global capitalist economy. As such, alternative configurations of gender are subsumed under and rendered secondary to what is deemed more useful to China's capitalist development.

Gender is never conceptualized abstractly—rather, the embodiment of gender takes place in the context of political economy. Although political economy does not determine the possibilities of what can enter the field of discourse as gender, it creates a regime of differentiation—between useful and useless bodies, proper and improper desires, modern and backward beliefs, and the like—under which gendered lives find and carve out spaces of survival. The story of how China's capitalist transformations subsumed sexuality, however, is not about the mistranslations or appropriations of an original "Western feminism." Instead, I emphasize the location of China to show that global feminist theories of gender have been crafted through their encounters with China and its material contexts.

The Sex/Gender Distinction

Originally formulated to dispute biologically deterministic explanations of women's subordination, the sex/gender distinction has developed in unexpected ways in transitions from one language to another. Drawing on a wide range of sources, from John Money's sexological writings to Simone de Beauvoir's dictum, "One is not born a woman, but rather becomes one," anglophone feminists in the 1970s developed the theoretical distinction between sex (understood as anatomy) and gender (understood as cultural identity) to argue that a woman's biological sex ought not to dictate the kind of work she should do or the kind of life she should live.[5] Arguing that having a uterus does not mean a woman must become a wife and a mother, early 1970s feminists contested the causal relation between sex and gender. At this point in anglophone feminist theory, *gender* essentially meant *gender roles*. In her 1975 essay "The Traffic in Women," Gayle S. Rubin coined the phrase *sex/gender system* to examine "the set of arrangements by which a society transforms biological sexuality into products of human activity, and in which these transformed sexual needs are satisfied."[6] Just as the capitalist subsumption restructures the labor process to suit its needs, the sex/gender system rearranges the biological raw material of human sex into a hierarchical realm of men and women called *gender*. Because the sex/gender system in Rubin is an impersonal structure, analogous to the Marxist notion of political economy, her usage departed significantly from that of earlier feminist theorists of gender. For Rubin, gender is not a cultural identity (which individuals can freely choose and express). Instead, gender is the social consequence of an impersonal and intrinsically oppressive structure of power (*system* in Rubin's parlance). In Rubin's theory, gender refers to the workings of culture that transform perceived differences of sex into hierarchies and structures of domination. Hence, Rubin's usage of *gender* is closer to *gender inequality* than *gender roles*. Feminist theorists in the 1970s and 1980s, especially those seeking to develop a feminist historical materialism, were universally indebted to Rubin's sex/gender system but did not necessarily agree with her arguments. Influential thinkers, including Juliet Mitchell, Heidi Hartmann, Iris Marion Young, Moira Gatens, Patricia Collins, Nancy Hartsock, Donna J. Haraway, and Sandra Harding, have all adopted Rubin's concept of the sex/gender system into their own work while registering their own differences.[7]

In certain versions of feminist and queer scholarship influenced by Michel Foucault, this distinction is reversed. Whereas 1970s feminists saw sex as the raw material from which gender was wrought, Foucauldians argue that the opposite is true: sexuality is what constructs sex. Judith Butler's oft-cited dictum in *Gender Trouble* (quoting Friedrich Nietzsche rather than Foucault), "There is no 'being' behind doing," summarizes the view that there is no such thing as a preexisting biological sex from which a cultural gender is constructed.[8] Instead, a person is assigned to a given sex as a consequence of the acts, dispositions, and expressions that person is perceived to be performing in the social domain. For critics in this tradition, sex is a function of sexuality, a consequence of powerful narratives—which Eve Kosofsky Sedgwick calls "nonce taxonomy" for mapping out the human landscape—that retroactively establish the illusion of an interior core that we call *gender*.[9]

In recent years the distinction between sex and gender has taken on yet another entirely different definition as it comes to inform transgender movements and politics seeking to decouple a person's sex assignment at birth from their future gender identity. However, this does not mean that the sex/gender distinction has congealed into a uniform understanding within the field of transgender movements and politics. In the introduction to the inaugural issue of *Transgender Studies Quarterly* (*TSQ*) in 2014, Susan Stryker and Paisley Currah describe transgender as a capacious and mercurial concept that "carries its own antinomies": transgender can refer to either an identification or an analytic method, a way of being gendered or a way of doing gender, a form of gender crossing or a way of occupying genders that confound the gender binary, and a basis for identity-based rights claims or a tool to critically explore the distribution of inequality.[10] Institutionally, the concept of transgender can also impose its own set of norms in ways that render other nonbinary subjects invisible and delegitimize their access to health care.[11] As these developments have demonstrated, gender has exceeded and destabilized the sociological category of women. The life of gender—in academic theory, politics, and social movements—has confounded the original intentions of its American theorists. It is clear that there is no singular or stable account of gender; rather, gender is always in a state of flux, incessantly rethought and reforged by the demands of a globalized capitalist system.[12]

Gender is always a translation—from one discipline, context, or language to another—ineluctably intertwined with the geopolitical problems created by the violences of imperialism, colonialism, and transnational capitalism. Reflecting on an invitation to contribute to a Marxist dictionary project on gender in languages she was not familiar with (she referred to the Chinese example as ideogram and transcription), Donna J. Haraway offered these thoughts: "The value of an analytical category is not necessarily annulled by critical consciousness of its historical specificity and cultural limits. But feminist concepts of gender raise sharply the problems of cultural comparison, linguistic translation, and political solidarity."[13] It seems that there is no way to extricate the translation of gender from the problem of colonialism and political economy.[14] Indeed, the translation of *gender* into non-European languages, such as Chinese, raises questions about whether spaces previously resistant or exterior to world capitalism are now being assimilated and enfolded into the structure of neoliberal globalization defined by the Washington Consensus, or whether new gender thinking in China indexes the nation's precipitous ascent as an alternative model of development that can be termed the Beijing Consensus. Considering how *gender* has entered different languages, including Chinese, to create new coinages that may at times appear as instruments of an imperial takeover, Judith Butler argues that the translation of *gender* actually offers a path of linguistic humility for English, a reminder that we cohabit a multilingual world in which no one ever owned the term.[15] But how exactly do we describe that complex, multilingual world, and how does gender transform it? How is the translation of *gender* inflected by local concerns and the material conditions of a world that is not simply multilingual but deeply unequal?

Gender became a useful category for global feminist scholarship because of an encounter in and with China—the 1995 UN Fourth World Conference on Women in Beijing. The conference was noteworthy for the heated debates that arose between feminists espousing contradictory notions of gender as well as conservative and religious organizations insisting on strictly biological definitions. As several scholars working at the nexus of translation studies and gender theory have noted, this landmark event catapulted the notion of gender to the forefront of global debates by generating the Beijing Declaration and Platform for Action, a special report from the Vatican City and other conservative states concerned about the radical implications of the term, a special report from the UN, and global feminist responses to the controversy.[16]

The importance of the 1995 Beijing conference and its related documents for a global reorientation of feminist discourse has been thoroughly analyzed by scholars including Joan W. Scott, who reads the UN documents produced in preparation for and in response to the Beijing conference as the symptomatic expression of the emptiness of the term *gender* as a universal, abstract formulation.[17] For Scott, this emptiness or indeterminacy also signifies a radical potential for gender to challenge the established meanings of sex difference. While the Beijing conference's contributions to and implications for the development of gender theory are well documented, in this chapter I want to ask a different question: What was the role of the location of Beijing in this story of feminism's reorientation from biological sex to gender?

Though the translation of the term *gender* into French and other European languages has also caused significant controversies, and continues to do so, it was the encounter between gender theory and what appeared to be its most radical and unassimilable Other, China, that brought into crisis attempts to legislate a globally unified understanding of gender.[18] What was it about an encounter with China, Chinese feminism, and the Chinese language that precipitated global anxieties about gender theory's presumed provenance in Western thought, the term's linguistic nontranslatability and complicity with Western cultural imperialism, and its radical implications for transnational feminism? How was China consistently configured as an exotic and impenetrable tradition in the gender wars in the UN? What was the role of Chinese thinkers (feminist or antifeminist, Marxist or anti-Marxist) in the creation of a global, multilingual feminist politics (and the resistance to it), and what was the historical context in which Chinese thinkers coinvented their own concepts of gender?

I bridge these gaps by retheorizing the Beijing Consensus as a context for the contradictory strategies undertaken by Chinese academic feminists, workers in nongovernmental organizations, and state actors to translate, legislate, advocate, oppose, or erase the analytic distinction between sex and gender. In my usage of the concept throughout this book, the Beijing Consensus is not a state ideology or a structure of political economy that encompasses specific social actors but not others. Rather, the Beijing Consensus signifies an interpretative problem in relation to which contradictory discourses of gender/sexuality in contemporary China—both feminist and antifeminist, state controlled and civil society based, academic and popular, native to and imported from outside China—are constantly evolving. The concept of the Beijing Consensus names the complex debates about China's postsocialist modernity, asking whether China offers an alternative model of development to the Washington Consensus or is actually a neocolonial power competing with the advanced capitalist countries for mining rights and investments in the extractive industries of the global South. I characterize the Beijing Consensus as a same-but-different cultural logic that has also shaped the discourse around gender. I highlight the parallels between the Beijing Consensus and Chinese conceptions of gender as same-but-different "glocalizations" to show that gender thinking in China is not merely a discursive formation. It is also a material, geopolitical practice embedded in a larger struggle to define China's socialist legacy, its status in the world capitalist economy, its relation to the global South, and its search for alternative principles of political legitimacy and economic development.

This intimacy between political economy and gendered life has both desirable and oppressive consequences. While the Chinese examples I discuss demonstrate the need to consider the intersectionality of gender and geopolitics in a transnational context, the emphasis on China's alternative model and countermodernity has also led to gender-mainstreaming policies that exclude queer and trans subjects. Since the 1995 Beijing conference, the UN mandate to "mainstream gender" has guided Chinese feminist scholars as well as antifeminist state bureaucrats.[19] While the conference brought about a surge of academic interest in previously unexplored areas of women's history, it also strengthened the presence of international funding agencies such as the Ford Foundation, the Henry Luce Foundation, and Oxfam with vested interests in gender and development projects. In addition to making gender (understood as women's role in economic development) central to the Chinese state's postsocialist agenda, the 1995 conference also broadened the scope of feminist organizations led by the CCP, including the All-China Women's Federation, which had compiled source materials on Chinese women's contribution to the Communist Revolution and the strides they had made toward liberation under CCP leadership.[20]

In this chapter I discuss some instances of gender mainstreaming that result in a three-part constriction of Chinese discourse: the reduction of sex to gender, of gender to women, and of women to an index of development. While I emphasize analyzing political economy as the site of gender struggles, I also highlight the importance of gender and sexuality for understanding China's relations with the global South. China's investments in and interactions with other countries in the global South have been the subject of much media attention and academic study. However, issues of gender and sexuality have been largely ignored. My analysis shows that gender mainstreaming is one of the strategies that the Chinese state has adopted to support the thesis of the Beijing Consensus and justify its leadership in the global South. For the most part, gender mainstreaming means equality between women and men as biologically and sociologically distinct populations. This ossified view does not expand the field of gendered possibilities to lesbian/gay parenting, non-normative sexual practices, trans rights to medical care, reproductive freedom, or gender-variant subjects.[21] However, the Chinese state has embraced gender mainstreaming because it is compatible with China's own claim that socialism has created true equality between women and men. In other words, gender mainstreaming, rather than gender pluralism, supports the Beijing Consensus thesis that China is still a socialist country developing within the parameters of a revolutionary culture. This characterization of China as the site of a countermodernity and an alternative to Washington-led capitalism qualifies the People's Republic of China (PRC) to provide leadership in the global South. But the wide range of competing translations of *gender* that I discuss in this chapter challenges this instrumental view, bearing evidence that the possibilities of gender embodiment, morphology, and schemata cannot be so easily disciplined or domesticated.

From Sex/Gender to *Shengli Xingbie* and *Shehui Xingbie*

In July 2017 I was invited to give a keynote speech at the Sixth International Sexuality Studies Conference in Ha'erbin, China. Before the main events, the conference organizers (Huang Yingying and Pan Suiming, two leading sexologists at Renmin University) put together a three-day preconference training workshop for students, teachers, workers in nongovernmental organizations, and activists in gender and sexual rights movements. The participants, who came from different parts of China as well as Hong Kong and Taiwan, were joined by international scholars from the United States and the United Kingdom. While our working language was Chinese, most of the participants were well versed in the latest social issues and theoretical resources in North America. During one session the workshop leader asked the participants to explain their understandings of the differences between the English terms *sex* and *gender*. One person answered in Chinese that *shengli xingbie* (the most common Chinese translation of *sex*) is "the sex you are born with," while *shehui xingbie* (the most common Chinese translation of *gender*) is "the sex you choose for yourself."[22]

Both the workshop leader and the audience readily accepted this definition and moved on, but I was very struck by the conversation—by its underlying assumptions, by the elisions that went undetected and unchallenged, and by its invocation of categories that seemed self-evident to some of the most influential scholars and activists in contemporary Chinese sexual politics. These assumptions are not mistranslations or distortions. Rather, they signify a time-space compression of thoughts that originate in different discursive contexts. Crucially, the translation of the sex/gender distinction is not merely a matter of establishing hypothetical equivalence between words on a semantic level but one of negotiating contact zones mediated by the problems of political economy. The emergence of new lexicons for thinking about gender cannot be understood as linguistic accidents in a social vacuum. Instead of discussing how gender theory travels from one culture to another, my analysis focuses on this transcultural process itself as a theoretical problem for gender thinking in the age of the Beijing Consensus.

At the heart of this compression of thoughts lies a conceptual conflation of *choice* with *construction*. The question of choice is something we hear frequently in nature-versus-nurture debates about the origins of homosexuality—whether sexual orientations and preferences are acquired or innate. Speculations about the gay gene, social engineering, and environmental influences are found in homophobic institutions seeking to "cure" or prevent the development of homosexuality, but they are also important for antihomophobic legal defenses and activist strategies arguing that gay people were simply born this way. Chinese scholars have engaged this question since the publication of Li Yinhe and Wang Xiaobo's *Tamen de shijie: Zhongguo nan tongxinglian qunluo toushi* (Their world: A penetrating look into China's male homosexual community) in the early 1990s.

The question of construction, by contrast, refers to whether social categories such as gay and lesbian in English and their Chinese counterparts (*tongzhi* and *lala*) are transcultural or context dependent.[23] Influential cultural critics, such as Chou Wah-shan, argue that *tongzhi* are not gay in the Western sense because the basic sociological unit of Chinese society is the family rather than the individual.[24] Building on accounts of Chinese emperors and their male favorites (*nanchong*) in Xiaomingxiong's *Zhongguo tongxing'ai shilu* (A history of homosexual love in China) and Bret Hinsch's *Passions of the Cut Sleeve*, Chou maintains that both homosexuality and homophobia are modern Western imports with no commensurable roots in traditional Chinese culture's "silent tolerance" of same-sex relations. Without necessarily endorsing Chou's essentializing thesis, numerous scholars have further reinforced the narrative that China enjoyed a rich tradition of homoeroticism before the intrusion of the West.[25] Directly or indirectly, Chinese scholars making such arguments reveal a strong influence of Foucault's thesis in *The History of Sexuality* that "the sodomite had been a temporary aberration; the homosexual was now a species."[26] It is important to note, however, that Foucault's suggestion is that modern culture created the category of homosexuality as we understand it, through which an act (sodomy) was irreversibly transformed into an identity (homosexuality). Social constructionist theories argue that categories that appear to be immutable and biological—such as homosexuality—are discursive products of human definition and interpretation.

Theories of the social construction of sexuality and gender do not claim that sexual orientation or gender is actually a choice, but the Ha'erbin conference speaker's interpretation of *shehui xingbie* clearly conflates these two. According to this view, while sex is biologically given, gender is something one chooses at will to perform in the social domain. The Chinese translation of the sex/gender distinction as *shengli xingbie* and *shehui xingbie* registers a dichotomous understanding that divides a person's identity into a biological (*shengli*) facticity and a social (*shehui*) performance. This translation implies that while sex is immanent and immutable, in the social domain one is free to assume a different cultural gender. In this understanding the individual, not culture or language, becomes the agent of construction. Gender appears as a volitional choice, an identity that individuals freely author and perform. It is important to distinguish such a voluntarist conception of gender as an act of self-nomination from social construction theory, which refers to the structural and linguistic effects of social norms as well as institutions that have no single origins and that precede individual intentionality.

The speaker's definition thus produces an analytic elision in the sense that it interprets the social construction of gender as tantamount to an individual's ability to choose their own gender. By defining gender as "the sex you choose for yourself," the speaker conflates the nature/nurture debate about sexuality or homosexuality with the essentialism/constructivism debate about social gender—and both debates with contemporary transgender movements to decouple gender identity from sex assigned at birth. The speaker's conflation thus inherits and compresses the histories and residues of discourses about the origins of homosexuality, the existence of the "gay gene," and the fixity of sexual orientation from a much earlier era with a postmillennial vocabulary of gender choice and self-affirmation that has gradually entered

PRC culture through Taiwan.[27] While the speaker is not actually endorsing transgender rights in the PRC, the common Chinese translation of the sex/gender distinction blurs the vocabulary of historically distinct conversations and social movements. This shift embodies a curious desynchronization effect in the translation of critical concepts, while revealing gender to be an internally contradictory and eminently fungible concept within any given culture. In the remainder of this chapter, I demonstrate that these translation controversies—and their conflation of choice and construction—are not arbitrary linguistic accidents. Rather, they occur as efforts to define a same-but-different gender logic within the context of the Beijing Consensus. As such, theories of the sex/gender distinction in Chinese are best understood as part of the continuous debates about China's socialist legacy, market reforms, the rural-urban divide, and the possibility of developing an alternative social order to Washington-centered neoliberal capitalism.

Gender in Translation

In China there are currently two competing translations of *gender*. The more common translation today and the one used by the speaker at my conference, *shehui xingbie* (literally, "social sex difference"), was promoted in the 1990s by Wang Zheng, a diasporic feminist scholar who has collaborated with Chinese universities to develop various graduate programs in women's and gender studies. In "'Nüxing yishi,' 'shehui xingbie yishi' bianyi" (Distinguishing between "women's consciousness" and "gender consciousness"), Wang introduced North American theories of gender (mainly those of Gayle S. Rubin and Joan W. Scott) and proposed the phrase *shehui xingbie* to emphasize the constructed nature of gender, against essentialist notions of sex.[28] Wang's *shehui xingbie* was widely embraced by women scholars in China, especially those seeking a critical alternative to both gender essentialism and the official Chinese state discourse of *nannü pingdeng* (equality between men and women).[29]

The second strategy is to translate *gender* simply as *xingbie*, a term that began to appear in articles in China during the 1980s but did not gain prominence until the 1993 workshop "Chinese Women and Development" at Tianjin Normal University in China.[30] This approach was promoted by Li Xiaojiang, one of the most prominent feminist scholars of the post–Mao Zedong generation, who sought to develop an indigenous feminism distinct from both state ideology and Western feminism. Like Wang, Li has played a pivotal role in the institutionalization of feminist theory in China. Li is commonly regarded as the most representative figure of the 1980s women's studies movement because she organized the first women's studies association (1985) and established the academic discipline of women's studies (1986) in socialist China. These efforts carved out an independent space for Chinese women to express their voices and experiences outside the dictates of the socialist state, the official women's organization in China (the All-China Women's Federation), or the intellectual leadership of male Marxist humanists such as Li Zehou.[31]

Throughout the 1980s and 1990s, Li published a large quantity of theoretical writings that made two enduring arguments. First, she contests the story that socialism has liberated Chinese women and argues that for women to be free, they must first recover their real, natural, feminine singularity.[32] To counter the notion of women's liberation formulated by the party-state and transmitted by the All-China Women's Federation, Li maintains that women must develop their own gendered consciousness as distinct from that of men.[33] Second, she rejects Western feminism as a measure of Chinese women's progress and champions an indigenous Chinese feminism. While some critics such as Lisa Rofel generously describe the latter as Li's "refusal to make Chinese feminism appear to need Western feminism," others have accused Li of essentialism on both counts.[34] In other words, Li's translation of *gender* as *xingbie* encodes a double essentialism—the conviction that women's bodies and experiences express a natural and universal femininity that makes them distinct from men and that Chinese feminism forms a coherent and unified tradition that makes it distinct from Western feminism. Li's strategy to translate *gender* as *xingbie* is thus rooted in her belief in the incommensurability between Chinese and Western cultures.

Arguing that *xing* in traditional Chinese culture already encompasses both the social and natural dimensions of the English concept, Li criticizes the coinage of *shehui xingbie* as a redundant effort that overlooks the radical, feminist aspects of indigenous Chinese thought:

> In the Chinese language *nü* can only refer to the sex of a human being. The terms woman (*nüren*) and man (*nanren*) already reveal their social character, since they refer to "human beings who have a socialized sexual character." . . . Therefore, in China, no matter how far women's liberation is carried out, there is no need to launch another revolution in our conceptual scheme, because in our language the term woman (*nüren*) is not predicated on man. Furthermore, if it were not for the sake of facilitating communication

between China and the West, it would be redundant to introduce the notion of gender (*shehui xingbie*) to the Chinese language, since nü and nan are already understood as social, and not natural, beings.[35]

In Li's view, premodern China, before the importation of Marxism-Leninism, had already produced a progressive and sophisticated understanding of what Western scholars are now calling *gender*. Hence, Chinese women do not need Western feminism for their emancipation; quite to the contrary, a return to the traditional Chinese philosophy of *nan/nü* allows Chinese women to recover their true feminine essence against Maoist distortions and the official "May Fourth story" of how the Chinese Communists transformed women from oppressed victims into liberated modern subjects.

Li's view is shared by many PRC scholars. Gail Hershatter and Wang Zheng observe that "'gender' has been slow to catch on as an innovative concept precisely because it seems deceptively familiar to Chinese historians" who believe that "*nan/nü*, understood as a historical Chinese framing of gender, has a long and extensively elaborate textual record."[36] A case in point is the "Engendering China" conference at Harvard in 1992, which brought together renowned PRC scholars, feminist scholars from the United States and other English-speaking locations, and Chinese feminist scholars in diaspora associated with the Chinese Society for Women's Studies in preparation for the 1995 UN Fourth World Conference on Women in Beijing. Despite the ambition of the US organizers to "engender" the field of Chinese women's studies, the meaning and implications of gender "were basically opaque to the PRC participants" because "*xingbie* is a modern Chinese word for 'sex' that appears in household registration pamphlets and on many forms," so "people think that they know what *xingbie* is"; consequently, the conference title, "Engendering China," was simply translated as "Zhongguo zhi xingbie guannian" (The concept of sex in China).[37]

We can extrapolate two important points from the comparison of Wang's and Li's translations. First, while it is easy to see how these neologisms convey different understandings of the sex/gender distinction, what might escape our initial attention is how these differences actually issue from incommensurable interpretations of China's relations to the West and the legacy of Marxism-Leninism, or what I am describing as the dilemma of the Beijing Consensus. Li's theory and translation of gender essentialize traditional Chinese culture as a separate entity from the encroachments of Western thought. While the object of Li's analysis is premodern China, her claims are motivated by the problems of contemporary China in the age of the Beijing Consensus. Li's theory stems from a defensive nativism engendered by anxieties about postsocialist China's reintegration with the world economy. This nativism does not transcend the violent incorporation of China into an asymmetrical world capitalist system; rather, it presupposes and is precipitated by it.

By contrast, Wang's translation presents gender as a universal problem faced by feminists everywhere, and she finds Rubin's and Scott's formulations to be particularly useful for Chinese feminists. However, Wang's reading of Rubin and Scott remains somewhat conservative. As I have already discussed, neither Rubin nor Scott uses the term *gender* to mean simply women's gender roles or consciousness. Wang's translation of gender as women's consciousness overlooks the more radical implications of Rubin's and Scott's theories for transgender and nonbinary subjects. Indeed, both Rubin and Scott are foundational figures in queer theory, but Wang's translation deradicalizes the queerness of their theories and reheterosexualizes *gender* as a synonym for women—a position that Scott explicitly repudiates. Though Wang cites Scott as her influence, she ignores the poststructuralist and antipositivist dimensions of Scott's work.[38] In *Gender and the Politics of History*, Scott defines *gender* in her usage as "knowledge about sexual difference," and knowledge, "following Michel Foucault," as "the understanding produced by cultures and societies of human relationships" and "a way of ordering the world . . . that is inseparable from social organizations."[39] While Scott's concept of gender concerns the discursive transformation of perceived sexual difference into hierarchies of power, Wang's usage assimilates Scott's poststructuralist concept of sexual difference into the sociological meaning of gender roles in the service of empirical research on PRC women's history.

The second point to underscore from the comparison between the two rival translations is that both Wang and Li are primarily concerned with the Maoist ideology of *nannü pingdeng* (equality between men and women) and *funü jiefang* (women's liberation), which has constructed a narrative of "women holding up half of the sky" and asexual "iron girls" that masculinized rather than emancipated women.[40] While Li mobilizes an indigenous tradition of premodern writings on *nannü* to counter both Maoism and Western feminism, Wang reads Scott and other Western intellectuals as offering a theory of women's consciousness that can supplant the Maoist concept of gender equality in China.[41] That both Wang and Li read the translation of gender (theory) in terms of the PRC state's socialist formation and capitalist transformation, and that both critics erase the queer implications of gender, illustrates my larger point about the constraints that political economy places on cultural spaces for articulating a nonheteronormative notion of gender. Indeed, both Wang's use and Li's rejection of "Western theories of gender" are highly selective; these works represent only one particular view in a complex set of anglophone debates whose contexts involve a dialogue with queer theory that neither Wang nor Li considers.

As I argued in chapter 2, the distinction between sex and gender—in queer theory and gender-troubled feminism—refers to the debate over whether it is possible to extricate a biological notion of sex that is not in some way already gendered. Butler's *Gender Trouble* remains the authoritative text that cautions against the dichotomy between biological sex and cultural gender. Both Li and Wang accept this dichotomy as a point of departure despite their radically divergent conclusions. Translated as either *xingbie* or *shehui xingbie*, *gender* in these Chinese feminist discourses denotes a particular form of consciousness that is said to belong to women alone; that this consciousness has not surfaced earlier is explained as a consequence of Confucian patriarchy or Maoist suppression. But for scholars working in the Butlerian framework, the very idea that sex must be either male or female (as opposed to some other possibilities) signifies a binary concept of gender rooted in a dyadic heterosexism. Instead of denoting women, gender for Butler designates "the very apparatus of production whereby the sexes themselves are established."[42] The discourses of natural femininity (Li) or women's consciousness (Wang) may have empowered individuals who identify or qualify as women, but they risk imperiling and marginalizing those who live at a critical distance from gender norms. The conceptual separation between sex and gender as women's bodies and women's consciousness reproduces heteronormative assumptions that a theory of gender is supposed to contest.

Though both Wang and Li present Western feminism as a singular tradition, there is absolutely no consensus on this point in anglophone gender theory. While some critics, such as Eve Kosofsky Sedgwick and Gayle S. Rubin, argued that the study of sexuality must be separated from the study of gender, others, such as Moira Gatens, have criticized the sex/gender distinction itself as based in the "unreasoned, unargued assumption that both the body and the psyche are post-natally passive 'tabula rasa.'"[43] Given the internal disagreements within anglophone feminist discourses of gender, we can see that Wang's translation is merely a partial representation of a complex field rather than a systematic introduction to Western feminist theory. At the same time, Li's wholesale rejection of Western feminism risks reifying and simplifying

Chinese thought. Yet rather than choose the easy route of constructing a binary narrative of how Western theory entered China, we might remember that feminism has always been a transcultural practice. From the 1960s to the 1980s, well before the 1995 UN Fourth World Conference on Women in Beijing, Chinese feminist theory and practice exerted considerable influence on Western feminists.[44] Chinese "speaking bitterness" campaigns inspired the American feminist practices of consciousness-raising, while the experience of Chinese women provided important material for generations of feminist scholarship—from Julia Kristeva's psychoanalytic theory in the 1970s to the historical research of Kay Ann Johnson, Judith Stacey, and Phyllis Andors in the 1980s.[45]

Thus, neither Li's nor Wang's translation is fully satisfactory. Li's view overhomogenizes Chinese culture into a monolithic nativism, while Wang's approach conflates a particular argument with Western feminism tout court. Both translations are shaped by collective anxieties about the legacy of Maoist socialism, the specter of Marxism, and China's capitalist transformations. Instead of viewing gender as a Western concept that was first invented in North America and then translated and disseminated into China, as Li and Wang understand it, I characterize gender as a conceptual problematic that concerns feminists everywhere and a transcultural dialogue that builds on the historical experiences of different locations.[46] As Min Dongchao argues, the emergence of *xingbie/shehui xingbie* in the Chinese language need not be understood as the dissemination of a Western concept to the East; rather, it indicates an East-West form of cultural and political practice, a Chinese effort to connect (*jiegui*) to the world after decades of intellectual isolation.[47] Lydia H. Liu explains this process as a form of coauthorship, the invention and postulation of hypothetical equivalents between foreign words and concepts that *already exist* in Chinese, rather than a unidirectional form of cultural imperialism.[48] For both Min and Liu, translation should be analyzed and understood in the context of Chinese modernity rather than as the expansion of Western imperialism. My work extends these discussions by connecting translations of *gender* to a specific aspect of Chinese modernity, the problematic of the Beijing Consensus.

It is well known that in traditional Chinese culture, *xing* denoted (human) nature rather than sex or sexuality.[49] Only in the late Qing period and through the reverse translation of Japanese loanwords did *xing* gradually acquire its modern semantic meaning of referring to both human nature and sexuality. The conjoining of these two concepts, in turn, gave rise to various compound neologisms, including *nüxing* for "female" and *xingbie* for "gender." In his comprehensive examination of the historicity of *xing* from Mencius to the twentieth century, Leon Rocha argues that the conflation of "human nature" and "sexuality" occurred in a specific context: sex was reconceptualized "as *the* index to human character, *the* originary, psychical truth," as a consequence of China's colonial modernity.[50] Emphasizing similarly the impact of colonial modernity, Tani Barlow shows that *nüxing* was invented in the semifeudal, semicolonial 1920s "in the rhetoric of global sex and eugenic theory" to replace an earlier social category, *funü*. Whereas *funü* signified kin-based understandings of women as mothers and daughters in the patri-line, "the collectivity of kinswomen in the semiotics of Confucian family doctrine," the invention of *nüxing* represented a radically new understanding of women as "a fulcrum for upending Confucianism and the older forms of social theory" that established "sex as the core of an oppositional personal or individual identity and woman as a sexological category."[51] Under the Maoist state, however, the CCP once again reinstated *funü* as a political subject, one whose meaning now superseded both the Confucian understandings of the term and the eroticized subject *nüxing*.

In their criticism of Barlow's dating of *nüxing* to the 1920s, Lydia H. Liu, Rebecca Karl, and Dorothy Ko argue that the neologisms *nanxing* and *nüxing* appeared as early as beginning of the twentieth century in a large number of late Qing texts but, more important, were not taken to signify "male sex" and "female sex" at that time.[52] Instead, in the feminist writings of late Qing thinkers such as He-Yin Zhen, *nüxing* indicates something close to the character of woman (women), to be molded and developed with education. Hence, in Liu and colleagues' view, the concept of *nüxing* was still coded by the Confucian understanding of *xing* and remained distinct from its modern meanings of "female sex" or "femininity." Although precise dating of the modern use of *xing* remains controversial, it is clear that *xing* and *xingbie* have no singular origins that can be traced back to a stable Chinese tradition. Rather, they have been evolving concepts all along, multiply constituted and overdetermined by China's encounters with the West. Before the contemporary battles over *shehui/shengli xingbie*, *xingbie* already contained a heterogeneity that was deeply embedded in China's quest for an alternative modernity and a same-but-different cultural order that eventually would become the discourse of the Beijing Consensus.

Min Dongchao argues that the translation of *gender* into Chinese has since the early twentieth century been embedded in and constrained by a developmentalist discourse, framed in a Marxist vocabulary, and much of the thinking about gender has involved reaffirming, distancing oneself from, or redefining the tradition of Chinese socialism and Marxism. As Min recounts, in response to the codification of gender as an analytic category at the Beijing conference, leading voices such as Huang Qizhao and Chen Muhua began to argue for making gender a mainstream issue in Chinese policy in response to its codification as an analytic category at the Beijing conference. However, Chen Muhua argues that the analysis of "the problem of women" in Chinese Marxism had already assimilated the perspective that now traveled under the name of gender and that the Beijing conference simply reaffirmed the tenets of Marxist feminism.[53] In Chen's view, the notion of gender in the Beijing Platform for Action was synonymous with the equality of men and women in Chinese Marxist feminism. This debate quickly turned into a discussion of the compatibility between the Anglo-American discourse of gender and Chinese Marxism.

Li Huiying pushed past the boundaries of this debate with the essay "Jiang xingbie yishi naru jueche zhuliu de taolun" (The discussion of gender consciousness in mainstream policymaking), which rejected the conflation of gender with equality between men and women. Li interpreted the notion of gender in the Beijing Declaration and Platform for Action as "gender consciousness," distinct from formal or legal equality between women and men. Li's interpretation represented a culturalist turn in the translation of gender, which focused on consciousness-raising as feminism's goal. Min argues that this interpretation of gender prevailed in China because the end of socialism created a theoretical and cultural vacuum. With the rapid economic transformation in the postreform era, Chinese women in urban areas are no longer struggling with basic issues such as the right to work or the right to own property. However, native theoretical development has not caught up with these changes, and the old, Marxist-derived conceptual framework focused on legal and economic obstacles to gender parity has proved inadequate. At this juncture, the importation of the Anglo-American notion of gender provided a welcome opportunity to broaden the discussion of women's issues beyond legal inequalities. *Gender* then became a buzzword for feminist consciousness-raising programs and other efforts to advance women's cultural rights. The concept of gender in Chinese has provided feminists with a framework for discussing gender justice that surpasses the mere absence of formal discrimination. This development shows that the translations of *gender* and the emergence of neologisms are never simply linguistic accidents or discursive formations. Rather, the translations of *gender* are products of political and economic changes best understood in the framework of China's transformation from promoting inward-looking socialism to contending for global influence and opportunities. Translations of *gender* are, in other words, vital participants in the debates on the Beijing Consensus.

Gender and Development in the Beijing Consensus

In September 2017, together with several other researchers with whom I have been collaborating on this topic, I attended a conference with the theme "China in the Global South: The Central Role of Gender and Sexuality" in Beijing. A representative from UN Women China gave one of the town-hall speeches at this event. In her address she emphasized the importance of recognizing China's successes in improving women's lives. China, she argued, has enjoyed unparalleled, sustained growth rates in the postreform era, because it has achieved gender parity in three key areas: leadership and political participation, access to education, and the workplace. According to this speaker, women have made vital contributions to "China's transformation" from a poverty-stricken country to the world's second-largest economy, which would not have been possible if Chinese women had not been incorporated into the paid labor force. In her view, China's progress on gender parity is a model for countries in the global South, and in order for China to become the new leader in South-South Cooperation programs, the international community must first recognize the success of China's gender reforms. Gender, conceptualized this way, is not a structure of inequality or difference but the source of moral legitimation for China's leadership in South-South Cooperation. This speaker expressed her frustration with a male mainstream economist who had once suggested that gender had nothing to do with development because Japan had achieved high economic growth rates despite the persistence of patriarchy. Furious with this view, the UN representative argued that Japan's bubble economy was nothing but a mirage, whereas feminist economics had already proved that China's gender equality was indispensable to its economic growth. In light of these feminist discoveries, the UN representative urged policy makers to recognize and learn from China's strategies for achieving such progress.

But *economic development* and *gender equality* are both controversial terms that mean quite different things for different populations. To begin with, there is absolutely no consensus that China has achieved greater gender equality than other countries in the global South.[54] This assertion relies on simplistic sociological categories that generate statistics on women-men ratios, such as the number of female politicians or college graduates, as China's "key performance indicators" of gender equality. It ignores, for example, the state's 2015 arrest and detention of prominent women's rights activists (China's "Feminist Five"), its repressive marriage property laws, assaults on women's reproductive freedom (from the one-child policy to the current three-child policy), the moral panic over the so-called leftover women (*sheng nü*), controversies over China Netcasting Services Association's 2017 ban on online media depictions of homosexuality and other so-called abnormal sexual relationships and behaviors, and the most recent (announced in September 2021) government crackdown on effeminate men in China's celebrity culture, to name just a few.[55] In a recent report based on research published by Chinese scholars, China fell to 106th place in the World Economic Forum's Gender Gap Index for 2020, behind Brazil and Russia.[56]

As already mentioned, Chinese feminists such as Li Xiaojiang have vehemently rejected the well-worn narrative that the Maoist state liberated women and created gender equality. Instead, Chinese feminists argue that the socialist state created a desexualized Maoist woman whose femininity and subjectivity have been erased or else pressed into service as revolutionary subjects.[57] In 1980s feminism in China, these voices were so strong that Tani Barlow concluded that "virtually everyone involved in the debate rejected the Communist Party's claim to have established social, political, and legal equality for Chinese women."[58] Setting aside the problematic assertion that China has indeed become a model of gender equality for all countries in the global South, what interests me about the UN representative's address is her reduction, first, of gender to women and, subsequently, of women to an instrument of China's capitalist development. While the speaker understands her address to be a feminist intervention that calls attention to women's contributions to China's transformation, her analysis in fact proposes no *intrinsic* value for women's issues. Her framework does not explain why feminists should be concerned with topics that do not pertain to capitalist development, such as women's bodily autonomy and reproductive freedom; regulations of intimacy, pleasure, and sexuality; or rigidified norms of femininity and masculinity. This narrow conception of feminist interests explains why, although she was invited to speak on the topic "China in the Global South: The Central Role of Gender and Sexuality," her presentation in fact made no mention of sexuality at all.

The UN speaker's evacuation of sexuality from her feminist analysis of China's postreform economic miracle indicates an unresolved tension between sex and gender in international feminist theory and practice. To fully illustrate this problem, I briefly return to Butler's argument against the "proper objects" of feminist and queer analysis. Invoking Foucault's understanding of sex as "a regime of identity or a fictional ideal by which sex as anatomy, sensation, acts, and practice are arbitrarily unified," Butler argues against a chiasmic splitting of the semantic content of *sex* whereby feminism is presumed to be concerned with only one aspect of it (putative anatomical identity, the kind of sex one *is*), while gay and lesbian studies is assigned a different aspect (sexuality, the kind of sex one *does*).[59] That we use the word *sex* to denote both gender (male/female) and sexuality (act) is not simply a matter of linguistic convention or confusion but the historical consequence of the transformation of sex into a "fictitious unity" and a "causal principle" that assumes that a certain form of gender (characteristics) must lead to a certain kind of sexuality. Conversely, the kind of sexual acts one engages in (or fantasizes about) retroactively establishes a "regime of truth" about a person, the inner essence that we call *gender*. But instead of exploring and critiquing the discursive regimes that produce sex as a fictitious unity and a causal principle, scholars commonly split the semantic ambiguity of sex into "proper" assignments for feminism and gay and lesbian studies. For example, in their introduction to a field-defining volume, *The Lesbian and Gay Studies Reader*, the editors suggest that "lesbian/gay studies does for sex and sexuality approximately what women's studies does for gender."[60] Butler considers this disciplinary assignment as a mutual impoverishment of feminist and gay/lesbian projects and argues that both should be concerned with gender and sex/sexuality. This disciplinary divide reduces the rich semantic ambiguity of *sex* into monolithic definitions that foreclose, precisely, an investigation of how sex (as gender) comes to be seen as a function or consequence of sex (as sexuality) and how normative gender is consolidated through normative sexuality.

The UN representative's understanding of sex as gender and her dismissal of sexuality as a feminist concern follow the methodological divide that Butler criticizes, whereby sex (understood as gender) is assigned to feminism, while sex (understood as sexuality) is assigned to gay and lesbian studies and removed from feminist analysis. But in the case of China, the construction of sexuality as external to feminism is specifically fortified by the kind of Chinese developmentalism commended by the UN representative. Chinese feminist researchers have pointed out that women's studies in China is "characteristically policy-oriented" and "geared to practical concerns and moral urgency."[61] According to Lin Chun, the reason for this lies in "China's unique historical trajectory," namely, the fact that the Communist Party's early incorporation of the "women question" into its revolutionary struggles against feudalism and imperialism has paradoxically precluded the emergence of a separate feminist movement attendant to questions of sexuality, gendered subjectivity, and gender consciousness. Therefore, women's research programs and feminist movements became possible only in the 1980s as a result of "two parallel contradictory processes: a significant retreat of the state and a rapid expansion of the market."[62]

Lin's analysis helps explain why, between Maoist modernization theory and the social impact of postsocialism, women's studies and women's movements in China have been mired in the conundrum of different forms of developmentalism. Sexuality appears to be a useless consideration from this perspective, and the importance of policy matters is determined by their fit with a growth-centered agenda. Issues that do not have a demonstrable connection to economic growth are cast aside, and gender is considered important only insofar as capitalist development is first deemed beneficial to all. Using the Chinese example as a model to teach third-world countries how to think of women as untapped resources for accelerated modernization, the UN speaker conflates the importance of gender with the importance of understanding women's role in development. To be sure, feminist arguments that investing in women and girls leads to more effective development outcomes are neither new nor exclusive to China. The UN speaker's view is neither singular nor personal but part of broader currents in development studies and UN efforts that collapse women/gender/development, a line of thinking that has been critically examined by Nalini Visvanathan, Naila Kabeer, Sylvia Chant, and Sylvanna M. Falcón, to name just a few.[63]

The Chinese State Develops Women

As Lisa Rofel and I have argued, China's investments in Africa and reemergence as a world power reflect transformations that are not just economic but also cultural.[64] As such, these changes are sustained through a specifically gendered and sexual set of representations and images.[65] It is critical to understand the nuanced functions performed by the translation of gender in this process. Moreover, what I am calling translation is a two-way street—just as the translations of *gender* from English to Chinese are consistently inflected with the developmentalist logic of the Beijing Consensus, the same is true when Chinese concepts are translated back into English.

On September 27, 2015, President Xi Jinping delivered a high-profile speech at the UN Global Leaders' Meeting on Gender Equality and Women's Empowerment, which was also the twentieth anniversary of the 1995 Fourth World Conference on Women in Beijing. Titled "Promoting Women's All-Round Development and Building a Better World for All" ("促进妇女全面发展 共建共享美好世界") the speech exemplifies a particular political vision, one that treats women as both the instrument and the object of development—a population to be educated, molded, assimilated, and put to use in accordance with the state's productionist ideology in an expeditious fashion ("促进").[66] In the speech Xi announces that it is the state's responsibility to "develop" women and that the development of women will lead to "a better world for all." This developmentalist argument connects women to a specific slogan in Chinese diplomacy. Xi's phrase, "gong jian gong xiang meihao shijie," is translated as "building a better world for all" in official UN documents, but a more accurate translation might be "building a beautiful world that we can all share in harmony." This phrase is part of the Chinese state's rhetoric of Great Harmony and a cognate for "China's peaceful rise" or "peaceful development," the official policy adopted during the Hu Jintao era. Over the years since the end of socialism, China has invented a variety of nearly synonymous slogans, such as the "Chinese Dream," "One World, One Dream," "Harmonious Society," and "Scientific Development Concept." These synonyms for Great Harmony serve the same rhetorical purpose of assuaging Western anxieties about the "China threat." According to this vision, China's ascendancy on the world stage as an economic and military power will lead to the "peaceful co-rise" of and benefits for all nations, rather than the "clash of civilizations" predicted by the bipolar vision of Samuel Huntington and other Washington critics.[67] While the doctrine of peaceful co-rise is not new, Xi's 2015 speech was the first to assign women a central role in the country's long march toward a new world order under the coleadership of Beijing and Washington. Xi observes, "Women and children are the ones who suffer most when peace or tranquility is disrupted. We must stand firmly for peace, development and win-win cooperation, cherish peace dearly and uphold it so that every woman and child will enjoy the sunshine of happiness and tranquility."

While Xi's speech paints a picture of China's "peaceful co-rise" and "win-win cooperation" with Western countries, a crucial gap remains between Chinese and international understandings of gender. The international media described the speech as China's promise to "reaffirm [its] commitment to gender equality."[68] In the original Chinese, however, Xi makes clear that China is committed only to "women's rights" and not "gender equality." In Chinese, Xi uses the word *gender* (*xingbie*) only once, in reference to something called the "UN agenda" and "UN perspective." The English translation reads, "In the Post-2015 Development Agenda we have just adopted, gender perspective has been included in all the items on the agenda. Let us reaffirm the spirit of the Beijing Conference with renewed commitment and pledge greater efforts to promote gender equality and women's all-round development." But in Xi's original Chinese speech, the Chinese pledge is made to *nannü pingdeng*, the Maoist state slogan for "equality between men and women." Although both *xingbie* and *nannü pingdeng* are translated as "gender" in the official English document, Xi is careful not to confuse them. In the body of the speech, Xi further elaborates on the connection between women and development:

> Women are creators of material and spiritual wealth and represent an important force driving social development and progress. Without women, there would be no continuity of the human race or the human society.
>
> The pursuit of gender equality is a great cause. A review of history shows that without women's liberation and progress, the liberation and progress of mankind would not be attainable. To achieve the lofty goal of gender equality, we have gone through an extraordinary and uphill journey.[69]

Once again, the English translation uses "gender equality" in both places where, in Chinese, Xi said "equality between men and women." Given that the word *xingbie* was actually used in the same speech in reference to the UN agenda, Xi clearly understood the difference between these terms and made a strategic choice to reaffirm China's commitment to equality between men and women but not to gender as defined by Western nations.

The difference is clear. *Nannü pingdeng*, equality between men and women, has been one of the key principles of the CCP's platform since the Maoist era. It is perceived as an appropriately Chinese, even socialist-revolutionary concept and fully compatible with the doctrine of the Beijing Consensus. It rests on a binary understanding that there are only two sexes and prioritizes the male perspective (hence, it's "equality between men and women" rather than "equality between women and men"). This framework extends legal protection and rights only to heteronormative relations between individuals identifying as women and men. Gender equality, on the other hand, is seen as a Western liberal idea in China. Broadly construed, gender equality could include transgender rights, same-sex marriage, and battles against femmephobia and other social policing of gender expressions, as well as new configurations of family and kinship. Indeed, the flexibility of the notion of gender was why, in preparation for the 1995 UN Fourth World Conference on Women in Beijing, the Vatican City and other conservative countries launched a campaign to prevent UN policy-drafting committees from using the word *gender*, seeing it as a euphemistic expression for homosexuality, bestiality, and the destruction of the family. In this strategically crafted memorial speech at the twenty-year anniversary of the 1995 conference, Xi's reaffirmation of China's commitment to "equality between men and women" conveyed a strong message to the Chinese public that China is not endorsing transgender or homosexual rights. This distinction, however, was lost in the English translation and to the international media.

Xi's circumlocution is not unique among state actors. Rather, the Chinese state's translation of *gender* signals a determinate response to a rift in the international community. While Xi attributes gender (*xingbie*) to a UN agenda and emphasizes its distinction from the Chinese notion of *nannü pingdeng*, in fact the UN itself does not have a uniform understanding of gender: whether it refers to the essential differences between women and men or is a more progressive concept that encompasses sexual preferences and gender identities. The official UN stance is that *gender* ought to remain undefined. As Jane Adolphe's detailed research on UN initiatives for women reveals, state-negotiated documents have consistently and intentionally rejected the radical feminist concept of gender as a social construct. Indeed, the UN's various historical attempts to integrate the term *gender* into policy papers, including the Convention on the Elimination of All Forms of Discrimination against Women (CEDAW) and the Beijing Declaration and Platform for Action, have been subject to a high degree of tension internal to the organization. Adolphe identifies four competing understandings of gender within the UN system: (1) "gender as a social construct"; (2) "gender as a cultural aspect of femininity and masculinity, but based on the biological sexes, male and female"; (3) "gender as synonymous with women and sex, or women and children"; and (4) "gender meaning the two sexes, male and female, within the context of society."[70] As mentioned, the 1995 Beijing conference, as the first event in the history of the UN to rigorously engage with the concept of gender, brought the term *gender* into a definitional crisis. It produced, among other things, the first UN document that employed the term *gender* extensively—233 times.[71]

Per a position paper published by the UN Research Institute for Social Development in preparation for the Fourth World Conference on Women in Beijing in 1995, the significance of the conference lies in nothing less than having brought about a paradigm shift in policy discourse from women in development (WID) to gender and development (GAD).[72] Whereas the women-in-development framework treats women as an economic unit, with their claims to social justice hinging on economic-efficiency arguments about what they can contribute to the development process, the gender-and-development perspective gives analytic weight to the conflictual and cooperative dimensions between women and men, the cultural ideologies of maleness and femaleness, and their relationality. Globally, the Beijing conference became a pivotal event for the rising visibility of the term *gender*, which for some seemed to threaten to displace traditional notions of sex under the influence of "new gender theorists" such as Judith Butler. As already mentioned, the concept of gender caused a great deal of alarm among members of the UN. Several states, spearheaded by the Vatican City, objected that the influence of radical feminist theory would alter the meaning of *gender* from its "ordinary, generally acceptable usage" as a synonym for *women* to include homosexuality and even bestiality. In response to the Beijing Declaration and Platform for Action, the Vatican City, several countries with large Catholic populations, and Arab states produced counterdocuments of their own to ensure that use of the term *gender* would not imply rights based on sexual orientation.

The UN convened a special committee to resolve this issue. After investigating the matter, the UN Commission on the Status of Women concluded that *gender* should be understood in its "ordinary, generally accepted usage" but did not define what that usage is. In "Annex V: Statement on the Commonly Understood Meaning of Gender" in the *Report of the United Nations Conference on Human Settlements (Habitat II), Istanbul, 3–14 June 1996*, the UN Commission on the Status of Women explains:

1. During the 19th meeting of the Commission on the Status of Women, acting as preparatory body for the Fourth World Conference on Women, an issue arose concerning the meaning of the word "gender" in the context of the Platform for Action of the Conference. . . . The Commission mandated the informal contact group to seek agreement on the commonly understood meaning of "gender" in the context of the Platform for Action and to report directly to the Conference in Beijing. 2. Having considered the issue thoroughly, the contact group noted that: (1) the word "gender" had been

commonly used and understood in its ordinary, generally accepted usage in numerous other United Nations forums and conferences; (2) there was no indication that any new meaning or connotation of the term, different from accepted prior usage, was intended in the Platform for Action. 3. Accordingly, the contact group reaffirmed that the word "gender" as used in the Platform for Action was intended to be interpreted and understood as it was in ordinary, generally accepted usage.[73]

The UN solution was essentially a tautology. By defining the meaning of *gender* as its "ordinary, generally accepted usage" in past UN forums and conferences throughout the world, and stating that this meaning of *gender* would serve as a guideline for future UN documents and conferences, the committee in fact offered no definition at all. What the document offered, instead, was a circular logic. Elizabeth Weed notes that the statement offers "a stunningly candid glimpse at the *aporia* that is gender . . . a language that stands in for a referent that can't be named."[74] In the end, the gender wars that resulted from the Beijing conference were inconclusive, and the term remained undefined in the UN system. Since state parties never agreed to define gender as a social construct, the UN adopted a nondefinitional approach as a solution, an act that attempted to "settle controversy by denying that it exists."[75]

The story of the "crisis of gender" resulting from the 1995 Beijing conference raises several important points for transnational feminist and queer theories and practices in the age of the Beijing Consensus.[76] First, rather than creating meaningful structural changes and redistribution of resources, the UN is only able to register national differences and promote their harmonious coexistence. While the UN world conferences promote the transnationalization of feminist struggles and create an imagined space of collective action for feminists to engage in advocacy and lobbying efforts beyond domestic singularity, they largely promote an image of a deracialized universal woman at the expense of acknowledging differences based on race, culture, economic standing, national origins, language, and sexuality.[77]

Second, the UN does not reflect a consensus among nations. Rather, it only monitors state parties and represents a compromise among governmental bodies that are themselves embedded in political interests and bureaucratic structures that are largely incongruent with the societies they claim to represent. As the UN itself is a fusion of politics and values, the political economy of feminisms at the UN level is shaped by asymmetrical power relations, dynamics, and realities.[78] As Joanne Sandler and Anne Marie Goetz have recently pointed out, the "crisis of multilateralism" among the United States, Russia, and China—the same problem I describe through the notion of the Beijing Consensus—has further stalled feminist progress and intensified the polarization of feminist projects.[79]

Third, the documents produced by the UN are nonbinding recommendations only and as such may or may not translate into meaningful actions.[80] Finally, even the so-called radical notion of gender opposed by those who insist on its "ordinary, generally accepted usage" is not truly radical. Readings of gender as a "social construct" or "femininity and masculinity" refer to gender *roles* in the household, politics, and the sex-segregated market, or how policies affect men and women differently. At best, these interpretations merely reinforce the 1970s feminist distinction between women's biological sex and women's socially assigned roles, responsibilities, and expectations, rather than arriving at a more transformative view of sex itself as a gendered category.

Conclusion

There is now a vast body of literature on how the 1995 Fourth World Conference on Women in Beijing and its documents redefined gender for transnational feminist theory and practice. What has not been sufficiently discussed is how the encounter in and with Beijing produced these controversies, how Chinese feminists and policy makers themselves responded to this event, or how these responses constitute an example of the subsumption of sexuality under capitalism. The Chinese turn to gender was not a simple consequence of the 1995 UN world conference. Rather, it occurred because of a complex dialogue between Chinese and Anglo-American intellectual currents, mediated by the century-long search for sovereignty, self-determination, and alternatives to the Western capitalist model that eventually became the thesis of the Beijing Consensus. Because the Beijing Consensus is a political paradox, one that emphasizes both China's leadership in global affairs and its distinction from Washington-led neoliberal capitalism, the trajectory of contemporary Chinese debates about sex/gender has been subsumed under the same-but-different cultural logic that undergirds the country's capitalist development. While some writers believe that Western theories of gender cannot sufficiently account for the uniqueness of Chinese women and the legacy of Marxism-Leninism, others embrace the concept of gender consciousness as an opportunity for postsocialist China to reconnect with the world. In both instances, however, the conversation is invariably eclipsed by the broader questions of China's neoliberal experiments and economic development, while more transformative and queer understandings of sex/gender remain occluded from view.

Gender, in both Chinese and anglophone theories, is a multiply constituted and internally contradictory notion, the meanings of which vary according to contexts and political purposes. There is no story to tell about how gender "travels" from one culture to another; specifically, I want to resist the narrative that a theory of gender construction or gender consciousness was first invented in North America and then translated into China during the 1980s and 1990s in order to replace a Marxist-feminist concept of gender equality espoused by party ideology. Instead of this narrative, I offer an account of the contradictory claims that are made in the name of gender and situate them as cultural articulations within the context of China's search for a new world order that has been described as the Beijing Consensus. Though I emphasize the mutual embeddedness of gender and political economy and describe capitalism as having the capacity to subsume sexuality, my ultimate hope is that gender will be freed from such constraints. This resistance to the subsumption of sexuality is central to the formation of an alternative politics that can nourish the possibilities of gendered life.

Conclusion

TOWARD A TRANSNATIONAL

QUEER MARXISM

The first draft of *The Specter of Materialism* was written during the COVID-19 crisis, when a global pandemic—joined by the fallout of Brexit, anti-Black murders, climate disasters, the farmers' strike in India, Hong Kong protests, and unprecedented hostility between China and the United States—irreversibly altered the terms we used to measure the distance between self and others. As I learned, along with others, how to improvise makeshift solutions in a new contactless world, I also discovered new ways to imagine our global engagement and sociality. I realized that to inhabit a human body is to be given over to mortality, vulnerability, and precarity. How to situate queer survival and persistence within the contradictions between the mobility of capital and the immobility of labor became a primary political and theoretical task for me.

While capitalist production has become rationalized and globalized, our regime of accountability has not. What is unevenly distributed is not just our vulnerability but also our sense of proximity—whose lives matter, whose lives are worth protection and recognition, and who belongs to the collective "us" versus "them." Bodies come together, sometimes erotically, across borders. But bodies are also laboring and producing use values that we consume, living in relation to hierarchies we helped create, and thinking in differentially valued traditions and languages. Queer bodies exist in a state of constant tension with the instruments of capital accumulation, including a citizenship system that confers legal rights based on birth accidents and monogamous marriages, an institution of private property enshrined in idealized forms of kinship and descent, the reproduction of families as neoliberal consumers, and racially segregated access to health care, housing, and means of subsistence. To be queer, to inhabit a queer body, means that one must rebel against capitalism's laws of value and their regulation of gender and sexual norms. But to do this work, we cannot reduce the definition of capitalism to the ideology of US corporations. Instead, it is imperative to develop an analytic of capitalism as a transnational regime of accumulation and dispossession. Shifting the question from queer theory's applicability to non-Western societies to what we can learn from their historical experiences, we can begin to reconceptualize US-based queer theory as a minority participant in a multilingual conversation. Instead of thinking of non-European sexual subjects as underrepresented victims in need of search and rescue, I turn to them as differently situated knowledge producers in the history of the uneven accumulation of capital. While my own work is certainly not truly global in scope, I hope that this book's arguments and findings—no matter how exploratory and provisional they may seem at times—will expand our archive of references for a global queer Marxism that has yet to be born.

The Specter of Materialism is a theoretically promiscuous book that brings together three areas of humanistic inquiry that are rarely discussed together: queer theory's materialist turn from questions of representation to those of precarity, dispossession, and the maldistribution of life chances; contemporary Marxism's reconceptualization of race, gender, and sexuality as material differences that capital requires for its expanded reproduction; and the subsumption of social differences within the political economy of post-socialist China. Through analyses of the various dimensions of the so-called Beijing Consensus—the financialization of China's agrarian hinterlands, the creation of a novel hegemony and South-South Cooperation programs, the privatization of its socialist institutions, and the subsumption of gendered and sexual relations under new regimes of value accumulation—*The Specter of Materialism* provides a historically grounded understanding of capitalism's concrete effects in order to expand the materialist framework of contemporary queer theory.

In writing this book, I understand my project to be performing a threefold intervention: decentering Marxism, provincializing queer theory, and pluralizing epistemologies rather than examples. The focus on the Beijing Consensus allows me to tell the story of China's incorporation into global capital and the politics of queer precarity without turning Asia into either an impenetrable tradition or a carbon copy of the West. China does not signify a set of exotic or unassimilable customs. It is, rather, a perspective on inter-penetrating colonialisms and violences, partitioned loyalties and geographies, fractured families, and lost memories. Sexuality emerges in this context as a powerful framework for understanding the production of affect and subjec-tivities under regimes of capital accumulation and colonial plunder. The study of sexuality allows us to situate the formation of the subject within the violent history that produced Asia as an object of thought. In so doing, the study of sexuality also provides a way for us to think beyond the antinomy of cultural and economic life that has dominated some strands of leftist thought. The workings of culture are not purely imagined, fantasized, or projected at will. Rather, culture itself is made possible by concrete exercises of power, by those who take away and sustain lives.

My analysis of the production of precarity and the subsumption of social differences in this book aims to show that the reconfigurations of gender and sexuality are not secondary effects of the primitive accumulation of capital. Rather, the hierarchical valuation of gendered life is part of the same process that allows certain human bodies to materialize as intelligible social subjects while denying others access to clean water, food, shelter, or the right to imag-ine and speak in ways that matter to the public. Rather than dismissing ma-terialism as a phantasm, queer theory and Marxism provide overlapping and indispensable perspectives on the materiality of the body. With these insights we can begin the difficult labor of constructing a global queer Marxism. The purpose of this book is not to create a new intellectual orthodoxy or to birth a new movement. It is, rather, an invitation for new ways of imagining queer futures and transformative politics.

Notes

INTRODUCTION

1 Hung, "America's Head Servant?" As Ho-fung Hung pointed out, the viability of the fiscal remedies employed by the United States to stabilize its post-2008 economy depended on China's willingness to keep purchasing US Treasury bonds—a situation that was simply unimaginable a decade ago.

2 R. Brenner, *Economics of Global Turbulence*.

3 Minqi Li has characterized the contemporary world order as a system of unequal exchange that allowed the United States to "purchase" trillions of dollars' worth of Chinese goods by printing Treasury bonds. Without China, Li estimated, about 38 percent of the total US labor force would have to be withdrawn from service sectors and transferred to material production sectors. "China's reserve assets, rather than being a part of China's imperialist wealth, essentially constitute China's informal tribute to U.S. imperialism by paying for the latter's 'seigniorage privilege.'" M. Li, "China: Imperialism or Semi-periphery?"

4 Dirlik, *After the Revolution*; Guthrie, *China and Globalization*; Hung, *China and the Transformation*; and Naughton, *Growing out of the Plan*.

5 Au, *China's Rise*, 119.

6 Ching Kwan Lee, *Against the Law*.

7 Rofel and Yanagisako, *Fabricating Transnational Capitalism*.

8 While an earlier generation of Marxist feminists understood patriarchy as a feature of capitalism without making it specific to capitalism, scholars in more recent years have proposed a displacement of the transhistorical understanding of gender as "domination" by historicizing it as a "real abstraction" in the reproduction of the social totality. See *Endnotes*, "Logic of Gender."

9 As Colleen Lye has reminded us, identity politics, though sometimes dismissed as parochial or essentializing, originated from third-worldist revolutionary practices that were emphatically international. Lye, "Identity Politics."

10 Ramo, *Beijing Consensus*.

11 Arrighi and Zhang, "Beyond the Washington Consensus."

12 Connery, "Revolutionary China," 259; and Andreas, "Changing Colours in China," 127. See chapter 1 for a fuller discussion.

13 Some of these debates have been translated and made available in C. Wang, *One China, Many Paths*.

14 Rojas and Litzinger, *Ghost Protocol*, 3–4.

15 Halper, *Beijing Consensus*.

16 See chapter 1 for a more detailed discussion of this point.

17 In this context it is also useful to remind ourselves of Sara Ahmed's trenchant critique of how the language of diversity, now ritualistically chanted by university authorities, works to normalize and displace more critical terms such as *equality* and *social justice*. Ahmed, *On Being Included*.

18 Marx, *German Ideology*, 574.

19 Marx, *Capital*, 3:968–69.

20 Louis Althusser captures this point by suggesting that capital is an "absent cause." As a structure that is both overdetermining ("determination-in-the-last-instance") and perpetually absent, capital can never be captured by a priori assumptions. Instead, capital is visible only through its traces and historical effectivity, which Althusser proposes to uncover through the interpretive procedure he terms *symptomatic reading*. See Althusser, *Reading Capital*, 99, 188.

21 The translation of this fragment is available as an appendix in the Penguin edition of Marx, *Capital*, vol. 1.

22 Marx, *Economic Manuscripts of 1861–63*, 146–47.

23 *Endnotes*, "History of Subsumption."

24 Marx, *Capital*, 1:952.

25 Marx, *Capital*, 1:956.

26 Marx, *Capital*, 1:986.

27 Marx, *Capital*, 1:975.

28 Marx, *Capital*, 1:980.

29 Althusser, "Ideology and Ideological State Apparatuses," 143.

30 Hardt and Negri, *Labor of Dionysus*, 15.

31 Karl, *Magic of Concepts*, 120–23.

32 Harootunian, *Marx after Marx*, 78.

33 Harootunian, *Marx after Marx*, 9.

34 Harootunian's thesis was presented in his "Deprovincializing Marx: Reflections on a Cultural Dominant" and debated at an international conference at National Chiao-Tung University, Taiwan, in June 2012, the proceedings of which were subsequently published as *East Asian Marxisms and Their Trajectories* (edited by Joyce C. H. Liu and Viren Murthy) and featured the opinions of prominent Marxists from the region and from without (such as

Wang Hui, Kojin Karatani, and Moishe Postone). In contrast to Harootunian's view, Postone argues that "actually existing socialisms" such as China and the Soviet Union represent "a critique of capitalism from the standpoint of labor," which must be distinguished from Marx's "critique of labor in capitalism" in his mature theory. Postone, "Marx, Temporality and Modernity," 30, 32.

CHAPTER ONE. ALTERITY IN QUEER THEORY AND THE POLITICAL ECONOMY OF THE BEIJING CONSENSUS

1 Irving and Lewis, "Special Issue on Trans-Political Economy."
2 Currah and Stryker, "General Editors' Introduction," 2.
3 For an investigation of this issue, see Patel, "Seeding Debt."
4 Marx, *Capital*, 1:1019, emphasis and square brackets in the original.
5 See Nealon, "Price of Value," 103.
6 Clover, "Value/Theory/Crisis"; *Endnotes*, "Misery and the Value Form"; Larsen et al., *Marxism and the Critique of Value*; Lye and Nealon, *After Marx*; Nesbitt, "Value as Symptom"; and R. Martin, *Financialization of Daily Life*.
7 Fabian, *Time and the Other*.
8 Sedgwick, *Epistemology of the Closet*, 45.
9 In a recent special issue of the *Journal of Asian Studies* on the reception or "appropriation" of *Gender Trouble* in Asian studies, Geeta Patel explains that *Gender Trouble* has empowered students and faculty in South Asia with a new set of "grammar and vocabulary through which they could parse sexuality and desire," while Gail Hershatter explores conversations this text enabled "not as a blueprint but as an incubator of locally grounded thinking" for Chinese feminists and China studies scholars. Patel, "*Gender Trouble* in South Asia," 952; and Hershatter, "*Gender Trouble*'s Afterlife," 911. Judith Butler offers these useful comments: "The question is no longer whether what *Gender Trouble* says is true for all times and places (it never made that claim), but whether its lexicon can, transposed and translated, introduce helpful perspectives to those who seek to understand sex/gender in different systematic configurations." Butler, "Reflections on *Gender Trouble*," 972.
10 My thinking on this topic has benefited from Hentyle Yapp's critical reading of liberalism's curation of multicultural differences within a monocultural frame. As Yapp points out, minority subjects are often framed as worthy of inclusion only for demonstrating alterity and resistance, while the United States remains the tacit benchmark against which progress is measured. Writing more specifically on the global circulation of non-Western art, Yapp considers three common frameworks within which non-Western artists come to be seen as embodiments of political resistance against the authoritarian state: humanization, intersubjectivity, and relationality. Yapp, *Minor China*, 75.

11 This definition continues to be central to contemporary queer theory and politics. For a renewed exploration of the queer as a nonontological position rather than an identitarian category that came out of a recent symposium on the topic in Berlin, see the essays in Brilmyer, Trentin, and Xiang, "Ontology of the Couple."

12 Kadji Amin reminds us that the term *queer*, founded on anti-identitarianism and an aspirational horizon of being always elsewhere, remains affectively haunted by the political moment of the 1990s in which it emerged. Hence, Amin proposes that rather than continuing to celebrate queer mobility and lack of definition, we ground queer in its multiple inheritances and attachments. Amin, "Haunted by the 1990s."

13 Butler, Laclau, and Žižek, *Contingency, Hegemony, Universality*. The concept of the constitutive outside, first formulated by Jacques Derrida, was elaborated as central to the radical democracy project by Ernesto Laclau and Chantal Mouffe in *Hegemony and Socialist Strategy* and further by Mouffe in *The Democratic Paradox*. For a comparison of Butler's use of the constitutive outside to Elizabeth Grosz's understanding of the generative violence of difference in the constitution of corporeality, see Cheah, "Mattering."

14 Extending this point on the distinction between queer and identity categories such as gay and lesbian, Heather Love has productively constructed an alternative genealogy of US-based queer theory as rooted in a broader form of mid-twentieth-century deviance studies of prostitutes, alcoholics, juvenile delinquents, and other underdog figures. Recognizing queer theory's intellectual debts to deviance studies, Love suggests, is key to the stigma-centric solidarity politics of queer studies. Love, *Underdogs*, esp. ch. 4.

15 Berlant and Warner, "What Does Queer Theory Teach Us," 344.

16 In a brilliant essay, J. Keith Vincent explains early queer theory's preoccupation with the figure of the Other—how and why questions of sexuality always become punitive, projective, and paranoid readings of what we think we know about other people's desires—as pivoting on an "inside/outside question." Some versions of psychoanalytic queer theory treat sexual desire and sexual orientation as internal phenomena originating within the self and "accessible to others only through confession, coming out, psychoanalysis, outing, or other modes of externalization." Other versions of queer theory problematize this assumption, insisting that these are "intersubjective both in their origins and in their immediacy." Vincent, "Sex on the Mind," 200. Vincent's own work, which utilizes the perspective of non-Western literature to rethink the notion of interiority in queer theory in relation to cognitive theory, instantiates the paradigm shift in transnational queer theory's engagement with the Other that I describe in this chapter.

17 See Cornell, *Transformations*, for an early formulation of this view. The concept of queer futurity has been reelaborated in the context of Lee Edelman's

critique of reproductive futurism, the antisocial thesis debate, and Lauren Berlant's analysis of the present's "crisis ordinariness" and the promise of the good life. See Edelman, *No Future*; Caserio et al., "Antisocial Thesis"; and Berlant, *Cruel Optimism*, 222–48.

18 Connery, "End of the Sixties," 184.

19 On archiving the past, see Cvetkovich, *Depression*; Freeman, *Time Binds*; Love, *Feeling Backwards*; and F. Martin, *Backward Glances*. On African articulations as queer customary reworkings of temporality, see Fiereck, Hoad, and Mupotsa, "Queering-to-Come."

20 Keeling, *Queer Times, Black Futures*, 82, 99.

21 Muñoz, *Cruising Utopia*, 45.

22 Muñoz, *Cruising Utopia*, 54.

23 Wittig, "One Is Not Born a Woman," 12.

24 Irigaray, *This Sex Which Is Not One*.

25 Butler, *Gender Trouble*, 107–27.

26 The emergence of queer-of-color scholarship has critically challenged the additive and inclusionary framework of liberal queer theory from the position of the unthought, though the point has not been developed with equal force in relation to lifeworlds and research paradigms outside the anglophone academy. See, among others, Hartman, *Wayward Lives, Beautiful Experiments*; and Nyong'o, *Afro-Fabulations*.

27 Halperin, *How to Do the History of Sexuality*, 20.

28 *How to Do the History of Sexuality*, written as a sequel to *One Hundred Years of Homosexuality and Other Essays on Greek Love*, revises the argument by making greater allowances for continuities between past and present while upholding Halperin's historicist commitments. Halperin does not use the word *sex* in the same sense I am employing it: for Halperin, sex is a natural fact outside of history, whereas sexuality is historically and culturally produced. Halperin further emphasizes that the description of other societies need not imply a normative valuation of our own experiences.

29 Foucault, *History of Sexuality*, 23.

30 Davidson, "Sex and the Emergence of Sexuality"; Hacking, "Making Up People"; Chauncey, *Gay New York*; *and* Halperin, *One Hundred Years of Homosexuality*.

31 Foucault, *History of Sexuality*, 154.

32 Foucault, *History of Sexuality*, 57–58. I elaborated this argument in P. Liu, *Queer Marxism in Two Chinas*, 21–30. For an illuminating analysis of Foucault's use of cultural differences, see Lazreg, *Foucault's Orient*. Ann Laura Stoler's classic study of the racial context of Foucault's theory, *Race and the Education of Desire*, remains indispensable for our understanding of the role played by sexual epistemologies in the creation of colonial categories and vice versa. See also Boone, *Homoerotics of Orientalism*, for an argument that refuses the neat demarcations between these discourses.

33 For sure, Foucault's Eurocentrism does not mean that his ideas cannot be pressed into service as tools for antiracist thinking. The special issue "Foucault and Race" in *Foucault Studies* 12 (October 2011), for example, features five essays defending the political value of Foucault's work as carving out a heterotopic space for racial resistance and epistemic pluralism. In a recent work, Rey Chow delineates the possibilities of "thinking race with Foucault" to develop an alternative to the Saidian critique of Foucault's blindness to the imperial contexts of disciplinary institutions. R. Chow, *Face Drawn in Sand*, 87–112.

34 Savci, *Queer in Translation*, 3.

35 Sedgwick, *Epistemology of the Closet*, 1.

36 Sedgwick, *Epistemology of the Closet*, 13–14, emphasis added.

37 Rubin, "Thinking Sex," 157.

38 In an interview Rubin explains how her thinking on universalism evolved from "The Traffic in Women" to "Thinking Sex": "In 'Traffic,' I simply absorbed the idioms and innocent universalism of the time. By the time I wrote 'Thinking Sex,' I wanted to make more modest claims. That was part of why, in 'Thinking Sex,' I noted that the Lévi-Straussian/Lacanian formulations might or might not be accurate for other societies, even as I was certain that they had limited applicability to our own. I had acquired some skepticism about the universality of those models." Rubin, "Sexual Traffic," 301.

39 Roscoe, *Changing Ones*; Almaguer, "Chicano Men"; and Massad, *Desiring Arabs*.

40 A comprehensive survey of this literature may be found in Tamara Loos's "Reading *Gender Trouble* in Southeast Asia." Loos considers several works in depth, including J. Neil Garcia's *Performing the Self*, Michael Peletz's *Gender Pluralism*, Sharyn Graham Davies's *Gender Diversity in Indonesia*, Rosalind Morris's "Three Sexes and Four Sexualities," and Megan Sinnott's *Toms and Dees* to chart the limits of the applicability of the "Foucauldian archive" to Southeast Asian contexts.

41 In his study of the *thù xú* phenomenon (male-male amorous relations in the then newly emerging French-Vietnamese secondary schools) based on newspapers published in the late 1920s in Vietnam, for example, Richard Quang-Anh Tran recharacterizes Vietnamese same-sex sexuality as a cathectic object onto which different interlocutors projected both their anxieties and aspirations. Tran, "Sexuality as Translation."

42 In addition to the equivalence between *tongzhi* and homosexuality, another point of contention in Chinese studies concerned the so-called great paradigm shift—whether a moment of rupture similar to Foucault's concept of the speciation of the modern homosexual has ever occurred in Chinese history. See Sang, *Emerging Lesbian*, 99–126; Kang, *Obsession*; Rojas, "'New Species'"; L. Shi, "Constructing a New Sexual Paradigm"; and D. Wong, "Hybridization." I return to this debate in greater detail in chapter 5.

43 Indeed, anthropological research is central to the type of transnational queer theory that I describe and develop in this book. For an illuminating analysis of anthropology's place in the intellectual movements from a restrictive *queer* (focused on sex and sexuality) to queer as a challenge to categorical legibility and a way to think vitalities between bio- and necropolitics, see Weiss, "Queer Theory from Elsewhere."

44 Recent critical explorations of location-specific approaches to queer studies include Currier and Migraine-George, "Queer Studies/African Studies"; El-Tayeb, *European Others*; Henry, "Queer/Korean Studies as Critique"; Hoad, "Re: Thinking Sex"; Horton, "Queer Turn"; Matebeni and Msibi, "Vocabularies of the Non-normative"; Meghani and Saeed, "Postcolonial/Sexuality"; Méndez, "Notes toward a Decolonial Feminist Methodology"; Pereira, *Queer in the Tropics*; Rao, *Out of Time*, esp. ch. 2; and Tellis and Bala, *Global Trajectories of Queerness*. On the concept of queer Asia as a decolonizing epistemology, see Luther and Ung Loh, *Queer Asia*; Sinnott, "Border, Diaspora and Regional Connections"; Henry, "Introduction"; and Wilson, "Queering Asia."

45 Arondekar and Patel, "Area Impossible," 155.

46 Arondekar and Patel, "Area Impossible," 152.

47 Sedgwick, *Epistemology of the Closet*, 85.

48 Sedgwick, *Epistemology of the Closet*, 71–72, 1.

49 Spivak, "Bonding in Difference," 28.

50 Mandel, *Late Capitalism*, 274–77.

51 Postone, *Time, Labor, and Social Domination*, 347.

52 The argument that socialist China, along with other developmentalist states, was shaped by a global treadmill effect that was capitalist in nature should be carefully distinguished from the state capitalist thesis, which is predicated on the formation of an internal capitalist class. For a recent reassessment of the latter debate (and defense of China's socialist characteristics), see Meyskens, "Rethinking the Political Economy."

53 Chuǎng, "Sorghum and Steel."

54 Chuǎng, "Sorghum and Steel."

55 Karl, "Engaging Gerth's Sleights (of Hand)."

56 Arrighi, *Adam Smith in Beijing*.

57 Though those scholars' aim is in part to dispel the myth of the Chinese path as evolutionary cul-de-sac and developmental stasis, in more recent years the "great divergence" thesis has been challenged by scholars who conduct multisite research to show how overlapping circuits of economic competition within Asia over the course of the nineteenth and twentieth centuries produced increasingly abstract notions of value, production, and labor in global capitalism. See A. Liu, *Tea War*.

58 Arrighi, *Adam Smith in Beijing*.

59 Hung, *China and the Transformation*, 12. See also Hung, *China Boom*, ch. 3.

60 Dirlik, "Rise of China," 534.

61 Goodman and Zang, "New Rich in China."

62 Wang H., *China's New Order*, 54–55.

63 Silver and Zhang, "China as an Emerging Epicenter," 175. Hence, Beverly Silver and Lu Zhang argue that rather than unleashing a "race to the bottom," the growth of manufacturing in China has proved that where capital goes, labor-capital conflict shortly follows. For broad accounts of China's rural and urban labor protests since the abolition of socialist institutions, see O'Brien and Li, *Rightful Resistance;* and Ching Kwan Lee, *Against the Law.*

64 Wen, "Centenary Reflections."

65 A. Day, *Peasant in Postsocialist China;* A. Zhang, "Invisible Labouring Bodies"; and Liebman and Lee, "Garbage as Value."

66 Zhan, *Land Question in China*, 38.

67 DeMare, *Land Wars*; Huayin Li, *Village China*; and Shue, *Peasant China in Transition*.

68 Selden, *Political Economy of Chinese Socialism*, 52.

69 P. Ho, "Who Owns China's Land," 396. See also Brandt et al., "Land Rights in Rural China"; and Q. Zhang and Donaldson, "Rise of Agrarian Capitalism."

70 Hayward, "China's Land Reforms."

71 For an analysis of the connections between the superexploitation of migrant labor and China's capitalist globalization, see Foster and McChesney, *Endless Crisis*.

72 Au, *China's Rise*, 183–98.

73 Chuang, *Beneath the China Boom*.

74 A. Day, *Peasant in Postsocialist China*, ch. 1.

75 Federici, *Patriarchy of the Wage*.

76 Pun, "Discursive Dyslexia and the Articulation of Class," 80. See also Pun, *Made in China*; Yan, *New Masters, New Servants*; L. Zhang, *Strangers in the City*; O'Donnell, "*Dagongmei*"; and Solinger, *Contesting Citizenship in Urban China*.

77 C. Wu, *Mapping China*.

78 Kong, "Reinventing the Self," 286.

79 Bao, *Queer Media in China*; and L. Ho, *Gay and Lesbian Subcultures*.

80 Yan, "Neoliberal Governmentality and Neohumanism"; Anagnost, "Corporeal Politics of Quality (*Suzhi*)"; and Kipnis, "Neoliberalism Reified."

81 Rofel, *Desiring China*, ch. 3; and J. Wei, *Queer Chinese Cultures and Mobilities*, ch. 4.

82 B. Lu, "Rethinking Queer Value."

83 Refusing to separate queerness and family relations, Lin Song argues in a recent study that China's economic-driven growth in the media sector has brought about new modes of queer becoming and kinship that are at once assimilationist and subversive: "Queer culture *is* public culture in the PRC,

and constitutes a pivotal site of negotiation with state-sanctioned notions of Chineseness." Song, *Queering Chinese Kinship*, 130.

84 J. Wei, *Queer Chinese Cultures and Mobilities*, 99.

85 Brautigam, *Dragon's Gift*.

86 Yun Sun, "China's Aid to Africa."

87 Begu et al., "China-Angola Investment Model."

88 Abegunrin and Manyeruke, *China's Power in Africa*.

89 For a historical account of the changing relations between China and Africa from the Bandung era to the Beijing Consensus, see Volland, "Turning the Tables." See also Moyo, "Perspectives on South-South Relations"; and Lovell, *Maoism*, ch. 6.

90 French, *China's Second Continent*; Corkin, "Competition or Collaboration?"; and Habib, "Seeing the New African Scramble."

91 Sautman and Yan, "Discourse of Racialization of Labor"; and Castillo, "'Race' and 'Racism.'"

92 Cheru and Obi, *Rise of China and India*.

93 M. Ye, *Belt Road and Beyond*. With the state-mobilized globalization framework, Min Ye proposes that we shift the question from why autocratic leaders launch nationalist strategies to how subnational and commercial actors interpret and implement such strategies.

94 See Baik, "'One Belt One Road.'"

95 This point is well underscored by the contributors to a recent issue of *Made in China Journal*. See Franceschini and Loubere, "Archaeologies."

96 Brautigam, "Critical Look."

97 Ching Kwan Lee, *Specter of Global China*.

98 Huynh, "Black Marxism." See also Sheridan, "Prehistories of China-Tanzania," for an analysis that complicates the dichotomy of colonizer and colonized by attending to the history of Chinese migration, which preceded the rise of China and its state projects.

99 Lin C., *China and Global Capitalism*.

100 Wen, *Ten Crises*, 30, 170.

101 M. Li, *Rise of China*.

102 M. Li, "China: Imperialism or Semi-periphery?"

103 Arrighi, *Adam Smith in Beijing*, 361, 24.

104 Bolinaga, "From the Washington Consensus," 49.

105 Dieng, "'Gone Native?'"

106 S. Cheng, "Choreography of Masculinity."

107 Bao, *Queer Media in China*, 155–79.

108 Rofel, *Desiring China*. Building on Lisa Rofel's innovative analysis, Alvin K. Wong has more recently coined the term *perverse use-value* to describe the coding of queer bodies as risky and socially nonreproductive. For Wong, however, perversion also functions as a form of queer potentiality against the

developmental logic of neoliberalism in the Sinosphere. A. Wong, "Queering the Quality of Desire."

CHAPTER TWO. THE SPECTER OF MATERIALISM

An earlier version of this chapter appeared as "Queer Theory and the Specter of Materialism," *Social Text* 38, no. 4 (145) (2020): 25–47.

1 For a sobering analysis of the "Kafkaesque web of official identity contradiction and chaos" state institutions defining sex in the United States have created for transgender people, see Currah, *Sex Is as Sex Does*, 8. Focusing on sex classifications as a technology of government, Currah displaces arguments about what sex and gender really are with the question of what sex does for a particular state project in order to reveal the limits of identity-based transgender rights movements.

2 Puar, *Right to Maim*, 34.

3 Ghaziani and Brim, introduction, 13.

4 This debate is well known. For helpful commentaries and expositions, see Love, "Feminist Criticism and Queer Theory"; and Jagose, "Feminism's Queer Theory."

5 On racial mattering, see Mel Chen, *Animacies*. For new works exploring intercorporeal embodiment, materialism, and crip theory, see McRuer, *Crip Times*; Shildrick, *Dangerous Discourses*; and Kafer, *Feminist, Queer, Crip*.

6 My formulation is indebted to Christopher Nealon's reading of poetic writing as matter—both as a material product of the capitalism's transitional moments and as what's the matter in times of capitalist crisis. Through its experience with financial and political upheavals, poetry becomes the material medium for registering obliterable life as well as the imagination of textual authority in addressing such crises. Nealon, *Matter of Capital*.

7 Jackson, *Becoming Human*.

8 Nyong'o, "Opacity, Narration, and 'The Fathomless Word.'"

9 Xiang, "Transdualism," 437. Xiang develops the concept of transdualism through a theorization of the hexagram Tai of the *Yi Jing* to offer reasons why the body-of-orifices is neither a dualism of men and women nor a function of social construction. On embodiment and materialist critiques of queer theory in this context, see also Prosser, "Judith Butler"; and Salamon, *Assuming a Body*.

10 Gleeson and O'Rourke, introduction, 9, 18–20. See also Gabriel, "Gender as Accumulation Strategy," for a reading of gender as social form, a subjective imprint of the symbolization of sexual difference that serves as an instrument by which capital compels and exploits labor.

11 For a radical reconceptualization of the material ground for colonialism and its transformation, see Byrd, *Transit of Empire*; Morgensen, *Spaces between Us*; and I. Day, *Alien Capital*. For an exploration of queer theory's turn to objects through Marxist critiques of settler colonialism and financial capitalism,

see Rosenberg, "Molecularization of Sexuality." Emma Heaney's *The New Woman* develops a "materialist trans feminism" (253) that reveals the basis of the social category of woman in historical relations of labor and usefully reminds us that woman has never been a cis category.

12 Mortimer-Sandilands and Erickson, *Queer Ecologies*, introduction, 4. See also Nyong'o, "Back to the Garden," for a queer-materialist approach to ecotheory; and Moore, *Capitalism in the Web of Life*, for a reinterpretation of capitalism as a "world-ecology" that accumulates through a fundamental reorganization of nature.

13 Rosenberg, "Afterword," 283–85.

14 Butler has also commented on the first sense of the material I outline here, most notably in the published exchange between Butler and Nancy Fraser. In "Merely Cultural," Butler responds to a neoconservative Marxist critique that new social movements have produced a cultural politics that is factionalizing, identitarian, and particularistic at the expense of a systemic analysis of the interrelatedness of social and economic conditions. In her response, "Heterosexism, Misrecognition, and Capitalism," Fraser critiques Butler's conflation of the material and the economic to defend her own view that gay men and lesbians mainly suffer from "injustices of misrecognition" that are analytically distinct from "injustices of maldistribution" (280).

15 Butler, *Gender Trouble*, 11.

16 Wendy Brown offers a related formulation of the problem by locating the basis of identity in a sense of woundedness. For Brown, a state of injury is a necessary condition for a state of being. Unlike Butler, however, Brown insists that the ontological problem of the states of injury must be understood in the context of the liberal state's regulation and protection of life. W. Brown, *States of Injury*.

17 Laclau and Mouffe's *Hegemony and Socialist Strategy* is widely seen as a manifesto of post-Marxism. Against the Marxist postulation of the proletariat as a universal subject, Laclau and Mouffe argue that the contemporary world witnesses a proliferation of partial and fragmented identities, each with its own role to play in the pursuit of radical democracy.

18 As David L. Eng and Jasbir K. Puar put it, "The politics of subjectless critique today demands an explicit acknowledgment of how the political referent of queer studies has often presumed an ever-expanding sphere of identifiable subjects laying claim to liberal rights, recognition, normalization, and inclusion." Eng and Puar, "Introduction," 5.

19 Rubin, "Traffic in Women," 35.

20 Hartmann, "Unhappy Marriage," 97. For representative critiques and responses, see Sargent, *Women and Revolution*.

21 J. Brenner, "Review," 698. Some writers propose that Marx has been reckoned to have had too little to say about not gender but social reproduction,

which warrants a rereading of key passages such as chapter 23 of the first volume of *Capital*. See Cammack, "Marx on Social Reproduction"; and Floyd, "Automatic Subjects." An annotated translation of He Yin-Zhen's work is available in L. Liu, Karl, and Ko, *Birth of Chinese Feminism*.

22 Haraway, "'Gender' for a Marxist Dictionary," 131.

23 Engels, *Origin of the Family*, 56.

24 Engels, *Origin of the Family*, 56.

25 See Hennessy, *Profit and Pleasure*; Hennessy, "Thinking Sex Materially"; and Hennessy, "Queer Theory, Left Politics."

26 Hartsock, *Money, Sex, and Power*.

27 Harding, "Why Has the Sex/Gender System," 321–22.

28 Tadiar, *Fantasy-Production*.

29 Contemporary social reproduction theory draws on Lise Vogel's *Marxism and the Oppression of Women* to make this point. See Weeks, *Problem with Work*; S. Ferguson and McNally, "Precarious Migrants"; and Federici, *Revolution at Point Zero*. For an extension of social reproduction theory to queer-materialist analysis, see Sears, "Situating Sexuality." Alan Sears argues that "the construction of the homosexual was made possible by the transformation of social reproduction brought about by the rise of capitalism, including the distinction between the public realm of social production and the private realm of the household. The subsequent history of homosexuality has been organised around changes in the matrix of production and reproduction through processes of capitalist restructuring" (144).

30 Ebert, *Ludic Feminism and After*; and Penny, *After Queer Theory*.

31 Jameson, *Political Unconscious*, 62.

32 Žižek, "Class Struggle or Postmodernism?"

33 In addition to Parker's work considered here, see also Klotz, "Alienation, Labor, and Sexuality."

34 Parker, "Unthinking Sex," 19.

35 Ngai, *Theory of the Gimmick*, 177.

36 C. Cohen, "What Is This Movement," 116.

37 C. Cohen, "Punks, Bulldaggers, and Welfare Queens," 438, 440.

38 On queer identity and mass culture, see Doty, *Making Things Perfectly Queer*. For classic discussions of homonationalism and queer liberalism, see Puar, *Terrorist Assemblages*; and Eng, *Feeling of Kinship*. For a superb analysis of pinkwashing and homonationalism in the context of Singapore's creative-economy discourse, see Treat, "Rise and Fall of Homonationalism." Rahul Rao's *Out of Time* powerfully reveals the workings of what he calls "homocapitalism," a system in which international financial institutions and development industries actively adopt LGBT-friendly initiatives to demonstrate their commitment to a kinder, more inclusive and humane approach to economic growth (136).

39 Duggan, "New Homonormativity," 179, 178. For a useful historicization of homonormative formations that organized LGBT people into polarities such as "the same-sex married couple vs. the 'welfare queen'"; "the gay/lesbian consumer-citizen vs. the poor queer"; and "the gay gentrifier vs. the 'dangerous' other," see Weiss, "Queer Politics in Neoliberal Times," 107.

40 Hemmings, "Sexuality, Subjectivity . . . and Political Economy?," 128.

41 Aizura, "Trans Feminine Value," 133.

42 Bogdan Popa's work stands as a significant exception and counter to this trend. Rather than seeing the industrial mode of production as historically obsolete or analytically superseded by Foucauldian biopolitics and immaterial labor, Popa finds the productive body and Communist sexualities—as theorized by eastern European Marxist writers—to be precisely what contemporary queer theory needs in order to avoid the pitfalls of gender-focused analysis. Popa, *De-centering Queer Theory*.

43 See Lukács, *History and Class Consciousness*; and Marcuse, *Eros and Civilization*.

44 Other works exploring these connections include Alderson, *Sex, Needs and Queer Culture*; Bao, *Queer China*; Cover, "Material/Queer Theory"; Drucker, *Warped*; D. Evans, *Sexual Citizenship*; Henderson, *Love and Money*; Holcomb, *Claude McKay*; Morton, *Material Queer*; Rosenberg and Villarejo, "Queer Studies"; Sears, "Queer Anti-capitalism"; Wesling, "Queer Value"; A. Wong, "Queering the Quality of Desire"; Yapp, *Minor China*; and Zavarzadeh, Ebert, and Morton, *Marxism, Queer Theory, Gender*.

45 Hardt and Negri, *Empire*.

46 McRuer, "As Good as It Gets."

47 Lewis, *Politics of Everybody*, 91, 202.

48 See, among others, Meyer, "Intersectional Analysis"; Camfield, "Theoretical Foundations"; and Valocchi, "Class-Inflected Nature of Gay Identity."

49 Muñoz, *Disidentifications*.

50 R. Ferguson, *Aberrations in Black*.

51 Brim, *Poor Queer Studies*.

52 See Lanser, *Sexuality of History*, esp. ch. 4; Padgug, "Sexual Matters"; and Escoffier, "Political Economy of the Closet."

53 D'Emilio, "Capitalism and Gay Identity," 102. Other early theorizations of this connection include Greenberg and Bystryn, "Capitalism, Bureaucracy, and Male Homosexuality." D'Emilio's thesis has shaped subsequent discussions of the connections among US labor history, working-class politics, and sexual minorities, including M. Frank, *Out in the Union*; Tinkcom, *Working like a Homosexual*; Valocchi, "Capitalism and Gay Identities"; and Wolf, *Sexuality and Socialism*. Outside the US context, Sophie Chamas has examined how Lebanese revolutionary-socialist organizations produced a Marxist theoretical discourse of queer utopia. Chamas, "Reading Marx in Beirut."

54 Martin Duberman's *Stonewall* is arguably the work that cemented the event's reputation as the birth of the gay liberation movement. See also Adam, *Rise of a Gay and Lesbian Movement*. For a critique of Stonewall as a site of historical metalepsis, an effect that was miscast as a cause in global histories of sexuality, see Arondekar, "Sex of History."

55 Chauncey, *Gay New York*; Manalansan, *Global Divas*; and Muñoz, *Disidentifications*.

56 The idea of the "spread" has been taken up by Altman, "Global Gaze/Global Gays." For a dissenting view, see Rofel, *Desiring China*, 89–91. For a different intervention through the concept of "glocalqueering," see Lim, *Brown Boys and Rice Queens*.

57 J. Ho, "Is Global Governance Bad."

58 As Martin F. Manalansan usefully reminds us, "In the shadows of Stonewall lurk multiple engagements and negotiations. Conversations about globalizing tendencies of gay identity, politics, and culture are disrupted by local dialogues of people who speak from the margins." Manalansan, "In the Shadows of Stonewall," 436.

59 Symons and Altman, "International Norm Polarization," 65.

60 Kahan, "Conjectures on the Sexual World-System," 327.

61 Drucker, *Warped*, 84.

62 For an example of this position, see Arruzza, "Gender as Social Temporality," which critiques Butler's theory of gender performativity as an abstract temporality without history.

63 Nussbaum, "Professor of Parody," 38.

64 Floyd, *Reification of Desire*, 2.

65 Goldstein, *Post-Marxist Theory*, 73, 72.

66 Butler, *Undoing Gender*, 29.

67 This view reflects Butler's revision of their argument: "I have also made use of psychoanalysis to curb the occasional voluntarism of my view of performativity without thereby undermining a more general theory of agency. *Gender Trouble* sometimes reads as if gender is simply a self-invention or that the psychic meaning of a gendered presentation might be read directly off its surface. . . . Moreover, my theory sometimes waffles between understanding performativity as linguistic and casting it as theatrical." Butler, "Preface 1999," in *Gender Trouble*, xxv.

68 Butler, *Undoing Gender*, 19.

69 Butler further develops these ideas in *Senses of the Subject*, 149–70.

70 Butler, *Undoing Gender*, 1.

71 Butler, *Undoing Gender*, 18.

72 In *The Force of Nonviolence*, Butler further develops the argument for the importance of social bonds and interdependency for understanding a *nonindividualist* account of equality.

73 Butler, *Undoing Gender*, 20. Rosa Lee considers Butler's theory of gender performativity to have provided a scientific foundation for a "transsexual Marxism." Lee argues that Butler "inaugurated, or at least consolidated and proposed, a scientific paradigm shift in the analysis of gender, a shift analogous to the shifts inaugurated by Copernicus and Marx. . . . Because it is her materialist assertion that not only gender but the sexed body is social rather than natural . . . that opens up the possibility of us seriously thinking through both gender and sex transition on a personal level—and the possibility of collective transition to communism as a process of undoing, remaking, or even substantively abolishing gender." R. Lee, "Judith Butler's Scientific Revolution," 63, 65–66.

74 For explorations of dispossession in Indigenous studies, see Byrd, Goldstein, and Reddy, "Economies of Dispossession."

75 Tilley, Kumar, and Cowan, "Introduction," 420.

76 D. Harvey, *New Imperialism*, 153.

77 Butler and Athanasiou, *Dispossession*, 3. The quotations are from a part of the text by Butler alone.

78 Butler and Athanasiou, *Dispossession*, 20.

79 Marx, *Economic and Philosophic Manuscripts of 1844*, 141.

80 Butler, "Inorganic Body," 15.

81 Ricardo, *Principles of Political Economy*.

82 Although Butler does not normally name Marx or Marxists as their interlocutors, the theory of gender performativity in *Gender Trouble*, which argues that gender acquires a naturalized presence through a substantializing grammar of the heterosexual matrix, is clearly indebted to Lukács's concept of reification, which explains how external social relations come to be perceived as the inherent attributes of the people involved with them. Louis Althusser's essay "Ideology and Ideological State Apparatuses" provides the theory of interpellation that Butler reworks into a new understanding of the paradox of *assujetissement* (subjection/subjectivation)—the process whereby a subject comes into being in and through its subjection to power.

CHAPTER THREE. THE SUBSUMPTION OF LITERATURE

A portion of chapter 3 appeared as "Lu Xun's Literary Revolution in Chinese Marxism," in *After Marx: Literature, Theory, and Value in the Twenty-First Century*, edited by Colleen Lye and Christopher Nealon (Cambridge, UK: Cambridge University Press, 2022), 161–75.

1 Cai, *Revolution and Its Narratives*.

2 Bao, *Queer Comrades*.

3 Huang Y. and Pan, *Xing zhi bian*. For a broad survey of new forms of sexual thought and gender discourses since the 1949 revolution, see H. Evans, *Women and Sexuality in China*.

4 Indeed, this tradition is so strong that it led Gloria Davies, Christian Sorace, and Haun Saussy—in a recent special issue of *Critical Inquiry* on aesthetic practice and the Chinese state that contained a substantial discussion of Lu Xun—to offer these remarks: "The CCP's reflexive awareness of the relationship between political power and aesthetic plasticity poses a complex challenge for critical theoretical approaches predicated on exposing and unmasking how power operates in general. If the discovery that art and language inherently interpellate us into political formations is supposed to be a mark of the post-structural turn, then Chinese subjects needed no turning directions because the political was always already aesthetic in its conceptualization and practice." G. Davies, Sorace, and Saussy, "Political Enchantment," 481.

5 For a different interpretation of Lu Xun's work as a transformative engagement with China's past rather than its total rejection, see E. Cheng, *Literary Remains*. On Chinese Marxist historians' efforts in the 1920s and 1930s to domesticate the concept of feudalism as a feature of China's own history, see Dirlik, "Universalisation of a Concept." Lin Chun notes that in Chinese Marxist theory, "'feudalism,' adapted from European and Japanese usage, is a politically and linguistically handy label for denoting China's rural social relations. Whether elements of a typical feudal system had ever developed in China is largely irrelevant, insofar as the term signals the country's major social-class structure for revolutionary mobilization." Lin C., *China and Global Capitalism*, 20.

6 T. Chow, *May Fourth Movement*, 269–88; and K. Liu, *Aesthetics and Marxism*, 7–9. For a contemporary Chinese iteration of this view that casts Marxism as a cultural revolution of everyday life and a localization of the national imaginary through literature, see Cai, *Revolution and Its Narratives*.

7 Jameson, "Third-World Literature," 69. For Chinese responses to Jameson's reading of Lu Xun, see Gu, "Lu Xun, Jameson."

8 Barmé, "True Story of Lu Xun."

9 G. Davies, "Chinese Literary Studies," 75. Lu Xun's own discussion of Nietzsche can be found in two essays, "Wenhua pianzhi lun" (On cultural extremism) and "Moluo shili shuo" (On the power of Mara poetry), both published in Japan in 1908. For a discussion of Nietzsche's influence on Lu Xun, see Cheung, *Lu Xun*; Mabel Lee, "From Chuang-tzu to Nietzsche"; and K. Wong and Tu, "Retroactive Lyricism/Eternal Return."

10 Qu, *Lu Xun zagan xuanji*.

11 Takeuchi, *What Is Modernity?*, 51.

12 Wang Xiaoming, "Manifesto for Cultural Studies," 282.

13 Goldman, "Political Use of Lu Xun," 446.

14 Mao, "Xin minzhu zhuyi lun," 920.

15 Yu, *China in Ten Words*, 98.

16 G. Davies, "Lu Xun in 1966," 518; and Mao, "Mao Zedong gei Jiang Qing de xin."

17 Goldman, "Political Use of Lu Xun," 451. For a more recent account of the Maoist appropriations of Lu Xun, see Lovell, "Afterlife of Lu Xun."

18 G. Davies, *Lu Xun's Revolution*, 5. On the debates between Lu Xun and the Communists between 1927 and 1932, see Sylvia Chan, "Realism or Socialist Realism?"

19 The identification of 1927 as the date of Lu Xun's "Marxist turn" was established by Li Zehou's authoritative study. See Li Z., "Lu Xun sixiang de fazhan," 455.

20 Mills, "Lu Xun," 210.

21 On the importance of Lu Xun in contemporary Chinese political and economic debates, see X. Zhong, "Who Is Afraid of Lu Xun?"

22 Wang H., *End of the Revolution*, 191–210.

23 Wang Xiaoming, "Introduction," 737.

24 Qian, "Refusing to Forget," 292.

25 Nan, "Difficult Breakthrough," 196.

26 For this reading of Lukács, see Esty and Lye, "Peripheral Realisms Now," 277. In a different context, Anna Kornbluh also draws on Marxist theory to suggest why we need to turn away from the traditional definition of realism as mimesis (representation of the existing world). In Kornbluh's view, realism "drafts and constructs worlds": it "designs and erects socialities, imagines the grounds of collectivities . . . [and] . . . modulates institutions and productions beyond the scope of the given." Kornbluh, "Realist Blueprint," 199.

27 On Lu Xun as a realist writer, see D. Wang, *Fictional Realism*; M. Anderson, *Limits of Realism*; Lyell, *Lu Hsun's Vision of Reality*; and Button, *Configurations of the Real*.

28 L. Lee, *Voices from the Iron House*, 49–68. See also X. Tang, "Lu Xun's 'Diary of a Madman'"; L. Liu, *Translingual Practice*; and Shih, *Lure of the Modern*. For a revisionist account that rejects both categories, see S. Sun, *Beyond the Iron House*.

29 Shih, *Lure of the Modern*, 74.

30 Jones, *Developmental Fairy Tales*, 34. On Lu Xun's relation to evolutionary science and Darwinism, see also Pusey, *Lu Xun and Evolution*, 37–66; L. Liu, "Life as Form"; and Qin Wang, "Literary Evolutionism and Its Discontents." A new translation of Lu Xun's essay "Ren zhi lishi" ["The Evolution of Men"] (1933) is available in Lu Xun, *Jottings under Lamplight*, 177–78.

31 Chen D., "On Literary Revolution," 141.

32 See G. Davies, *Lu Xun's Revolution*, 170–75; W. Wong, *Politics and Literature in Shanghai*, 9–38; Pickowicz, *Marxist Literary Thought in China*, 91–94; and Yin, *Politics of Art*.

33 Meisner, *Li Ta-chao*, 91. Li's essay was originally published in *Xin Qingnian* (New youth) in November 1919.

34 K. Liu, *Aesthetics and Marxism*, 2.

35 K. Liu, *Aesthetics and Marxism*, xii.

36 Pickowicz, *Marxist Literary Thought in China*, 171.

37 On the relationship between China's language reforms and modernization, see Tsu, *Kingdom of Characters*.
38 Barlow, *In the Event of Women*, ch. 2.
39 Lu Xun, "Guanyu xin wenzi" (On new writing), 165. For critical commentary, see Y. Zhong, *Chinese Grammatology*, 16, 69; Mullaney, *Chinese Typewriter*, 13; and Hill, "New Script."
40 Lu Xun, "Nahan zixu."
41 For discussion of this incident's impact on Lu Xun's thinking, see R. Chow, *Primitive Passions*, 4–9; L. Lee, *Voices from the Iron House*, 17–19; L. Liu, *Translingual Practice*, 62–64; and Shih, *Lure of the Modern*, 78.
42 Lu Xun, *Diary of a Madman*, 23–24.
43 Lu Xun, *Diary of a Madman*, 29.
44 Lu Xun, *Diary of a Madman*, 29.
45 Lu Xun, *Diary of a Madman*, 32.
46 Lu Xun, *Diary of a Madman*, 41, 30.
47 Gu, *Modern Chinese Literature*, 23.
48 Rojas, *Homesickness*, 98.
49 Rojas, *Homesickness*, 98.
50 Lu Xun, *Diary of a Madman*, 41.
51 For an innovative reading of Lu Xun's complex modernist configurations of his characters' relationships to ideologies, see Kaldis, "Aesthetic Cognition."
52 Stuckey, "Female Relations"; and T. Tang, "Two Portrayals of Chinese Women."
53 L. Lee, *Voices from the Iron House*, 248.
54 P. Zhu, *Gender and Subjectivities*, 168.
55 McDougall, *Love Letters and Privacy*, 18.
56 See C. Brown, "Woman as Trope"; Stephen Chan, "Language of Despair"; Chang, *Shishang xiandai xing*, 300–303; E. Cheng, *Literary Remains*, 81–110; Chien, "Feminism and China's New 'Nora'"; M. Chu, "Lu Xun's Women Characters"; Feng, *New Woman*, 40–59; Xia Li, "Nora and Her Sisters"; and P. Zhu, *Gender and Subjectivities*, 45–58.
57 E. Cheng, "Gendered Spectacles."
58 Heinrich, "Zoology," 446.
59 For a different interpretation that similarly places the story (translated as "The Misanthrope") in the context of Lu Xun's views on evolutionary biology, see Jones, *Developmental Fairy Tales*, 63–65.
60 Lu Xun, "Lun zhaoxiang zhilei," 187.
61 D. Wang, "'Popular Literature and National Representation,'" 210. See also D. Wang, "Impersonating China."
62 Lu Xun is credited as the cultural critic who introduced Henrik Ibsen to China, having mentioned the Norwegian playwright in "On the Power of Mara Poetry" and "On Cultural Extremism" in 1908. In the 1930s, under Qu Qiubai's influence, Marxist interpretations of Ibsen as a critic of capitalist

exploitation of women and minorities became mainstream in China. Despite alternative proposals that Ibsen's individualism was incompatible with socialist collectivism, Lu Xun's understanding of Ibsenism as a materialist account of women's oppression defined the tenets of Chinese Marxism through the 1950s. See Tam, *Chinese Ibsenism*, 160–64.

63   Quotations from "What Happens after Nora Walks Out" are from the translation in Lu Xun, *Jottings under Lamplight*, here from p. 256. An earlier translation of this speech is available in Barlow, *Power of Weakness*, 84–92.

64   Lu Xun, *Jottings under Lamplight*, 257.

65   Lu Xun, *Jottings under Lamplight*, 258.

66   Lu Xun, *Jottings under Lamplight*, 258.

67   Lu Xun reiterates this view in a 1933 essay, "On Women's Liberation" ("Guanyu funü jiefang").

68   Lu Xun, *Jottings under Lamplight*, 260.

69   Lu Xun, *Jottings under Lamplight*, 256.

70   Althusser, *Reading Capital*, 21–24.

71   L. Liu, *Translingual Practice*, 37.

72   Various critics have described Sister Xianglin as a madwoman and a gendered variant of the Madman in the 1918 story. See Fitzgerald, "'Diary of a Madwoman'"; and Hockx, "Mad Women and Mad Men."

73   Lu Xun, *Diary of a Madman*, 236.

74   Lu Xun, *Diary of a Madman*, 225.

75   Lu Xun, *Diary of a Madman*, 222.

76   Lu Xun, *Diary of a Madman*, 241.

77   R. Chow, *Woman and Chinese Modernity*, 110–11.

78   Lu Xun, *Diary of a Madman*, 223.

79   Lu Xun, *Diary of a Madman*, 48, 173, 360.

80   Lu Xun, *Diary of a Madman*, 221.

81   Chang, "Asia as Counter-method."

82   Takeuchi, *What Is Modernity?*, 49.

83   On Takeuchi's critique of modernist writers in general, see Takeuchi, *What Is Modernity?*, 30, 40. On Takeuchi as a reader of Sōseki, see Tansman and Vincent, "Sōseki Great and Small," 9; and Harb, "Penning the Mad Man," 99, 107.

84   Veg, "On the Margins of Modernity," 36.

85   Von Kowallis, "Takeuchi's Lu Xun/China's Takeuchi."

86   K.-H. Chen and Chua, "Introduction."

87   K.-H. Chen, *Asia as Method*, 21.

88   In 2001, shortly after the journal's launch, the prominent queer activist Wang Ping published "Why Inter-Asia? The Tongzhi Movement," a position paper on the relationship between LGBT movements and the inter-Asia cultural studies movement. A special issue titled "Global Queer, Local Theories," edited by Wei-cheng Chu and Fran Martin, appeared as *Inter-Asia Cultural*

Studies 8, no. 4 (December 2007). Other significant queer projects in *Inter-Asia Cultural Studies* include Chang, "Taiwan Queer Valentines" (1996); F. Martin, "Perfect Lie" (2003); and Aizura, "Of Borders and Homes" (2006). For a more recent assessment of the interreferencing practices of Asia as method, see Tan, "Networking Asia Pacific."

89 "As I see it, one of the lasting legacies of this period is the installation of the anticommunism-pro-Americanism structure in the capitalist zone of East Asia, whose overwhelming consequences are still with us today." K.-H. Chen, *Asia as Method*, 7. Chen describes this problem variously as "a set of cultural forms and structures of feelings" (111), a "structure of sentiment" (119, 124, 133, in dialogue with Ding Naifei's coinage of the term but also with reference to Raymond Williams), a "psychic structure" (79, in the context of Frantz Fanon), and "a structure of the cultural imaginary" (108, 111).

90 K.-H. Chen, *Asia as Method*, 65–68.

91 K.-H. Chen, *Asia as Method*, 72.

92 In "Imagining Asia," Viren Murthy traces Takeuchi, Wang Hui, and K.-H. Chen as representative figures forming a common intellectual lineage of Marxism in Asia, while criticizing Chen for misinterpreting Marxist conceptions of class. See also Murthy, "Resistance to Modernity."

93 See Bernards, "Malaysia as Method"; Dutton, "Cultural Revolution as Method"; De Kloet, Chow, and Chong, *Trans-Asia as Method*; and the essays in the recent special issue of *Prism*, "Method as Method," edited by Carlos Rojas.

CHAPTER FOUR. THE SUBSUMPTION OF THE COLD WAR

An earlier version of this chapter appeared as "Cold War as Method," *Prism: Theory and Modern Chinese Literature* 16, no. 2 (2019): 408–31.

1 D. Harvey, *New Imperialism*, 39; Ren, *Mao Zedong xin minzhu zhuyi*, 104.

2 Wen, *Ten Crises*, 12.

3 J. Chen, *Mao's China*, 240.

4 Deng X., "Zenme huifu nongye shengchan," 323.

5 Hung, *China Boom*, 53.

6 The literature is too vast to cite here, but some representative works include T. Day and Liem, *Cultures at War*; Fu, "Cold War Politics"; Chris Lee, "Rhythm and the Cold War Imaginary"; S. Lee, *Cinema and the Cultural Cold War*; Lee P. and Wong, *Lengzhan yu Xianggang dianying*; Taylor and Xu, *Chineseness and the Cold War*; L. Wong, *Transpacific Attachments*; and Xiaojue Wang, *Modernity with a Cold War Face*. Several major international conferences held in recent years reflect this trend: "Sights and Sounds of the Cold War in the Sinophone World," Washington University in St. Louis, March 25–26, 2017; "Unlearning Cold War Narratives: Toward Alternative Understandings of the Cold War," National University of Singapore,

May 27–28, 2016; "Literature and Cultural Translation in China, Hong Kong, and Taiwan during the Cold War," Lingnan University, March 6–7, 2015; and "Transpacific China in the Cold War," University of Texas at Austin, April 18–19, 2013.

7 In addition to Kuan-Hsing Chen's work discussed in the previous chapter, see Y. Chen, "What the 'Third World' Means"; G. Sun, "How Does Asia Mean?"; Chao, "Languages of Social Movements"; Dai, *After the Post–Cold War*; and Wang H., *End of the Revolution*.

8 The process was started by the June 15th North-South Joint Declaration in June 2000 and reaffirmed by the Panmunjom Declaration for Peace, Prosperity and Unification of the Korean Peninsula in April 2018. For recent reflections and assessments, see Kim, "Cultural Question"; and Moonyoung Lee, "Landscape of the Minds." For the concept of the division system, see Paik, *Division System in Crisis*. We Jung Yi has developed the innovative concept of "worm-time" to describe the "trans-memory" of the Cold War among those living in the shadow of the unfinished war. For Yi, South Korea's culture industry—fiction, movie blockbusters, and even internet "webtoons" (web cartoons)—encodes somewhat obsessive attempts to work through the traumatic origins of the nation's founding, while offering a mode of collective remembering in the absence of closure, reconciliation, and international justice. See Yi, "Division Literature."

9 Jameson, "Actually Existing Marxism," 15.

10 Flair Donglai Shi offers a compelling intervention within current debates on the sinophone, a concept that has been deployed by scholars such as Shu-mei Shih in support of the localization of Taiwan and other Sinitic-language cultures and communities against Sinocentrism. While Shi acknowledges the value of Shih's antidiaspora politics, he contends that an exclusive conceptualization of the sinophone vis-à-vis the PRC overlooks the significance of the history of the Cold War and can easily get mixed up with anti-PRC sentiments—in other words, sinophone becomes sinophobe. F. Shi, "Reconsidering Sinophone Studies."

11 Cronin, *World the Cold War Made*, 115.

12 The point I am making stems from a broader conversation about the conditions of knowledge production that began with Paul A. Cohen's call (in *Discovering History in China*) to develop a China-centered alternative to the "impact-response" framework, the critique of the area studies model in China studies, and the invention of "Asian studies in Asia." Specifically in the context of Cold War studies, many interventionist works have already reconfigured Asia as the protagonist of history. See, among others, J. Chen, *Mao's China*; Masuda, *Cold War Crucible*; Szonyi, *Cold War Island*; H. Liu, Szonyi, and Zheng, *Cold War in Asia*; and Jager and Mitter, *Ruptured Histories*.

13 See Roh, Huang, and Niu, *Techno-Orientalism*, for an analysis of the construction of Asians as cogs of hyperproduction and dehumanized labor—the
antithesis of Western liberal humanism.

14 Adorno, "Cultural Criticism and Society," 34.

15 Cumings, *Parallax Visions*, 45.

16 Fukuyama, *End of History*, 211.

17 In "The 'Post-colonialism' of Cold War Discourse," William Pietz argues
that while the primary theoretical anchor of Cold War discourse is the specter of totalitarianism, it gained wide acceptance among the general public
through a conflation of Communism and fascism, despite the fact that
Communism emerged historically as an antifascist movement. Pietz further
shows that this picture of totalitarianism actually derived its vocabulary
from an earlier colonialist fantasy about totalitarianism outside of Europe,
such as the so-called tribal societies of uncivilized peoples and "oriental
despotism."

18 Kwon, *Other Cold War*, 19.

19 As Christine Hong and other scholars have argued, the Cold War in Asia has
always been a product of US militarism, even though some of the events have
presented themselves as "local" struggles against Communism or colonialism. "For the inhabitants of Asia and the Pacific, the postwar Pax Americana,
the American military 'peace' that settled the region in the wake of Japan's
defeat, would introduce an anti-Communist necropolitical order in which
unfreedom would be presented as freedom, democratization as democracy,
and militarism as the basis for life itself." Hong, *Violent Peace*, 3.

20 H. Lin, *Accidental State*.

21 Political parties in Taiwan are divided into two color-coded blocs. The pan-
Green camp supports Taiwanese independence, while the pan-Blue camp
favors greater economic linkage with the PRC. On the Club 51 phenomenon,
see K.-H. Chen, *Asia as Method*, 161–73.

22 P. Anderson, "Stand-Off in Taiwan."

23 Pletsch, "Three Worlds."

24 Pletsch, "Three Worlds," 577–78.

25 R. Chow, introduction, 3.

26 Sakai, *End of Pax Americana*, 91–128.

27 G. Walker, "Accumulation of Difference."

28 *Xiao ao jianghu* was first serialized in *Ming Pao* from April 20, 1967, to
October 12, 1969. It was also serialized in Singapore's *Shin Min Daily News*
(*Xin ming ribao*). In 1973 Jin Yong announced that he would "seal his
pen" (*fengbi*) and spend the rest of his career revising his published novels
instead of writing new ones, a decision that resulted in multiple editions of
all of his works. The editions that appeared after 2000, in particular, feature
radical changes. In this chapter I cite the most commonly read and histori-

cally influential version (usually referred to as *liuxing ban*, or the popular edition), published by Yuanliu Press in Taiwan.

29 The film was an enormous success at the box office (grossing HK$34,460,000) and became an "instant classic" in Hong Kong cinema. Dou, *Jian xiao jianghu*, 130.

30 On Tsui as a technological innovator of Hong Kong martial arts cinema, see Chen Mo, *Zhongguo wuxia dianying shi*, 271; Jia, *Zhongguo wuxia dianying shi*, 103; and Schroeder, *Tsui Hark's Zu*.

31 Teo, *Chinese Martial Arts Cinema*, 164–69.

32 Jin Yong, *Xiao ao jianghu*, 4:1279.

33 Jin Yong, *Xiao ao jianghu*, 3:1255.

34 Using *Swordsman II* as a key example, Travis S. K. Kong emphasizes that the growing "gay visibility" in Hong Kong since the 1990s is indeed a contradictory phenomenon that both offers new cultural icons for LGBTQ youths, charting new paths of recognition and civil rights, and transforms subversive resistance to capitalist consumption. Contesting that queer is always polysemic, Kong argues that *Swordsman II* succeeds in creating "a space for the visibility of gay sexuality on screen" while following "the capitalist logic of profit making." Kong, "Queering Masculinity," 57–58, 68.

35 *China News*, "Xu Ke toulu Lin Qingxia"; *Entertainment*, "Jin Yong biaoshi bu xihuan"; and *Entertainment*, "Wei shenme Lin Qingxia."

36 To date, the story has also been adapted for television eight times, with both male and female actors portraying Asia: in 1984 (by Television Broadcast Limited, Hong Kong), 1985 (by Taiwan Television Limited), 1996 (by TVB, Hong Kong), 2000 (by China Television Company, Ltd., Taiwan; and by Mediacorp, Singapore), 2001 (by China Central Television, China), 2013 (by Hunan Satellite TV, China), and 2018 (by Youku, China). Other adaptations, including an earlier film version (1978, Shaw Brothers, Hong Kong), radio shows (1981, Hong Kong), a musical (2007, Hong Kong), comics, music, and video games, have further consolidated the story's iconic status in Chinese popular culture.

37 Zhou, "Dongfang Bubai, Online Fandom," 113.

38 Leung, "Homosexuality and Queer Aesthetics," 522. See also Leung, "Unsung Heroes."

39 See, for example, Marchetti, "Hong Kong New Wave," 109. For a compelling reading of *Swordsman II* as expressing utopian longings for an unknown and unknowable future beyond 1997, see Stephen Chan, "Figures of Hope." For a brilliant interpretation of Tsui's work as part of a "kung fu cultural imaginary" that denies its own modernity in order to intervene in Hong Kong's anxiety-ridden return to China, see S.-L. Li, "Kung Fu."

40 Chou, *Tongzhi lun*, 299–302.

41 See Leung, *Undercurrents*, 71–77, for a powerful reading of the film's transsexual agency and self-fashioning. For an alternative argument for the coexistence

of prohibited same-sex desire and naturalized heterosexual romance in this film, see Yau C., *Xingbie guangying*.

42 Gina Marchetti characterizes Lin and Maggie Cheung as the female queer icons that are counterparts to Leslie Cheung, and the three as the "queer connections" of Hong Kong New Wave cinema. Marchetti, "Hong Kong New Wave," 109–10. Travis S. K. Kong similarly emphasizes that Lin launched her career through cross-dressing roles; *Swordsman II*, in particular, established Lin as "Hong Kong's Marlene Dietrich." Kong, "Queering Masculinity," 69.

43 Zhou, "Dongfang Bubai, Online Fandom," 111. See also Teo, "Tsui Hark," 153–54, for an analysis of the importance of Lin's performance as the androgynous Dongfang Bubai in the creation of "the Tsui Hark cult," which Stephen Teo sees as indicative of the fusion of gender fluidity and national identity.

44 For a discussion of these allusions, see Chen F., "Xiao'ao jianghu zhong de yishu yu renwu." In the afterword Jin Yong claims that the novel is not an allusion to the Cultural Revolution but merely an attempt to depict human nature in Chinese society. Jin Yong, *Xiao ao jianghu*, 4:1682. This disclaimer is unpersuasive and certainly not how the novel has been received by the reading public.

45 The original Chinese (as spoken by Asia in the film) is as follows: "江山如此多娇／引无数英雄竞折腰."

46 In reference to Asia in Jin Yong's original text, I retain the use of *he/him/his* pronouns. In reference to the film version, I use *she/her/hers* pronouns in contexts where the post-metamorphosis Asia embraces a female identity, and *they/them/their* pronouns when referring to the character in general.

47 X. Chen, *Staging Chinese Revolution*, 64.

48 Jin Yong, *Xiao ao jianghu*, 4:1265.

49 Further information on this story can be found in various biographies and critical studies of Jin Yong. See, for example, Zhang G., *Jin Yong yu Ming Pao chuanqi*, 116–49; Sun Yixue, *Jin Yong zhuan*, 124–36; and P. Liu, *Stateless Subjects*, 141–48.

50 *Ta Kung Pao* 大公報, October 28, 1964.

51 For a detailed account of the discrepancies between the historical diffusion of Manichaeism into China and Jin Yong's fictional representations, see Lieu, "Fact or Fiction," 62–63; and Lin W., "Jin Yong bi xia de Mingjiao," 66–67.

52 Jin Yong, *Yi tian tu long ji*, 1017.

53 Schein, *Minority Rules*.

CHAPTER FIVE. THE SUBSUMPTION OF SEXUALITY

An earlier version of this chapter appeared as "Thinking Gender in the Age of the Beijing Consensus," *Feminist Studies* 47, no. 2 (2021): 341–71.

1 T. Wei, "Look at the Beijing Conference."

2 Rofel, *Desiring China*; and Engebretsen, Schroeder, and Bao, *Queer/Tongzhi China*.

3 The historian Wenqing Kang has argued that the much lauded "decriminalization" and "depathologization" of homosexuality in China are mischaracterizations of the problem because technically, homosexuality was never criminalized and medicalized in China. Instead, the Chinese state from the Qing to the Republican and PRC periods has consistently denied the existence of homosexuals. For this reason, male same-sex relations were prosecuted under the name of "hooliganism" (*liumang zui*) or social disturbance, but never under the category of homosexuality as such. According to Kang, although the 1997 decriminalization of homosexuality was hailed as a legal milestone, it was really a secondary by-product of a broader effort to standardize the Chinese legal system after the end of the Cultural Revolution. Similarly, the removal of the category of homosexuality from CCMD-III in 2001 was the paradoxical result of Chinese psychiatric professionals' efforts to meet international standards of medical practice. Kang, "Decriminalization and Depathologization of Homosexuality in China." For a comprehensive analysis of the status of homosexuality in Chinese law, see Guo, *Zhongguo fa shiye de tongxinglian*.

4 "Women hold up half of the sky" was the slogan of the Communist Party-led women's liberation movement during the Mao Zedong era. For a study of the origins and mutations of the slogan, see Zhong, "Four Interpretations for the Slogan."

5 Beauvoir, *Second Sex*, 281. For an account of feminist reformulations of John Money and Robert Stoller, see Germon, *Gender*. See also Edholm, Harris, and Young, "Conceptualizing Women."

6 Rubin, "Traffic in Women," 34. It is worth mentioning that *sex* in Rubin's sex/gender system refers to sexual practice rather than the distinction between male and female. This understanding forms the basis of her theoretical disagreements with Judith Butler, who preserves the semantic ambiguity of *sex* (as both gender and sexuality) as the point of departure for a different kind of feminist inquiry. See Rubin, "Interview," 67.

7 I discuss these debates in chapter 2.

8 Nietzsche, quoted in Butler, *Gender Trouble*, 34.

9 Sedgwick, *Epistemology of the Closet*, 23.

10 Stryker and Currah, "Introduction," 1.

11 Jarrín, "Untranslatable Subjects."

12 See Love, "Rethinking Sex." This collection of essays conveys a sense of how Rubin's methodological distinction between sex and gender has given rise to new ways of thinking across different disciplines about sex radicalism, crip sexuality, Black feminism, and sex trafficking.

13 Haraway, "'Gender' for a Marxist Dictionary," 130.

14 The translation of *queer* (and queer theory) has been a particularly thorny example. For recent scholarship exploring the intersection between the translation of *queer* and political economy, see Baer and Kaindl, *Queering Translation, Translating the Queer*; Epstein and Gillett, *Queer in Translation*; Ruvalcaba, *Translating the Queer*; and Savci, *Queer in Translation*.

15 Butler, "Gender in Translation," 9. While Butler often worries that the translation and dissemination of (anglophone) gender theory might become a form of cultural imperialism, we should also remind ourselves that such cross-cultural dialogues, as J. Keith Vincent wisely put it in the case of Takemura Kazuko, Butler's Japanese translator, also instantiate modes of resistance and cultural activism. Vincent, "Takemura Kazuko," 255.

16 See Bunch and Fried, "Beijing '95"; E. Chow, "Making Waves, Moving Mountains"; and Goetz and Baden, "Who Needs [Sex]."

17 Scott, "Gender Studies and Translation Studies," 357–59; see also Scott, "Fictitious Unities."

18 Perreau, *Queer Theory*, ch. 1; and K. Harvey, *Intercultural Movements*.

19 F. Xu, "Chinese Feminisms Encounter International Feminisms," 203. On the 1995 Beijing conference as the starting point of gender mainstreaming in China, see Liu B., "95 shijie funü dahui he Zhongguo funü yanjiu"; Lin C., "Finding a Language," 12; and Spakowski, "Socialist Feminism in Postsocialist China," 566.

20 Hershatter and Wang, "Chinese History," 1413–14.

21 On the phenomenon of Chinese same-sex couples who become parents through assisted reproductive technology and transnational surrogacy, see W. Wei, "Queering the Rise of China." For a consideration of the reverse process, whereby the global North extracts the labor of assisted reproduction and gestational surrogacy in China, India, and eastern Europe to extend life, see Floyd, "Automatic Subjects"; and Pande, *Wombs in Labor*.

22 A transcript of this session is available in Huang Y. and Pan, *Jidian yu fansi*, 208–19.

23 For a detailed discussion of this conundrum, see P. Liu, *Queer Marxism in Two Chinas*, 41–48.

24 Chou, *Houzhimin tongzhi*, 319–47.

25 Vitiello, *Libertine's Friend*; and Ning, "Yangqi tongxinglian, fankai xin nanse."

26 Foucault, *History of Sexuality*, 23. Discussions of the emergence of homosexuality (*tongxing ai*) through sexological and psychiatric writings in Republican China include Dikötter, *Sex, Culture and Modernity*; Fang, *Tongxinglian zai zhongguo*; Sang, *Emerging Lesbian*; and Kang, *Obsession*. For a different account that traces the regulation of modern sexuality in China back to the eighteenth century, see Sommer, *Sex, Law, and Society*.

27 Transgender activism and social organizations, such as T/G Butterfly Garden, have flourished in Taiwan since the 1990s. See Ho C., *Kua xingbie*; Chu W., *Pipan de xing zhengzhi*; and F. Martin and Ho, "Trans/Asia, Trans/gender." For a discussion of the influence of Western and Taiwanese trans discourses on the PRC, see A. Huang, "On the Surface," 116–19. For studies of transgender subjects in the PRC, see Fang, *Zhongguo bianxingren xianxiang*; and S. Ye, "Reconstructing the Transgendered Self."

28 Wang Z., "'Nüxing yishi,' 'shehui xingbie yishi' bianyi."

29 Spakowski, "'Gender' Trouble," 34–35.

30 Min, *Translation and Travelling Theory*; and Lin C., "Finding a Language," 18.

31 Wang L., "Gender and Sexual Differences," 10.

32 Barlow, *Question of Women*, 253.

33 Hershatter, *Women and China's Revolutions*, 275.

34 Rofel, *Desiring China*, 68; Yang, "From Gender Erasure to Gender Difference," 57–58; Barlow, *Question of Women*, 253; and Wang Z., "Maoism, Feminism," 138.

35 Li Xiaojiang, "With What Discourse," 262.

36 Hershatter and Wang, "Chinese History," 1412.

37 Hershatter and Wang, "Chinese History," 1417.

38 See Scott's introduction to *Gender and the Politics of History*, 4–6, for her own account of her use of poststructuralism in the development of a "radical epistemology" for feminist history. For a broader contextualization of Scott's effort to advance poststructuralist arguments beyond their recognized place in literary criticism, see Meyerowitz, "History of 'Gender.'" Joanne Meyerowitz notes that some critics of Scott's poststructuralist approach went so far as to accuse her of having "undermined the 'traditional stage of historical fact-finding' for those groups of women whose history had not yet been written, and damaged political activism for women's rights" ("History of 'Gender,'" 1348), as Joan Hoff argued in "Gender as a Postmodern Category."

39 Scott, *Gender and the Politics of History*, 2.

40 Schaffer and Song, "Unruly Spaces," 19. See also Yihong Jin, "Rethinking the 'Iron Girls.'"

41 In their introduction to *Translating Feminisms in China*, Dorothy Ko and Wang Zheng further emphasize the importance of translation and cross-cultural dialogue in the development of an autonomous field of women's history against the legacy of the Maoist state. Ko and Wang note that although the CCP leaders initially endorsed May Fourth feminisms, *nüquan zhuyi* (feminism or the women's rights movement) became a taboo subject during the Maoist era, which "witnessed a closing-down of both intellectual space for debating *nüquan* and social spaces for women's spontaneous activism" (6).

42 Butler, *Gender Trouble*, 10.

43 Gatens, "Critique of the Sex/Gender Distinction," 144.

44 Rofel, *Other Modernities*, 41, 47.

45 Kristeva, *About Chinese Women*; Johnson, *Women, the Family, and Peasant Revolution*; Stacey, *Socialist Revolution in China*; and Andors, *Unfinished Liberation of Chinese Women*. The CCP launched speaking-bitterness campaigns to build the revolutionary subjectivity of the masses. By 1947 speaking bitterness had become a mainstay of the CCP's mobilization techniques. See G. Wu, "Speaking Bitterness"; F. Sun, *Social Suffering and Political Confession*; and Javed, "Speaking Bitterness."

46 See P. Liu, *Queer Marxism in Two Chinas*, ch. 2.

47 Min, "What about Other Translation Routes."

48 L. Liu, *Translingual Practice*, ch. 1.

49 L. Liu, Karl, and Ko, *Birth of Chinese Feminism*, 15; Dikötter, *Sex, Culture and Modernity*, 68; and Munro, *Concept of Man*.

50 Rocha, "Xing," 603. Concurring with Jai Ben-ray's research, Rocha identifies Ye Dehui's "Preface to The Classic of the Plain Girl" ("Sunü jing xu," 1907) as possibly containing the first occurrence of *xing* referring to sex and human nature. See Jai, "Zhongguoren xingguan chutan"; see also Ruan, *Sex in China*.

51 Barlow, *Question of Women*, 37, 53.

52 L. Liu, Karl, and Ko, *Birth of Chinese Feminism*, 16.

53 Min, *Quanqiuhua yu lilun lüxing*, 158.

54 See Q. Wang and Min, *Revisiting Gender Inequality*, for an analysis of how postsocialist economic reforms have widened the gender gap and inequalities for women.

55 On the Chinese state's 2015 detention of five feminists for organizing street-based advocacy against sexual harassment, see Tan, "Digital Masquerading"; Wang Z., "Detention of the Feminist Five"; Ye, "Drama of Chinese Feminism"; and C. Zhang, *Dreadful Desires*, 156. On leftover women, see Hong Fincher, *Leftover Women*; and Lake, *Leftover in China*. On the Chinese government crackdown on effeminate male celebrities, see C. Li, Chang Chien, and Stevenson, "China's Celebrity Culture Is Raucous"; and P. Liu, "Women and Children First." For a comprehensive analysis of the landscape of women's agitations and social subjects including the Feminist Five and leftover women, see A. Wu and Dong, "What Is Made-in-China Feminism(s)?"

56 R. Walker and Millar, "Is the Sky Falling In."

57 A representative collection of statements can be found in Meng and Dai, *Fuchu lishi dibiao*. For contextualizations of Chinese understandings of gender during the Maoist era, see H. Evans, *Women and Sexuality in China*; Dai, "Rewriting Chinese Women"; Honig, "Maoist Mappings of Gender"; and Manning, "Making a Great Leap Forward?"

58 Barlow, *Question of Women*, 255. For an account that shifts the question from "Was the revolution good for women?" to "What happens to our view of the revolutions when we place women at the center of the account?" see Hershatter, *Women and China's Revolutions*.

59 Butler, "Against Proper Objects," 2. For the original reference, see Foucault, *History of Sexuality*, 154. Important disagreements have been put forth by critics such as Sedgwick, whose *Epistemology of the Closet* famously claims, "The study of sexuality is not coextensive with the study of gender; correspondingly, antihomophobic inquiry is not coextensive with feminist inquiry" (27). For further elaboration, see Sedgwick, "Gender Criticism."

60 Butler, "Against Proper Objects," 1. Abelove, Barale, and Halperin, *Lesbian and Gay Studies Reader*.

61 Lin C., Liu, and Jin, "China," 108.

62 Lin C., "Finding a Language," 12–13.

63 Visvanathan et al., *Women, Gender, and Development Reader*; Kabeer, *Reversed Realities*; Chant, *Gender, Generation and Poverty*; and Falcón, *Power Interrupted*.

64 P. Liu and Rofel, "*Wolf Warrior II*."

65 Critics also note that China's Going Out strategies include the creation of culture industries and organs of soft power. See Huailiang Li, "Chinese Culture 'Going Out.'"

66 Chinese text from *Xinhuanet*, "Xi Jinping zai quanqiu funü fenghui shang de jianghua"; English translation from Embassy of the People's Republic of China in Ireland, "Remarks by President Xi."

67 Huntington, *Clash of Civilizations*.

68 Sengupta, "Xi Jinping Vows."

69 The original Chinese reads: "妇女是物质文明和精神文明的创造者，是推动社会发展和进步的重要力量。没有妇女，就没有人类，就没有社会。追求男女平等的事业是伟大的。纵观历史，没有妇女解放和进步，就没有人类解放和进步。为实现男女平等的崇高理想，人类走过了不平坦、不平凡的历程。"

70 Adolphe, "'Gender' Wars," 4–5.

71 Adolphe, "'Gender' Wars," 12.

72 Razavi and Miller, "From WID to GAD."

73 UN Commission on the Status of Women, *Report*, 229.

74 Weed, "From the 'Useful' to the 'Impossible,'" 289.

75 Scott, *Gender and the Politics of History*, x.

76 Though I am discussing only the 1995 Beijing conference and its immediate aftermath, it is important to note that these attacks on the concept of gender have not abated. See Corrêa, Paternotte, and Kuhar, "Globalization of Anti-gender Campaigns."

77 Falcón, *Power Interrupted*, 20.

78 Chowdhury, "Locating Global Feminisms Elsewhere."
79 Sandler and Goetz, "Can the United Nations Deliver."
80 See Zwingel, *Translating International Women's Rights*, for an analysis of how CEDAW norms translate or fail to translate into local feminist practices. Susanne Zwingel notes that CEDAW norms are fluid and fundamentally dependent on context-specific values and agency.

Bibliography

Abegunrin, Olayiwola, and Charity Manyeruke. *China's Power in Africa: A New Global Order*. London: Palgrave, 2019.

Abelove, Henry, Michèle Aina Barale, and David M. Halperin. Introduction to *The Lesbian and Gay Studies Reader*, edited by Henry Abelove, Michèle Aina Barale, and David M. Halperin, xv–xvii. New York: Routledge, 1993.

Adam, Barry. *The Rise of a Gay and Lesbian Movement*. Boston: G. K. Hall, 1987.

Adolphe, Jane. "'Gender' Wars at the United Nations." *Ave Maria Law Review* 11, no. 1 (2012): 1–31.

Adorno, Theodor W. "Cultural Criticism and Society." In *Prisms*, 17–34. Cambridge, MA: MIT Press, 1983.

Ahmed, Sara. *On Being Included: Racism and Diversity in Institutional Life*. Durham, NC: Duke University Press, 2012.

Aizura, Aren Z. "Of Borders and Homes: The Imaginary Community of (Trans) Sexual Citizenship." *Inter-Asia Cultural Studies* 7, no. 2 (2006): 289–309.

Aizura, Aren Z. "Trans Feminine Value, Racialized Others, and the Limits of Necropolitics." In *Queer Necropolitics*, edited by Jin Haritaworn, Adi Kuntsman, and Silvia Posocco, 129–47. New York: Routledge, 2014.

Alderson, David. *Sex, Needs and Queer Culture: From Liberation to the Post-gay*. London: Zed Books, 2016.

Almaguer, Tomás. "Chicano Men: A Cartography of Homosexual Identity and Behavior." In *The Lesbian and Gay Studies Reader*, edited by Henry Abelove, Michèle Aina Barale, and David M. Halperin, 255–73. New York: Routledge, 1993.

Althusser, Louis. "Ideology and Ideological State Apparatuses (Notes towards an Investigation)." In *Lenin and Philosophy and Other Essays*, 127–86. New York: Monthly Review Press, 2001.

Althusser, Louis. *Reading Capital*. London: Verso, 2016.

Altman, Dennis. "Global Gaze/Global Gays." *GLQ: A Journal of Gay and Lesbian Studies* 3, no. 4 (1997): 417–36.

Amin, Kadji. "Haunted by the 1990s: Queer Theory's Affective Histories." *WSQ: Women's Studies Quarterly* 44, nos. 3–4 (2016): 173–89.

Anagnost, Ann. "The Corporeal Politics of Quality (*Suzhi*)." *Public Culture* 16, no. 2 (2004): 189–208.

Anderson, Marston. *The Limits of Realism: Chinese Fiction in the Revolutionary Period*. Berkeley: University of California Press, 1990.

Anderson, Perry. "Stand-Off in Taiwan." *London Review of Books* 26, no. 11 (2004): 12–17.

Andors, Phyllis. *The Unfinished Liberation of Chinese Women, 1949–1980*. Bloomington: Indiana University Press, 1983.

Andreas, Joel. "Changing Colours in China." *New Left Review* 54 (November/ December 2008): 123–42.

Arondekar, Anjali. "The Sex of History, or Object/Matters." *History Workshop Journal* 89 (2020): 207–13.

Arondekar, Anjali, and Geeta Patel, eds. "Area Impossible: The Geopolitics of Queer Studies." Special issue, *GLQ: A Journal of Gay and Lesbian Studies* 22, no. 2 (2016).

Arondekar, Anjali, and Geeta Patel. "Area Impossible: Notes toward an Intro-duction." *GLQ: A Journal of Gay and Lesbian Studies* 22, no. 2 (2016): 151–71.

Arrighi, Giovanni. *Adam Smith in Beijing: Lineages of the Twenty-First Century*. London: Verso, 2007.

Arrighi, Giovanni, and Lu Zhang. "Beyond the Washington Consensus: A New Bandung?" In *Globalization and Beyond: New Examinations of Global Power and Its Alternatives*, edited by Jon Shefner and Patricia Fernández-Kelly, 25–57. University Park: Penn State University Press, 2011.

Arruzza, Cinzia. "Gender as Social Temporality: Butler (and Marx)." *Historical Materialism* 23, no. 1 (2015): 28–52.

Au, Loong Yu. *China's Rise: Strength and Fragility*. With contributions from Bai Ruixue, Bruno Jetin, and Pierre Rousset. Pontypool, UK: Merlin, 2012.

Baer, Brian James, and Klaus Kaindl, eds. *Queering Translation, Translating the Queer: Theory, Practice, Activism*. Abingdon, UK: Routledge, 2017.

Baik, Jiwoon. "'One Belt One Road' and the Geopolitics of Empire." *Inter-Asia Cultural Studies* 20, no. 3 (2019): 358–76.

Bao, Hongwei. *Queer China: Lesbian and Gay Literature and Visual Culture under Postsocialism*. London: Routledge, 2020.

Bao, Hongwei. *Queer Comrades: Gay Identity and Tongzhi Activism in Postsocial-ist China*. Copenhagen, Denmark: Nordic Institute of Asian Studies, 2018.

Bao, Hongwei. *Queer Media in China*. London: Routledge, 2021.

Barlow, Tani. *In the Event of Women*. Durham, NC: Duke University Press, 2021.

Barlow, Tani, ed. *The Power of Weakness: Four Stories of the Chinese Revolution*. New York: Feminist Press at CUNY, 2007.

Barlow, Tani. *The Question of Women in Chinese Feminism*. Durham, NC: Duke University Press, 2004.

Barmé, Geremie. "The True Story of Lu Xun." *New York Review*, November 23, 2017. https://www.nybooks.com/articles/2017/11/23/true-story-of-lu-xun/.

Beauvoir, Simone de. *The Second Sex*. 1949. New York: Knopf, 1993.

Begu, Liviu Stelian, Maria Denisa Vasilescu, Larisa Stanila, and Roxana Clodnitchi. "China-Angola Investment Model." *Sustainability* 10, no. 8 (2018): 2–17.

Berlant, Lauren. *Cruel Optimism*. Durham, NC: Duke University Press, 2011.

Berlant, Lauren, and Michael Warner. "What Does Queer Theory Teach Us about X?" *PMLA* 110, no. 3 (1995): 343–49.

Bernards, Brian. "Malaysia as Method: Xiao Hei and Ethnolinguistic Literary Taxonomy." In *The Oxford Handbook of Modern Chinese Literatures*, edited by Carlos Rojas and Andrea Bachner, 811–931. Oxford: Oxford University Press, 2016.

Bolinaga, Luciano Damián. "From the Washington Consensus to the Beijing Consensus: Latin America Facing the Rise of China as a Great Power." In *New World Orderings*, edited by Lisa Rofel and Carlos Rojas, 38–57. Durham, NC: Duke University Press, 2023.

Boone, Joseph Allen. *The Homoerotics of Orientalism*. New York: Columbia University Press, 2014.

Brandt, Loren, Jikun Huang, Guo Li, and Scott Rozelle. "Land Rights in Rural China: Facts, Fictions, and Issues." *China Journal* 47 (2002): 67–97.

Brautigam, Deborah. "A Critical Look at Chinese 'Debt-Trap Diplomacy': The Rise of a Meme." *Area Development and Policy* 5, no. 1 (2020): 1–14.

Brautigam, Deborah. *The Dragon's Gift: The Real Story of China in Africa*. Oxford: Oxford University Press, 2009.

Brenner, Johanna. "Review: Marxist Theory and the Woman Question." *Contemporary Sociology* 13, no. 6 (1984): 698–700.

Brenner, Robert. *The Economics of Global Turbulence: The Advanced Capitalist Economies from Long Boom to Long Downturn, 1945–2005*. London: Verso, 2006.

Brilmyer, S. Pearl, Filippo Trentin, and Zairong Xiang, eds. "The Ontology of the Couple." Special issue, *GLQ: A Journal of Gay and Lesbian Studies* 25, no. 2 (2019).

Brim, Matt. *Poor Queer Studies: Confronting Elitism in the University*. Durham, NC: Duke University Press, 2020.

Brown, Carolyn T. "Woman as Trope: Gender and Power in Lu Xun's 'Soap.'" In *Gender Politics in Modern China: Writing and Feminism*, edited by Tani E. Barlow, 74–89. Durham, NC: Duke University Press, 1993.

Brown, Wendy. *States of Injury: Power and Freedom in Late Modernity*. Princeton, NJ: Princeton University Press, 1995.

Bunch, Charlotte, and Susana Fried. "Beijing '95: Moving Women's Human Rights from Margin to Center." *Signs: Journal of Women in Culture and Society* 22, no. 1 (1996): 200–204.

Butler, Judith. "Against Proper Objects." *differences: A Journal of Feminist Cultural Studies* 6, nos. 2–3 (1994): 1–26.

Butler, Judith. *Bodies That Matter: On the Discursive Limits of "Sex."* New York: Routledge, 1993.

Butler, Judith. *The Force of Nonviolence*. London: Verso, 2020.

Butler, Judith. "Gender in Translation: Beyond Monolingualism." *philoSOPHIA* 9, no. 1 (2019): 1–25.

Butler, Judith. *Gender Trouble: Feminism and the Subversion of Identity*. 1990. New York: Routledge, 1999.

Butler, Judith. "The Inorganic Body in the Early Marx: A Limit-Concept of Anthropocentrism." *Radical Philosophy* 2, no. 6 (2019): 3–17.

Butler, Judith. "Merely Cultural." *Social Text* 15, nos. 3–4 (52–53) (1997): 265–77.

Butler, Judith. "Reflections on *Gender Trouble* Thirty Years Later: Reply to Hershatter, Loos, and Patel." *Journal of Asian Studies* 79, no. 4 (2020): 969–76.

Butler, Judith. *Senses of the Subject*. New York: Fordham University Press, 2015.

Butler, Judith. *Undoing Gender*. New York: Routledge, 2004.

Butler, Judith, and Athena Athanasiou. *Dispossession: The Performative in the Political*. Cambridge, UK: Polity, 2013.

Butler, Judith, Ernesto Laclau, and Slavoj Žižek. *Contingency, Hegemony, Universality: Contemporary Dialogues on the Left*. London: Verso, 2000.

Button, Peter. *Configurations of the Real in Chinese Literary and Aesthetic Modernity*. Leiden: Brill, 2009.

Byrd, Jodi. *The Transit of Empire: Indigenous Critiques of Colonialism*. Minneapolis: University of Minnesota Press, 2011.

Byrd, Jodi, Alyosha Goldstein, and Chandan Reddy, eds. "Economies of Dispossession: Indigeneity, Race, and Capitalism." Special issue, *Social Text* 36, no. 2 (135) (2018).

Cai Xiang. *Revolution and Its Narratives: China's Socialist Literary and Cultural Imaginaries, 1949–1966*. Translated by Rebecca Karl and Xueping Zhong. Durham, NC: Duke University Press, 2016.

Camfield, David. "Theoretical Foundations of an Anti-racist Queer Feminist Historical Materialism." *Critical Sociology* 42, no. 2 (2016): 289–306.

Cammack, Paul. "Marx on Social Reproduction." *Historical Materialism* 28, no. 2 (2020): 76–106.

Caserio, Robert L., Lee Edelman, Judith Halberstam, José Esteban Muñoz, and Tim Dean. "The Antisocial Thesis in Queer Theory." *PMLA* 121, no. 3 (2006): 819–28.

Castillo, Roberto. "'Race' and 'Racism' in Contemporary Africa-China Relations Research: Approaches, Controversies, and Reflections." *Inter-Asia Cultural Studies* 21, no. 3 (2020): 310–36.

Chamas, Sophie. "Reading Marx in Beirut: Disorganised Study and the Politics of Queer Utopia." *Middle East—Topics and Arguments* 14 (July 2020): 143–59.

Chan, Stephen Ching-kiu. "Figures of Hope and the Filmic Imaginary of Jianghu in Contemporary Hong Kong Cinema." *Cultural Studies* 15, nos. 3–4 (2001): 486–514.

Chan, Stephen Ching-kiu. "The Language of Despair: Ideological Representations of the 'New Woman' by May Fourth Writers." In *Gender Politics in Modern China: Writing and Feminism*, edited by Tani Barlow, 13–32. Durham, NC: Duke University Press, 1993.

Chan, Sylvia. "Realism or Socialist Realism? The 'Proletarian' Episode in Modern Chinese Literature, 1927–1932." *Australian Journal of Chinese Affairs* 9 (January 1983): 55–74.

Chang Hsiao-hung. "Asia as Counter-method." *Prism* 16, no. 2 (2019): 456–71.

Chang Hsiao-hung 張小虹. *Shishang xiandai xing* 時尚現代性 [Fashioning modernity]. Taipei: Lianjing, 2016.

Chang, Hsiao-hung 張小虹. "Tongzhi qingren, feichang yuwang" 同志情人, 非常慾望 [Taiwan queer valentines]. *Zhongwai wenxue* 中外文學 [Chung-Wai literary monthly] 25, no. 1 (1996): 6–25.

Chant, Sylvia. *Gender, Generation and Poverty: Exploring the "Feminisation of Poverty" in Africa, Asia and Latin America*. Cheltenham, UK: Elgar, 2007.

Chao, Kang. "The Languages of Social Movements." *International Critical Thought* 1, no. 4 (2011): 397–407.

Chauncey, George. *Gay New York: Gender, Urban Culture, and the Making of the Gay Male World, 1890–1940*. New York: Basic Books, 1994.

Cheah, Pheng. "Mattering." *Diacritics* 26, no. 1 (1996): 108–39.

Chen Duxiu. "On Literary Revolution." In *Modern Chinese Literary Thought: Writings on Literature, 1893–1945*, edited by Kirk Denton, 140–45. Stanford, CA: Stanford University Press, 1995.

Chen Fangying 陳芳英. "Xiao'ao Jianghu zhong de yishu yu renwu" 笑傲江湖中的藝術與人物 [The arts and characters in *The Smiling, Proud Wanderer*]. In *Jin Yong xiaoshuo guoji xueshu yantaohui lunwenji* 金庸小說國際學術研討會論文集 [Proceedings of the international conference on Jin Yong's novels], edited by Qiu Gui Wang, 221–35. Taipei: Yuan-Liou Publishing, 1999.

Chen, Jian. *Mao's China and the Cold War*. Chapel Hill: University of North Carolina Press, 2001.

Chen, Kuan-Hsing. *Asia as Method: Toward Deimperialization*. Durham, NC: Duke University Press, 2010.

Chen, Kuan-Hsing, and Beng Huat Chua. "An Introduction." *Inter-Asia Cultural Studies* 1, no. 1 (2000): 9–12.

Chen, Mel Y. *Animacies: Biopolitics, Racial Mattering, and Queer Affect*. Durham, NC: Duke University Press, 2012.

Chen Mo 陳墨. *Zhongguo wuxia dianying shi* 中國武俠電影史 [History of Chinese martial arts cinema]. Taipei: Fengyun, 2006.

Chen, Xiaomei. *Staging Chinese Revolution: Theater, Film, and the Afterlives of Propaganda*. New York: Columbia University Press, 2017.

Chen, Yingzhen. "What the 'Third World' Means to Me." Translated by Petrus Liu. *Inter-Asia Cultural Studies* 6, no. 4 (2005): 535–40.

Cheng, Eileen J. "Gendered Spectacles: Lu Xun on Gazing at Women." *Modern Chinese Literature and Culture* 16, no. 1 (2004): 1–36.

Cheng, Eileen J. *Literary Remains: Death, Trauma, and Lu Xun's Refusal to Mourn*. Honolulu: University of Hawai'i Press, 2013.

Cheng, Sealing. "Choreography of Masculinity: The Pursuit of Marriage by African Men in Forced Displacement in Hong Kong." *Feminist Studies* 47, no. 2 (2021): 282–311.

Cheru, Fantu, and Cyril Obi, eds. *The Rise of China and India in Africa: Challenges*. London: Zed Books, 2010.

Cheung, Chiu-yee. *Lu Xun: The Chinese "Gentle" Nietzsche*. Frankfurt am Main: Peter Lang, 2001.

Chien, Ying-Ying. "Feminism and China's New 'Nora': Ibsen, Hu Shi, and Lu Xun." *Comparatist* 19 (May 1995): 97–113.

China News 中國新聞網. "Xu Ke toulu Lin Qingxia mingan yiku; Jin Yong fandui ta yan Dongfang Bubai" 徐克透露林青霞敏感易哭 金庸反對她演東方不敗 [Tsui Hark reveals that the sensitive Brigitte Lin cries often; Jin Yong objects to the casting of Lin as Asia the Invincible]. July 21, 2008. http://www .chinanews.com/yl/mxzz/news/2008/07-21/1318813.shtml.

Ching Siu-tung 程小東, director. Produced by Tsui Hark. *Xiao ao jianghu zhi Dongfang Bubai* 笑傲江湖之東方不敗 [Swordsman II: Asia the Invincible]. Hong Kong: Long Shong Pictures, 1992.

Ching Siu-tung 程小東, director. Produced by Tsui Hark. *Xiao ao jianghu zhi fengyun zaiqi* 笑傲江湖之風雲再起 [Swordsman III: East is red]. Hong Kong: Long Shong Pictures, 1993.

Chitty, Christopher. *Sexual Hegemony: Statecraft, Sodomy, and Capital in the Rise of the World System*. Durham, NC: Duke University Press, 2020.

Chou Wah-shan 周華山. *Houzhimin tongzhi* 後殖民同志 [Postcolonial tongzhi]. Hong Kong: Xianggang tongzhi yanjiushe, 1997.

Chou Wah-shan 周華山. *Tongzhi lun* 同志論 [On tongzhi]. Hong Kong: Xianggang tongzhi yanjiushe, 1995.

Chow, Esther Ngan-Ling. "Making Waves, Moving Mountains: Reflections on Beijing '95 and Beyond." *Signs: Journal of Women in Culture and Society* 22, no. 1 (1996): 185–92.

Chow, Rey. *A Face Drawn in Sand: Humanistic Inquiry and Foucault in the Present*. New York: Columbia University Press, 2021.

Chow, Rey. Introduction to *Modern Chinese Literary and Cultural Studies in the Age of Theory: Reimagining a Field*, edited by Rey Chow, 1–25. Durham, NC: Duke University Press, 2000.

Chow, Rey. *Primitive Passions: Visuality, Sexuality, Ethnography, and Contemporary Chinese Cinema*. New York: Columbia University Press, 1995.

Chow, Rey. *Woman and Chinese Modernity: The Politics of Reading between West and East*. Minneapolis: University of Minnesota Press, 1991.

Chow, Tse-tsung. *The May Fourth Movement: Intellectual Revolution in Modern China*. Cambridge, MA: Harvard University Press, 2014.

Chowdhury, Elora H. "Locating Global Feminisms Elsewhere: Braiding US Women of Color and Transnational Feminisms." *Cultural Dynamics* 21, no. 1 (2009): 51–78.

Chu, Madeline. "Lu Xun's Women Characters." *Journal of Chinese Studies* 1, no. 1 (1984): 25–37.

Chu Wei-cheng 朱偉誠, ed. *Pipan de xing zhengzhi* 批判的性政治 [Critical sexual politics]. Taipei: Taishe, 2008.

Chu Wei-cheng and Fran Martin, eds. "Global Queer, Local Theories." Special issue, *Inter-Asia Cultural Studies* 8, no. 4 (December 2007).

Chuǎng. "Sorghum and Steel: The Socialist Developmental Regime and the Forging of China." *Chuǎng* no. 1 (2016). http://chuangcn.org/journal/one/sorghum-and-steel/.

Chuang, Julia. *Beneath the China Boom: Labor, Citizenship, and the Making of a Rural Land Market*. Oakland: University of California Press, 2020.

Clover, Joshua. "Value/Theory/Crisis." *PMLA* 127, no. 1 (2012): 107–14.

Cohen, Cathy J. "Punks, Bulldaggers, and Welfare Queens: The Radical Potential of Queer Politics?" *GLQ: A Journal of Gay and Lesbian Studies* 3, no. 4 (1997): 437–65.

Cohen, Cathy J. "What Is This Movement Doing to My Politics?" *Social Text* 17, no. 4 (61) (1999): 111–18.

Cohen, Paul A. *Discovering History in China: American Historical Writing on the Recent Chinese Past*. New York: Columbia University Press, 1984.

Collins, Cory G. "Drag Race to the Bottom? Updated Notes on the Aesthetic and Political Economy of *RuPaul's Drag Race*." *TSQ: Transgender Studies Quarterly* 4, no. 1 (2017): 128–34.

Connery, Christopher. "The End of the Sixties." *boundary 2* 36, no. 1 (2009): 183–210.

Connery, Christopher. "Revolutionary China and Its Late-Capitalist Fate." *Historical Materialism* 23, no. 2 (2015): 257–86.

Corkin, Lucy. "Competition or Collaboration? Chinese South African Transnational Companies in Africa." *Review of African Political Economy* 35, no. 115 (2008): 128–33.

Cornell, Drucilla. *Transformations: Recollective Imagination and Sexual Difference*. London: Routledge, 1993.

Corrêa, Sonia, David Paternotte, and Roman Kuhar. "The Globalization of Anti-gender Campaigns." *International Politics and Society*, May 31, 2018. https://www.ips-journal.eu/topics/human-rights/article/show/the -globalisation-of-anti-gender-campaigns-2761/.

Cover, Rob. "Material/Queer Theory: Performativity, Subjectivity, and Affinity-Based Struggles in the Culture of Late Capitalism." *Rethinking Marxism* 16, no. 3 (2004): 293–310.

Cronin, James. *The World the Cold War Made: Order, Chaos, and the Return of History*. London: Routledge, 1996.

Cumings, Bruce. *Parallax Visions: Making Sense of American–East Asian Relations at the End of the Century*. Durham, NC: Duke University Press, 2012.

Currah, Paisley. *Sex Is as Sex Does: Governing Transgender Identity*. New York: New York University Press, 2022.

Currah, Paisley, and Susan Stryker. "General Editors' Introduction." *TSQ: Transgender Studies Quarterly* 4, no. 1 (2017): 1–3.

Currier, Ashley, and Thérèse Migraine-George. "Queer Studies/African Studies: An (Im)Possible Transaction?" *GLQ: A Journal of Gay and Lesbian Studies* 22, no. 2 (2016): 281–305.

Cvetkovich, Ann. *Depression: A Public Feeling*. Durham, NC: Duke University Press, 2012.

Dai Jinhua. *After the Post–Cold War: The Future of Chinese History*. Edited by Lisa Rofel. Durham, NC: Duke University Press, 2018.

Dai Jinhua. "Rewriting Chinese Women: Gender Production and Cultural Space in the Eighties and Nineties." In *Spaces of Their Own: Women's Public Sphere in Transnational China*, edited by Mayfair Mei-hui Yang, 191–206. Minneapolis: University of Minnesota Press, 1999.

David, Emmanuel. "Capital T: Trans Visibility, Corporate Capitalism, and Commodity Culture." *TSQ: Transgender Studies Quarterly* 4, no. 1 (2017): 28–44.

Davidson, Arnold. "Sex and the Emergence of Sexuality." In *Forms of Desire: Sexual Orientation and the Social Constructionist Controversy*, edited by Edward Stein, 89–132. New York: Routledge, 1992.

Davies, Gloria. "Chinese Literary Studies and Post-structuralist Positions: What Next?" *Australian Journal of Chinese Affairs* 28 (July 1992): 67–86.

Davies, Gloria. "Lu Xun in 1966: On Valuing a Maoist Icon." *Critical Inquiry* 46, no. 3 (2020): 515–35.

Davies, Gloria. *Lu Xun's Revolution: Writing in a Time of Violence*. Cambridge, MA: Harvard University Press, 2013.

Davies, Gloria, Christian Sorace, and Haun Saussy. "Political Enchantment: Aesthetic Practices and the Chinese State." *Critical Inquiry* 46, no. 3 (2020): 475–81.

Davies, Sharyn Graham. *Gender Diversity in Indonesia: Sexuality, Islam and Queer Selves*. London: Routledge, 2010.

Day, Alexander F. *The Peasant in Postsocialist China: History, Politics, and Capitalism*. Cambridge: Cambridge University Press, 2013.

Day, Iyko. *Alien Capital*. Durham, NC: Duke University Press, 2016.

Day, Tony, and Maya H. T. Liem, eds. *Cultures at War: The Cold War and Cultural Expression in Southeast Asia*. Ithaca, NY: Cornell University Press, 2010.

De Kloet, Jeroen, Yiu-Fai Chow, and Gladys Pak Lei Chong, eds. *Trans-Asia as Method: Theory and Practice*. Lanham, MD: Rowman and Littlefield, 2019.

DeMare, Brian. *Land Wars: The Story of China's Agrarian Revolution*. Stanford, CA: Stanford University Press, 2019.

D'Emilio, John. "Capitalism and Gay Identity." In *Powers of Desire: The Politics of Sexuality*, edited by Ann Snitow, Christine Stansell, and Sharan Thompson, 100–13. New York: Monthly Review Press, 1983.

Deng Xiaoping 邓小平. "Zenme huifu nongye shengchan" 怎么恢复农业生产 [How to restore agricultural production]. In *Deng Xiaoping wenxuan* 邓小平文选 [Collected Works of Deng Xiaoping], 1: 322–27.

Diamond, Sigmund. *Compromised Campus: The Collaboration of Universities with the Intelligence Community, 1945–55*. Oxford: Oxford University Press, 1992.

Dieng, Rama Salla. "'Gone Native?': Reflections of a Feminist Tightrope Walker's Research on 'Land Grabbing' and the Dilemmas of 'Fieldworking' While Parenting." In *Women Researching in Africa: The Impact of Gender*, edited by Ruth Jackson and Max Kelly, 27–50. New York: Palgrave, 2018.

Dikötter, Frank. *Sex, Culture and Modernity in China: Medical Science and the Construction of Sexual Identities in the Early Republican Period*. Honolulu: University of Hawai'i Press, 1995.

Dirlik, Arif. *After the Revolution: Waking to Global Capitalism*. Hanover, NH: University of New England Press, 1994.

Dirlik, Arif. "The Rise of China and the End of the World as We Know It." *American Quarterly* 69, no. 3 (2017): 533–40.

Dirlik, Arif. "The Universalisation of a Concept: 'feudalism' to 'Feudalism' in Chinese Marxist Historiography." *Journal of Peasant Studies* 12, nos. 2–3 (1985): 197–227.

Doty, Alexander. *Making Things Perfectly Queer: Interpreting Mass Culture*. Minneapolis: University of Minnesota Press, 1993.

Dou Xinping 竇欣平. *Jian xiao jianghu: Xu Ke de shijie* 劍嘯江湖: 徐克的世界 [The resounding sword in *jianghu*: The world of Tsui Hark]. Beijing: Zhongguo guangbo dianshi chubanshe, 2007.

Drucker, Peter. *Warped: Gay Normality and Queer Anti-capitalism*. Chicago: Haymarket, 2015.

Duberman, Martin. *Stonewall: The Definitive Story of the LGBTQ Rights Uprising That Changed America*. New York: Dutton, 1993.

Duggan, Lisa. "The New Homonormativity: The Sexual Politics of Neoliberalism." In *Materializing Democracy: Toward a Revitalized Cultural Politics*, edited by Russ Castronovo and Dana D. Nelson, 175–94. Durham, NC: Duke University Press, 2002.

Dutton, Michael. "Cultural Revolution as Method." *China Quarterly* 227 (September 2016): 718–33.

Ebert, Teresa. *Ludic Feminism and After: Postmodernism, Desire, and Labor in Late Capitalism*. Ann Arbor: University of Michigan Press, 1996.

Edelman, Lee. *No Future: Queer Theory and the Death Drive*. Durham, NC: Duke University Press, 2004.

Edholm, Felicity, Olivia Harris, and Kate Young. "Conceptualizing Women." *Critique of Anthropology* 3, no. 9 (1976): 101–30.

El-Tayeb, Fatima. *European Others: Queering Ethnicity in Postnational Europe*. Minneapolis: University of Minnesota Press, 2011.

Embassy of the People's Republic of China in Ireland. "Remarks by President Xi on Gender Equality and Women's Empowerment." September 27, 2015. http://ie.china-embassy.org/eng/ztlt/2d2/t1321134.htm.

Endnotes. "The History of Subsumption." *Endnotes* 2 (April 2010). https://endnotes.org.uk/issues/2/en/endnotes-the-history-of-subsumption.

Endnotes. "The Logic of Gender: On the Separation of Spheres and the Process of Abjection." *Endnotes* 3 (September 2013). https://endnotes.org.uk/issues/3/en/endnotes-the-logic-of-gender.

Endnotes. "Misery and the Value Form." *Endnotes* 2 (April 2010). https://endnotes.org.uk/issues/2.

Eng, David L. *The Feeling of Kinship: Queer Liberalism and the Racialization of Intimacy*. Durham, NC: Duke University Press, 2001.

Eng, David L., and Jasbir K. Puar. "Introduction: Left of Queer." *Social Text* 38, no. 4 (145) (2020): 1–24.

Engebretsen, Elisabeth L., William F. Schroeder, and Hongwei Bao, eds. *Queer/Tongzhi China: New Perspectives on Research, Activism, and Media Cultures*. Copenhagen, Denmark: Nordic Institute of Asian Studies, 2015.

Engels, Friedrich. *The Origin of the Family, Private Property, and the State*. 1884. New York: Penguin, 2010.

Entertainment 娛樂. "Jin Yong biaoshi bu xihuan Xu Ke de Dongfang Bubai, shuo ta budong wuxia" 金庸表示不喜歡徐克的《東方不敗》，說他不懂武俠 [Jin Yong disapproved of Tsui Hark's *Asia the Invincible*, accusing the director of not understanding *wuxia*]. November 6, 2018. https://kknews.cc/entertainment/5zlp431.html.

Entertainment 娛樂. "Wei shenme Lin Qingxia ban de Dongfang Bubai shi Jin Yong zui bu xihuan de" 為什麼林青霞版的東方不敗是金庸最不喜歡的 [Why Brigitte Lin's version of Asia the Invincible is Jin Yong's least favorite]. November 5, 2018. https://kknews.cc/entertainment/xjp4qk9.html.

Epstein, B. J., and Robert Gillett, eds. *Queer in Translation*. New York: Routledge, 2017.

Escoffier, Jeffrey. "The Political Economy of the Closet: Notes towards an Economic History of Gay and Lesbian Life before Stonewall." In *Homo Economics: Capitalism, Community and Lesbian and Gay Life*, edited by Amy Gluckman and Betsy Reed, 123–34. London: Routledge, 1997.

Esty, Jed, and Colleen Lye, eds. "Peripheral Realisms Now." *Modern Language Quarterly* 73, no. 3 (2012): 269–88.

Evans, David. *Sexual Citizenship: The Material Construction of Sexualities*. London: Routledge, 1993.

Evans, Harriet. *Women and Sexuality in China: Dominant Discourses of Female Sexuality and Gender since 1949*. Cambridge, UK: Polity, 1997.

Fabian, Johannes. *Time and the Other: How Anthropology Makes Its Object*. New York: Columbia University Press, 2014.

Falcón, Sylvanna M. *Power Interrupted: Antiracist and Feminist Activism inside the United Nations*. Seattle: University of Washington Press, 2016.

Fang Gang 方刚. *Tongxinglian zai Zhongguo* 同性恋在中国 [Homosexuality in China]. Changchun: Jilin renmin chubanshe, 1995.

Fang Gang 方刚. *Zhongguo bianxingren xianxiang* 中国变性人现象 [Transgender in China]. Guangzhou: Guangzhou chubanshe, 1996.

Federici, Silvia. *Patriarchy of the Wage: Notes on Marx, Gender, and Feminism*. Oakland, CA: PM Press, 2021.

Federici, Silvia. *Revolution at Point Zero: Housework, Reproduction, and Feminist Struggle*. Oakland, CA: PM Press, 2020.

Feng, Jin. *The New Woman in Early Twentieth-Century Chinese Fiction*. West Lafayette, IN: Purdue University Press, 2004.

Ferguson, Roderick A. *Aberrations in Black: Toward a Queer of Color Critique*. Minneapolis: University of Minnesota Press, 2003.

Ferguson, Susan, and David McNally. "Precarious Migrants: Gender, Race, and the Social Reproduction of a Global Working Class." *Socialist Register* 51 (2015): 1–23.

Fiereck, Kirk, Neville Hoad, and Daniel S. Mupotsa. "A Queering-to-Come." *GLQ: A Journal of Gay and Lesbian Studies* 26, no. 3 (2020): 363–76.

Fitzgerald, Carolyn. "'Diary of a Madwoman' Traversing the Diaspora: Rewriting Lu Xun in Hualing Nieh's Mulberry and Peach." *Modern Chinese Literature and Culture* 26, no. 2 (2014): 38–88.

Floyd, Kevin. "Automatic Subjects: Gendered Labor and Abstract Life." *Historical Materialism* 24, no. 2 (2016): 61–86.

Floyd, Kevin. *The Reification of Desire: Toward a Queer Marxism*. Minneapolis: University of Minnesota Press, 2009.

Foster, John Bellamy, and Robert McChesney. *The Endless Crisis: How Monopoly-Finance Capital Produces Stagnation and Upheaval from the USA to China*. New York: Monthly Review Press, 2012.

Foucault, Michel. *The History of Sexuality*. Vol. 1. New York: Pantheon, 1978.

Franceschini, Ivan, and Nicholas Loubere, eds. "Archaeologies of the Belt and Road Initiative." Special issue, *Made in China Journal* 6, no. 2 (2021).

Frank, Andre Gunder. *ReOrient: Global Economy in the Asian Age*. Berkeley: University of California Press, 1998.

Frank, Miriam. *Out in the Union: A Labor History of Queer America*. Philadelphia: Temple University Press, 2015.

Fraser, Nancy. "Heterosexism, Misrecognition, and Capitalism: A Response to Judith Butler." *Social Text* 15, nos. 3–4 (52–53) (1997): 279–89.

Freeman, Elizabeth. *Time Binds: Queer Temporalities, Queer Histories*. Durham, NC: Duke University Press, 2010.

French, Howard W. *China's Second Continent: How a Million Migrants Are Building a New Empire in Africa*. New York: Knopf, 2014.

Fu, Poshek. "Cold War Politics and Hong Kong Mandarin Cinema." In *The Oxford Handbook of Chinese Cinemas*, edited by Carlos Rojas and Eileen Cheng-yin Chow, 116–33. Oxford: Oxford University Press, 2013.

Fukuyama, Francis. *The End of History and the Last Man*. New York: Free Press, 1992.

Gabriel, Kay. "Gender as Accumulation Strategy." *Invert Journal* 1 (n.d.). Accessed February 27, 2021. https://invertjournal.org.uk/posts?view =articles&post=7106265#gender-as-accumulation-strategy.

Garcia, J. Neil C. *Performing the Self: Occasional Prose*. Quezon City: University of the Philippines Press, 2003.

Gatens, Moira. "A Critique of the Sex/Gender Distinction." In *Beyond Marxism? Interventions after Marx*, edited by Judith Allen and Paul Patton, 142–61. Sydney: Intervention Publications, 1983.

Germon, Jennifer. *Gender: A Genealogy of an Idea*. New York: Palgrave Macmillan, 2009.

Ghaziani, Amin, and Matt Brim. Introduction to *Imagining Queer Methods*, edited by Amin Ghaziani and Matt Brim, 3–27. New York: New York University Press, 2019.

Gleeson, Jules Joanne, and Elle O'Rourke. Introduction to *Transgender Marxism*, edited by Jules Joanne Gleeson and Elle O'Rourke, 1–32. London: Pluto, 2021.

Goetz, Anne Marie, and Sally Baden. "Who Needs [Sex] When You Can Have [Gender]? Conflicting Discourses on Gender at Beijing." *Feminist Review* 56, no. 1 (1997): 3–25.

Goldman, Merle. "The Political Use of Lu Xun." *China Quarterly* 91 (1982): 446–61.

Goldstein, Philip. *Post-Marxist Theory: An Introduction*. Albany: State University of New York Press, 2005.

Goodman, David, and Xiaowei Zang. "The New Rich in China: The Dimensions of Social Change." In *The New Rich in China: Future Rulers, Present Lives*, edited by David S. G. Goodman, 1–20. New York: Routledge, 2008.

Greenberg, David F., and Marcia H. Bystryn. "Capitalism, Bureaucracy, and Male Homosexuality." *Crime, Law, and Social Change* 8, no. 1 (1984): 33–56.

Gu, Ming Dong. "Lu Xun, Jameson and Multiple Polysemia." *Canadian Review of Comparative Literature* 28, no. 4 (2001): 434–53.

Gu, Ming Dong, ed. *The Routledge Handbook of Modern Chinese Literature*. New York: Routledge, 2019.

Guo Xiaofei 郭晓飞. *Zhongguo fa shiye de tongxinglian* 中国法视野的同性恋 [Homosexuality in the purview of Chinese law]. Beijing: Zhishi chanquan chubanshe, 2007.

Guthrie, Doug. *China and Globalization: The Social, Economic, and Political Transformation of Chinese Society*. New York: Routledge, 2006.

Habib, Adam. "Seeing the New African Scramble for What It Really Is: Reflections on the United States and China." In *New Impulses from the South: China's Engagement of Africa*, edited by Hannah Edinger, Hayley Herman, and Johanna Jansson, 24–27. Stellenbosch, South Africa: Centre for Chinese Studies, Stellenbosch University, 2008.

Hacking, Ian. "Making Up People." In *Forms of Desire: Sexual Orientation and the Social Constructionist Controversy*, edited by Edward Stein, 69–88. New York: Routledge, 1992.

Halper, Stefan. *The Beijing Consensus: Legitimizing Authoritarianism in Our Time*. New York: Basic Books, 2010.

Halperin, David M. *How to Do the History of Sexuality*. Chicago: University of Chicago Press, 2002.

Halperin, David M. *One Hundred Years of Homosexuality and Other Essays on Greek Love*. New York: Routledge, 1990.

Haraway, Donna J. "'Gender' for a Marxist Dictionary." In *Simians, Cyborgs, and Women: The Reinvention of Nature*, 127–48. New York: Routledge, 1991.

Harb, Sayumi Takahashi. "Penning the Mad Man in the Attic: Queerness, Women Writers, and Race in Sōseki's *Sanshirō*." *Review of Japanese Culture and Society* 29 (2017): 92–108.

Harding, Sandra. "Why Has the Sex/Gender System Become Visible Only Now?" In *Discovering Reality: Feminist Perspectives on Epistemology, Metaphysics, Methodology, and Philosophy of Science*, edited by Sandra Harding and Merrill B. Hintikka, 311–24. New York: Kluwer, 2004.

Hardt, Michael, and Antonio Negri. *Empire*. Cambridge, MA: Harvard University Press, 2001.

Hardt, Michael, and Antonio Negri. *Labor of Dionysus: A Critique of the State-Form*. Minneapolis: University of Minnesota Press, 1994.

Harootunian, Harry. "Deprovincializing Marx: Reflections on a Cultural Dominant." In *East Asian Marxisms and Their Trajectories*, edited by Joyce C. H. Liu and Viren Murthy, 13–28. New York: Routledge, 2017.

Harootunian, Harry. *Marx after Marx: History and Time in the Expansion of Capitalism*. New York: Columbia University Press, 2017.

Hartman, Saidiya. *Wayward Lives, Beautiful Experiments: Intimate Histories of Social Upheaval*. New York: W. W. Norton, 2019.

Hartmann, Heidi. "The Unhappy Marriage of Marxism and Feminism: Towards a More Progressive Union." In *The Second Wave: A Reader in Feminist Theory*, edited by Linda Nicholson, 97–122. New York: Routledge, 1997.

Hartsock, Nancy. *Money, Sex, and Power: Toward a Feminist Historical Materialism*. New York: Longman, 1983.

Harvey, David. *The New Imperialism*. Oxford: Oxford University Press, 2003.

Harvey, Keith. *Intercultural Movements: American Gay in French Translation*. New York: Routledge, 2003.

Hayward, Jane. "China's Land Reforms and the Logic of Capital Accumulation." *Made in China Journal* 3, no. 4 (2018): 48–51.

Heaney, Emma. *The New Woman: Literary Modernism, Queer Theory, and the Trans Feminine Allegory*. Evanston, IL: Northwestern University Press, 2017.

Heinrich, Ari Larissa. "Zoology, Celibacy, and the Heterosexual Imperative: Notes on Teaching Lu Xun's 'Loner' as a Queer Text." *Frontiers of Literary Studies in China* 7, no. 3 (2013): 441–58.

Hemmings, Clare. "Sexuality, Subjectivity . . . and Political Economy?" *Subjectivity* 5, no. 2 (2012): 121–39.

Henderson, Lisa. *Love and Money: Queers, Class, and Cultural Production*. New York: New York University Press, 2013.

Hennessy, Rosemary. *Profit and Pleasure: Sexual Identities in Late Capitalism*. New York: Routledge, 2000.

Hennessy, Rosemary. "Queer Theory, Left Politics." *Rethinking Marxism* 7, no. 3 (1994): 85–111.

Hennessy, Rosemary. "Thinking Sex Materially: Marxist, Socialist, and Related Feminist Approaches." In *The Sage Handbook of Feminist Theory*, edited by Mary Evans, Clare Hemmings, Marsha Henry, Hazel Johnstone, Sumi Madhok, Ania Plomien, and Sadie Wearing, 308–26. Thousand Oaks, CA: Sage, 2014.

Henry, Todd A. "Introduction: Queer Korea; Toward a Field of Engagement." In *Queer Korea*, edited by Todd A. Henry, 1–52. Durham, NC: Duke University Press, 2020.

Henry, Todd A. "Queer/Korean Studies as Critique: A Provocation." *Korea Journal* 58, no. 2 (2018): 5–26.

Hershatter, Gail. "*Gender Trouble*'s Afterlife in Chinese Studies." *Journal of Asian Studies* 79, no. 4 (2020): 911–26.

Hershatter, Gail. *Women and China's Revolutions*. Lanham, MD: Rowman and Littlefield, 2018.

Hershatter, Gail, and Wang Zheng. "Chinese History: A Useful Category of Gender Analysis." *American Historical Review* 113, no. 5 (2008): 1404–21.

Hill, Michael G. "New Script and a New 'Madman's Diary.'" *Modern Chinese Literature and Culture* 27, no. 1 (2015): 75–104.

Hinsch, Bret. *Passions of the Cut Sleeve: The Male Homosexual Tradition in China*. Berkeley: University of California Press, 1990.

Ho Chung-rui 何春蕤, ed. *Kua xingbie* 跨性別 [Trans]. Chungli, Taiwan: Center for the Study of Gender/Sexuality, 2002.

Ho, Josephine Chung-rui. "Is Global Governance Bad for East Asian Queers?" *GLQ: A Journal of Lesbian and Gay Studies* 14, no. 4 (2008): 457–79.

Ho, Loretta Wing Wah. *Gay and Lesbian Subculture in Urban China*. London: Routledge, 2010.

Ho, Peter. "Who Owns China's Land? Policies, Property Rights and Deliberate Institutional Ambiguity." *China Quarterly* 166 (June 2001): 394–421.

Hoad, Neville. "Re: Thinking Sex from the Global South Africa." *GLQ: A Journal of Gay and Lesbian Studies* 17, no. 1 (2010): 119–24.

Hockx, Michel. "Mad Women and Mad Men: Intraliterary Contact in Early Republican Literature." In *Autumn Floods: Essays in Honour of Marian Galik*, edited by Raoul D. Gassmann and Robert H. Gassmann, 307–22. Bern: Peter Lang, 1997.

Hoff, Joan. "Gender as a Postmodern Category of Paralysis." *Women's History Review* 3, no. 2 (1994): 149–69.

Holcomb, Gary Edward. *Claude McKay, Code Name Sasha: Queer Black Marxism and the Harlem Renaissance*. Gainesville: University Press of Florida, 2009.

Hong, Christine. *A Violent Peace: Race, U.S. Militarism, and Cultures of Democratization in Cold War Asia and the Pacific*. Stanford, CA: Stanford University Press, 2020.

Hong Fincher, Leta. *Leftover Women: The Resurgence of Gender Inequality in China*. London: Zed Books, 2014.

Honig, Emily. "Maoist Mappings of Gender: Reassessing the Red Guards." In *Chinese Femininities/Chinese Masculinities: A Reader*, edited by Susan Brownell and Jeffrey N. Wasserstrom, 255–68. Berkeley: University of California Press, 2002.

Horton, Brian A. "The Queer Turn in South Asian Studies? or 'That's Over and Done Queen, On to the Next.'" *QED: A Journal in GLBTQ Worldmaking* 5, no. 3 (2018): 165–80.

Huang, Ana. "On the Surface: 'T' and Transgender Identity in Chinese Lesbian Culture." In Engebretsen, Schroeder, and Bao, *Queer/Tongzhi China*, 111–30.

Huang Yingying 黄盈盈 and Pan Suiming 潘绥铭, eds. *Jidian yu fansi: 2016–17 Zhongguo xing yanjiu* 积淀与反思：2016–2017 中国"性"研究 [Accumulation and reflection: Chinese "sex" studies in 2016–2017]. Hong Kong: 1908 youxian gongsi, 2018.

Huang Yingying 黄盈盈 and Pan Suiming 潘绥铭. *Xing zhi bian: Ershi shiji Zhongguo ren de xing shenghuo* 性之变：21 世纪中国人的性生活 [Sexual revolution: Sexual lives in twenty-first-century China]. Beijing: Renmin chubanshe, 2011.

Hung, Ho-fung. "America's Head Servant? The PRC's Dilemma in the Global Crisis." *New Left Review* 60 (November/December 2009): 5–25.

Hung, Ho-fung, ed. *China and the Transformation of Global Capitalism*. Baltimore: Johns Hopkins University Press, 2009.

Hung, Ho-fung. *The China Boom: Why China Will Not Rule the World*. New York: Columbia University Press, 2016.

Huntington, Samuel. *The Clash of Civilizations and the Remaking of World Order*. New York: Simon and Schuster, 1996.

Huynh, T. Tu. "Black Marxism: An Incorporated Analytical Framework for Rethinking Chinese Labour in South African Historiography." *African Identities* 11, no. 2 (2013): 1–15.

Ibsen, Henrik. *A Doll's House*. 1879. London: Penguin, 2016.

Irigaray, Luce. *This Sex Which Is Not One*. Ithaca, NY: Cornell University Press, 1985.

Irving, Dan, and Vek Lewis, eds. "Special Issue on Trans-Political Economy." *TSQ: Transgender Studies Quarterly* 4, no. 1 (February 2017).

Jackson, Zakiyyah Iman. *Becoming Human: Matter and Meaning in an Antiblack World*. New York: New York University Press, 2020.

Jager, Sheila Myoshi, and Rana Mitter, eds. *Ruptured Histories: War, Memory, and the Post–Cold War in Asia*. Cambridge, MA: Harvard University Press, 2007.

Jagose, Annamarie. "Feminism's Queer Theory." *Feminism and Psychology* 19, no. 2 (2009): 157–74.

Jai Ben-ray 翟本瑞. "Zhongguoren xingguan chutan" 中國人性觀初探 [A preliminary investigation of the Chinese view on sex]. *Si yu yan* 思與言 [Thought and language] 33, no. 3 (1996): 27–75.

Jameson, Fredric. "Actually Existing Marxism." In *Marxism beyond Marxism*, edited by Saree Makdisi, Cesare Casarino, and Rebecca Karl, 14–54. London: Routledge, 1996.

Jameson, Fredric. *The Political Unconscious: Narrative as a Socially Symbolic Act*. Ithaca, NY: Cornell University Press, 1982.

Jameson, Fredric. "Third-World Literature in the Era of Multinational Capitalism." *Social Text*, no. 15 (1986): 65–88.

Jarrín, Alvaro. "Untranslatable Subjects: Travesti Access to Public Health Care in Brazil." *TSQ: Transgender Studies Quarterly* 3, nos. 3–4 (November 2016): 357–75.

Javed, Jeffrey. "Speaking Bitterness." In *Afterlives of Chinese Communism: Political Concepts from Mao to Xi*, edited by Christian Sorace, Ivan Franceschini, and Nicolas Loubere, 257–62. Acton, Australia: Australian National University Press, 2019.

Jia Leilei 賈磊磊. *Zhongguo wuxia dianying shi* 中國武俠電影史 [History of Chinese martial arts cinema]. Beijing: Wenhua yishu chubanshe, 2005.

Jin, Yihong. "Rethinking the 'Iron Girls': Gender and Labour during the Chinese Cultural Revolution." In *Translating Feminisms in China*, edited by Dorothy Ko and Wang Zheng, 188–214. Malden, MA: Blackwell, 2007.

Jin Yong 金庸. *Xiao ao jianghu* 笑傲江湖 [The smiling, proud wanderer]. Taipei: Yuanliu, 1996.

Jin Yong 金庸. *Yi tian tu long ji* 倚天屠龍記 [Heavenly sword, dragon-slaying saber]. Taipei: Yuanliu, 1996.

Johnson, Kay Ann. *Women, the Family, and Peasant Revolution in China*. Chicago: University of Chicago Press, 1983.

Jones, Andrew F. *Developmental Fairy Tales: Evolutionary Thinking and Modern Chinese Culture*. Cambridge, MA: Harvard University Press, 2011.

Kabeer, Naila. *Reversed Realities: Gender Hierarchies in Development Thought*. London: Verso, 1994.

Kafer, Alison. *Feminist, Queer, Crip*. Bloomington: Indiana University Press, 2013.

Kahan, Benjamin. "Conjectures on the Sexual World-System." *GLQ: A Journal of Gay and Lesbian Studies* 23, no. 3 (2017): 327–57.

Kaldis, Nicholas. "Aesthetic Cognition and the Subject of Discourse in Lu Xun's Modern-Style Fiction." In *Remembering May Fourth: The Movement and Its Legacy*, edited by Carlos Yu-Kai Lin and Victor H. Mair, 207–26. Leiden: Brill, 2020.

Kang, Wenqing. "The Decriminalization and Depathologization of Homosexuality in China." In *China in and beyond the Headlines*, edited by Timothy Weston and Lionel Jensen, 231–48. Plymouth, UK: Rowman and Littlefield, 2012.

Kang, Wenqing. *Obsession: Male Same-Sex Relations in China, 1900–1950*. Hong Kong: Hong Kong University Press, 2009.

Karl, Rebecca E. "Engaging Gerth's Sleights (of Hand)." *PRC History Review* 5, no. 1 (2020): 1–25.

Karl, Rebecca E. *The Magic of Concepts: History and the Economic in Twentieth-Century China*. Durham, NC: Duke University Press, 2017.

Keeling, Kara. *Queer Times, Black Futures*. New York: New York University Press, 2019.

Kim, Sung Kyung. "A Cultural Question for the Division and Unification of the Korean Peninsula." *Inter-Asia Cultural Studies* 21, no. 3 (2020): 425–31.

Kipnis, Andrew. "Neoliberalism Reified: Suzhi Discourse and Tropes of Neoliberalism in the People's Republic of China." *Journal of the Royal Anthropology Institute* 13, no. 2 (2007): 383–499.

Klotz, Marcia. "Alienation, Labor, and Sexuality in Marx's 1844 Manuscripts." *Rethinking Marxism* 18, no. 3 (2006): 405–13.

Ko, Dorothy, and Wang Zheng. Introduction to *Translating Feminisms in China*, edited by Dorothy Ko and Wang Zheng, 1–12. Malden, MA: Blackwell, 2007.

Kong, Travis S. K. "Queering Masculinity in Hong Kong Movies." In *Masculinities and Hong Kong Cinema*, edited by Laikwan Pang and Day Wong, 57–80. Hong Kong: Hong Kong University Press, 2005.

Kong, Travis S. K. "Reinventing the Self under Socialism: Migrant Male Sex Workers ('Money Boys') in China." *Critical Asian Studies* 44, no. 2 (2012): 283–308.

Kornbluh, Anna. "The Realist Blueprint." *Henry James Review* 36 (2015): 199–211.

Kristeva, Julia. *About Chinese Women*. 1977. London: Marion Boyars, 2000.

Kwon, Heonik. *The Other Cold War*. New York: Columbia University Press, 2010.

Laclau, Ernesto, and Chantal Mouffe. *Hegemony and Socialist Strategy*. London: Verso, 1985.

Lake, Roseann. *Leftover in China: The Women Shaping the World's Next Superpower*. New York: Norton, 2018.

Lanser, Susan S. *The Sexuality of History: Modernity and the Sapphic, 1565–1830*. Chicago: University of Chicago Press, 2014.

Larsen, Neil, Mathias Nilges, Josh Robinson, and Nicholas Brown, eds. *Marxism and the Critique of Value*. Chicago: MCM Publishing, 2014.

Lazreg, Marnia. *Foucault's Orient: The Conundrum of Cultural Difference, from Tunisia to Japan*. New York: Berghahn, 2017.

Lee, Ching Kwan. *Against the Law: Labor Protests in China's Rustbelt and Sunbelt*. Berkeley: University of California Press, 2007.

Lee, Ching Kwan. *The Specter of Global China: Politics, Labor, and Foreign Investment in Africa*. Chicago: University of Chicago Press, 2018.

Lee, Chris. "Rhythm and the Cold War Imaginary: Listening to John Adams's *Nixon in China*." *differences: A Journal of Feminist Cultural Studies* 22, nos. 2–3 (2011): 190–210.

Lee, Leo Ou-fan. *Voices from the Iron House: A Study of Lu Xun*. Bloomington: Indiana University Press, 1987.

Lee, Mabel. "From Chuang-tzu to Nietzsche: On the Individualism of Lu Hsun." *Journal of Oriental Society of Australia* 17 (1985): 21–38.

Lee, Moonyoung. "Landscape of the Minds of South and North Koreans: Unification Perception, Mutual Recognition and the Possibility of Cultural Integration." *Inter-Asia Cultural Studies* 21, no. 3 (2020): 465–75.

Lee Pui Tak 李培德 and Wong Ain-ling 黃愛玲, eds. *Lengzhan yu Xianggang dianying* 冷戰與香港電影 [The Cold War and Hong Kong cinema]. Hong Kong: Hong Kong Film Archive, 2009.

Lee, Rosa. "Judith Butler's Scientific Revolution: Foundations for a Transsexual Marxism." In *Transgender Marxism*, edited by Jules Joanne Gleeson and Elle O'Rourke, 62–69. London: Pluto, 2021.

Lee, Sangjoon. *Cinema and the Cultural Cold War: US Diplomacy and the Origins of the Asian Cinema Network*. Ithaca, NY: Cornell University Press, 2020.

Leung, Helen Hok-Sze. "Homosexuality and Queer Aesthetics in Chinese Cinema." In *A Companion to Chinese Cinema*, edited by Yingjin Zhang, 518–34. Oxford: Blackwell, 2013.

Leung, Helen Hok-Sze. *Undercurrents: Queer Culture and Postcolonial Hong Kong*. Vancouver: University of British Columbia Press, 2009.

Leung, Helen Hok-Sze. "Unsung Heroes: Reading Transgender Subjectivities in Hong Kong Action Cinema." In *Masculinities and Hong Kong Cinema*, edited by Laikwan Pang and Day Wong, 81–98. Hong Kong: Hong Kong University Press, 2005.

Lewis, Holly. *The Politics of Everybody: Feminism, Queer Theory, and Marxism at the Intersection*. London: Zed Books, 2016.

Li, Cao, Amy Chang Chien, and Alexandra Stevenson. "China's Celebrity Culture Is Raucous. The Authorities Want to Change That." *New York Times*, August 27, 2021. https://www.nytimes.com/2021/08/27/business/media/china -celebrity-culture.html.

Li Dazhao 李大钊. "Wo de Makesi zhuyi guan" 我的馬克思主義觀 [My Marxist views]. *Xin qingnian* 新青年 [New youth] 6, no. 5 (May 1919): 521–37.

Li, Huailiang. "Chinese Culture 'Going Out': An Overview of Government Policies and an Analysis of Challenges and Opportunities for International Collaboration." In *Handbook of Cultural and Creative Industries in China*, edited by Michael Keane, 129–42. Cheltenham, UK: Edward Elgar, 2016.

Li, Huayin. *Village China under Socialism and Reform: A Micro-history, 1948–2008*. Stanford, CA: Stanford University Press, 2009.

Li Huiying 李慧英. "Jiang xingbie yishi naru jueche zhuliu de taolun" 将性别意识纳入决策主流的讨论 [The discussion of gender consciousness in mainstream policymaking]. *Funü yanjiu* 妇女研究 [Research on women] 3 (1996): 5–7.

Li, Minqi. "China: Imperialism or Semi-periphery?" *Monthly Review*, July 1, 2021. https://monthlyreview.org/2021/07/01/china-imperialism-or-semi -periphery/

Li, Minqi. *The Rise of China and the Demise of the Capitalist World Economy*. New York: Monthly Review Press, 2005.

Li, Siu-Leung. "Kung Fu: Negotiating Nationalism and Modernity." *Cultural Studies* 15, nos. 3–4 (2001): 515–42.

Li, Xia. "Nora and Her Sisters: Lu Xun's Reflections on the Role of Women in Chinese Society with Particular Reference to Elfriede Jelinek's *What Happened after Nora Left Her Husband or Pillars of Society* (1979)." *Neohelicon* 35, no. 2 (2008): 217–35.

Li Xiaojiang. "With What Discourse Do We Reflect on Chinese Women? Thoughts on Transnational Feminism in China." In *Spaces of Their Own: Women's Public Sphere in Transnational China*, edited by Mayfair Mei-hui Yang, 261–77. Minneapolis: University of Minnesota Press, 1999.

Li Yinhe 李银河 and Wang Xiaobo 王小波. *Tamen de shijie: Zhongguo nan tong-xinglian qunluo toushi* 他们的世界— 中国男同性恋群落透视 [Their world: A penetrating look into China's male homosexual community]. Hong Kong: Cosmos Books, 1992.

Li Zehou 李泽厚. "Lu Xun sixiang de fazhan" 鲁迅思想的发展 [A sketch of the development of Lu Xun's thought]. In *Zhongguo jindai sixiang shilun* 中国近代思想史论 [Essays on the history of modern Chinese thought], 439–71. Beijing: Renmin chubanshe, 1979.

Liebman, Adam, and Goeun Lee. "Garbage as Value and Sorting as Labour in China's New Waste Policy." *Made in China Journal* 5, no. 1 (2020): 56–63.

Lieu, Samuel. "Fact or Fiction: Ming-chiao (Manichaeism) in Jin Yong's *I-t'ien t'u-lung chi*." In *Proceedings of the International Conference on Jin Yong's Novels*, edited by Lin Lijun, 43–66. Hong Kong: Mingheshe, 2000.

Lim, Eng-Beng. *Brown Boys and Rice Queens: Spellbinding Performance in the Asias*. New York: New York University Press, 2014.

Lin Chun. *China and Global Capitalism: Reflections on Marxism, History, and Contemporary Politics*. New York: Palgrave, 2013.

Lin Chun. "Finding a Language: Feminism and Women's Movements in Contemporary China." In *Transitions, Environments, Translations: Feminisms in International Politics*, edited by Joan W. Scott, Cora Kaplan, and Debra Keates, 11–20. New York: Routledge, 1997.

Lin Chun, Liu Bohong, and Jin Yihong. "China." In *A Companion to Feminist Philosophy*, edited by Alison M. Jaggar and Iris Marion Young, 108–17. Oxford: Blackwell, 2017.

Lin, Hsiao-ting. *Accidental State: Chiang Kai-shek, the United States, and the Making of Taiwan*. Cambridge, MA: Harvard University Press, 2016.

Lin Wushu 林悟殊. "Jin Yong bi xia de Mingjiao yu lishi de zhenshi" 金庸筆下的明教與歷史的真實 [Jin Yong's Manichaeism versus historical reality]. *Lishi xuekan* 歷史月刊 [Historical monthly] 98 (1996): 62–67.

Liu, Andrew B. *Tea War: A History of Capitalism in China and India*. New Haven, CT: Yale University Press, 2020.

Liu Bohong 刘伯红. "95 shijie funü dahui he Zhongguo funü yanjiu" 95 世界妇女大会和中国妇女研究 [The 1995 World Conference on Women and China's women studies]. *Funü yanjiu* 妇女研究 [Research on women] no. 2 (1999): 46–51.

Liu, Hong, Michael Szonyi, and Zheng Yangwen, eds. *The Cold War in Asia: The Battle for Hearts and Minds*. Leiden: Brill, 2010.

Liu, Joyce C. H., and Viren Murthy, eds. *East Asian Marxisms and Their Trajectories*. New York: Routledge, 2017.

Liu, Kang. *Aesthetics and Marxism: Chinese Aesthetic Marxists and Their Western Contemporaries*. Durham, NC: Duke University Press, 2000.

Liu, Lydia H. "Life as Form: How Biomimesis Encountered Buddhism in Lu Xun." *Journal of Asian Studies* 68, no. 1 (2009): 21–54.

Liu, Lydia H. *Translingual Practice: Literature, National Culture, and Translated Modernity, China, 1900–1937*. Stanford, CA: Stanford University Press, 1995.

Liu, Lydia H., Rebecca Karl, and Dorothy Ko, eds. *The Birth of Chinese Feminism: Essential Texts in Transnational Theory*. New York: Columbia University Press, 2013.

Liu, Petrus. *Queer Marxism in Two Chinas*. Durham, NC: Duke University Press, 2015.

Liu, Petrus. *Stateless Subjects: Chinese Martial Arts Literature and Postcolonial History*. Ithaca, NY: Cornell East Asia Series, 2011.

Liu, Petrus. "Women and Children First—Jingoism, Ambivalence, and Crisis of Masculinity in *Wolf Warrior II*." *Refeng xueshu* 热风学术 [Refeng journal], no. 7 (December 2017): 80–83.

Liu, Petrus, and Lisa Rofel, eds. "*Wolf Warrior II*: The Rise of China and Sexual Politics." Special issue, *Refeng xueshu* 热风学术 [Refeng journal] no. 7 (December 2017).

Loos, Tamara. "Reading *Gender Trouble* in Southeast Asia." *Journal of Asian Studies* 79, no. 4 (2020): 927–46.

Love, Heather. *Feeling Backwards: Loss and the Politics of Queer History*. Cambridge, MA: Harvard University Press, 2009.

Love, Heather. "Feminist Criticism and Queer Theory." In *A History of Feminist Literary Criticism*, edited by Gill Plain and Susan Sellers, 301–21. Cambridge: Cambridge University Press, 2007.

Love, Heather, ed. "Rethinking Sex." Special issue, *GLQ: A Journal of Lesbian and Gay Studies* 17, no. 2 (2011).

Love, Heather. *Underdogs: Social Deviance and Queer Theory*. Chicago: University of Chicago Press, 2021.

Lovell, Julia. "The Afterlife of Lu Xun." *LA Review of Books*, China Channel, September 28, 2017. https://chinachannel.lareviewofbooks.org/2017/09/28/lu-xun-afterlife/.

Lovell, Julia. *Maoism: A Global History*. London: Bodley Head, 2019.

Lu, Ben Chia-hung. "Rethinking Queer Value: Money Boys and Value Struggles in Shanghai." *Situations: Cultural Studies in the Asian Context* 10, no. 2 (2017): 171–88.

Lu Xun 鲁迅. "Butian" 补天 [Mending heaven]. In *Lu Xun quanji* 鲁迅全集, 2:357–69.

Lu Xun. *Diary of a Madman and Other Stories*. Translated by William Lyell. Honolulu: University of Hawai'i Press, 1990.

Lu Xun 鲁迅. "Guanyu funü jiefang" 关于妇女解放 [On women's liberation]. In *Lu Xun quanji* 鲁迅全集, 4:614–16.

Lu Xun 鲁迅. "Guanyu xin wenzi" 关于新文字 [On new writing]. In *Lu Xun quanji* 鲁迅全集, 6:165–66.

Lu Xun. *Jottings under Lamplight*. Edited by Eileen J. Cheng and Kirk A. Denton. Cambridge, MA: Harvard University Press, 2017.

Lu Xun 鲁迅. "Lun zhaoxiang zhilei" 论照片之类 [On photography and related matters]. In *Lu Xun quanji* 鲁迅全集, 1:181–90.

Lu Xun 鲁迅. *Lu Xun quanji* 鲁迅全集 [Complete works of Lu Xun]. Beijing: Renmin wenxue, 1981.

Lu Xun 鲁迅. "Mingtian" 明天 [Tomorrow]. In *Lu Xun quanji* 鲁迅全集, 1:311–20.

Lu Xun 鲁迅. "Moluo shili shuo" 摩罗诗力说 [On the power of Mara poetry]. In *Lu Xun quanji* 鲁迅全集, 1:63–115.

Lu Xun 鲁迅. "Nahan zixu" 呐喊自序 [Preface to *Call to Arms*]. In *Lu Xun quanji* 鲁迅全集, 1:437–43.

Lu Xun 鲁迅. "Nala zouhou zenyang" 娜拉走后怎样 [What happens after Nora walks out]. In *Lu Xun quanji* 鲁迅全集, 1:143–51.

Lu Xun 鲁迅. "Nü diao" 女吊 [The hanging woman]. In *Lu Xun quanji* 鲁迅全集, 6:637–44.

Lu Xun 鲁迅. "Shangshi" 伤逝 [Regrets for the past]. In *Lu Xun quanji* 鲁迅全集, 2:113–34.

Lu Xun 鲁迅. "Sibada zhi hun" 斯巴达之魂 [The soul of Sparta]. In *Lu Xun quanji* 鲁迅全集, 7:9–20.

Lu Xun 鲁迅. "Wenhua pianzhi lun" 文化偏至论 [On cultural extremism]. In *Lu Xun quanji* 鲁迅全集, 1:44–62.

Lu Xun 鲁迅. "Wo zhi jielie guan" 我之节烈观 [My views on chastity]. In *Lu Xun quanji* 鲁迅全集, 1:121–33.

Lu Xun 鲁迅. "Zhufu" 祝福 [New year's sacrifice]. In *Lu Xun quanji* 鲁迅全集, 2:5–23.

Lukács, György [Georg]. *History and Class Consciousness: Studies in Marxist Dialectics*. Cambridge, MA: MIT Press, 1972.

Luther, J. Daniel, and Jennifer Ung Loh, eds. *Queer Asia: Decolonising and Reimagining Sexuality and Gender*. London: Zed Books, 2019.

Lye, Colleen. "Identity Politics, Criticism, and Self-Criticism." *South Atlantic Quarterly* 119, no. 4 (2020): 701–14.

Lye, Colleen, and Christopher Nealon, eds. *After Marx: Literature, Theory, and Value in the Twenty-First Century*. Cambridge, UK: Cambridge University Press, 2022.

Lyell, William. *Lu Hsun's Vision of Reality*. Berkeley: University of California Press, 1976.

Mackenzie, Lars Z. "The Afterlife of Data: Identity, Surveillance, and Capitalism in Trans Credit Reporting." *TSQ: Transgender Studies Quarterly* 4, no. 1 (2017): 45–60.

Manalansan, Martin F., IV. *Global Divas: Filipino Gay Men in the Diaspora*. Durham, NC: Duke University Press, 2003.

Manalansan, Martin F., IV. "In the Shadows of Stonewall: Examining Gay Transnational Politics and the Diasporic Dilemma." *GLQ: A Journal of Gay and Lesbian Studies* 2, no. 4 (1995): 425–38.

Mandel, Ernest. *Late Capitalism*. London: Verso, 1999.

Manning, Kimberley Ens. "Making a Great Leap Forward? The Politics of Women's Liberation in Maoist China." *Gender and History* 18, no. 3 (2006): 574–93.

Mao Zedong 毛泽东. "Qin yuan chun: xue" 沁园春·雪 [Snow—to the tune of *Qin Yuan Chun*]. In *Mao Zedong shici* 毛泽东诗词 [Poems of Mao Zedong], 424. Beijing: Renmin wenxue chubanshe, 2017.

Mao Zedong 毛泽东. "Mao Zedong gei Jiang Qing de xin" 毛泽东给江青的信 [Mao Zedong's letter to Jiang Qing]. July 8, 1966. Pipan yu zaizao, October 18, 2017. https://critiqueandtransformation.wordpress.com/2017/10/18/4630/.

Mao Zedong 毛泽东. "Xin minzhu zhuyi lun" 新民主主义论 [On new democracy]. January 1940. In *Mao Zedong xuanji* 毛泽东选集 [Selected works of Mao Zedong], 875–953. Beijing: Renmin chubanshe, 2011.

Mao Zedong 毛泽东. "Zai Yan'an yi zuo tan hui shang de jianghua" 在延安艺座谈会上的讲话 [Talks at the Yenan forum on literature and art]. May 1942. In *Mao Zedong xuanji* 毛泽东选集 [Selected works of Mao Zedong], 1377–85. Beijing: Renmin chubanshe, 2011.

Marchetti, Gina. "The Hong Kong New Wave." In *A Companion to Chinese Cinema*, edited by Yingjin Zhang, 95–117. Oxford: Blackwell, 2013.

Marcuse, Herbert. *Eros and Civilization: A Philosophical Inquiry into Freud*. Boston: Beacon Press, 1974.

Martin, Fran. *Backward Glances: Contemporary Chinese Queer Cultures and the Female Homoerotic Imaginary*. Durham, NC: Duke University Press, 2010.

Martin, Fran. "The Perfect Lie: Sandee Chan and Lesbian Representability in Mandarin Pop Music." *Inter-Asia Cultural Studies* 4, no. 2 (August 2003): 264–80.

Martin, Fran, and Josephine Ho, eds. "Trans/Asia, Trans/gender." Special issue, *Inter-Asia Cultural Studies* 7, no. 2 (2006).

Martin, Randy. *Financialization of Daily Life*. Philadelphia: Temple University Press, 2002.

Marx, Karl. *Capital*. Vol. 1. London: Penguin, 1976.

Marx, Karl. *Capital*. Vol. 3. London: Penguin, 1993.

Marx, Karl. *Economic Manuscripts of 1861–63*. New York: International Publishers, 1989.

Marx, Karl. *Economic and Philosophic Manuscripts of 1844*. New York: Dover, 2007.

Marx, Karl. *The German Ideology*. With Friedrich Engels. New York: Prometheus Books, 1998.

Marx, Karl. *Grundrisse: Foundations of the Critique of Political Economy*. London: Penguin, 1993.

Massad, Joseph. *Desiring Arabs*. Chicago: University of Chicago Press, 2007.

Masuda, Hajimu. *Cold War Crucible: The Korean Conflict and the Postwar World*. Cambridge, MA: Harvard University Press, 2015.

Matebeni, Zethu, and Thabo Msibi. "Vocabularies of the Non-normative." *Agenda* 29, no. 1 (2015): 3–9.

McDougall, Bonnie S. *Love Letters and Privacy in Modern China: The Intimate Lives of Lu Xun and Xu Guangping*. New York: Oxford University Press, 2002.

McRuer, Robert. "As Good as It Gets: Queer Theory and Critical Disability." *GLQ: A Journal of Gay and Lesbian Studies* 9, nos. 1–2 (2003): 79–105.

McRuer, Robert. *Crip Times: Disability, Globalization, and Resistance*. New York: New York University Press, 2018.

McWhorter, Ladelle, ed. "Foucault and Race." Special issue, *Foucault Studies* 12 (October 2011).

Meghani, Shamira A., and Humaira Saeed. "Postcolonial/Sexuality, or, Sexuality in 'Other' Contexts." *Journal of Postcolonial Writing* 55, no. 3 (2019): 293–307.

Meisner, Maurice. *Li Ta-chao and the Origins of Chinese Marxism*. Cambridge, MA: Harvard University Press, 1967.

Méndez, Xhercis. "Notes toward a Decolonial Feminist Methodology: Revisiting the Race/Gender Matrix." *Trans-Scripts* 5 (2015): 41–59.

Meng Yue 孟悦 and Dai Jinhua 戴锦华, eds. *Fuchu lishi dibiao* 浮出历史地表 [Emerging from the horizon of history]. Beijing: Zhongguo renmin daxue chubanshe, 2004.

Meyer, Doug. "An Intersectional Analysis of Lesbian, Gay, Bisexual, and Transgender (LGBT) People's Evaluations of Anti-queer Violence." *Gender and Society* 26, no. 6 (2012): 49–73.

Meyerowitz, Joanne. "A History of 'Gender.'" *American Historical Review* 113, no. 5 (2008): 1346–56.

Meyskens, Covell F. "Rethinking the Political Economy of Development in Mao's China." *positions: asia critique* 29, no. 4 (2021): 809–34.

Mills, Harriet. "Lu Xun: Literature and Revolution—from Mara to Marx." In *Modern Chinese Literature in the May Fourth Era*, edited by Merle Goldman, 161–220. Cambridge, MA: Harvard University Press, 1977.

Min Dongchao 闵冬潮. *Quanqiuhua yu lilun lüxing: Kuaguo nüxing zhuyi de zhishi shengchan* 全球化与理论旅行：跨国女性主义的知识生产 [Traveling theory within the context of globalization: Transnational feminism and knowledge production]. Tianjin: Tianjin renmin chubanshe. 2009.

Min Dongchao. *Translation and Travelling Theory: Feminist Theory and Praxis in China*. London: Routledge, 2017.

Min Dongchao. "What about Other Translation Routes (East-West)? The Concept of the Term 'Gender' Traveling into and throughout China." In *Gender and Globalization in Asia and the Pacific: Method, Practice and Theory*, edited by Kathy E. Ferguson and Monique Mironesco, 79–98. Honolulu: University of Hawai'i Press, 2008.

Moore, Jason W. *Capitalism in the Web of Life: Ecology and the Accumulation of Capital*. London: Verso, 2015.

Morgensen, Scott Lauria. *Spaces between Us: Queer Settler Colonialism and Indigenous Decolonization*. Minneapolis: University of Minnesota Press, 2011.

Morris, Rosalind. "Three Sexes and Four Sexualities: Redressing the Discourses on Gender and Sexuality in Contemporary Thailand." *positions: asia critique* 2, no. 1 (1994): 15–43.

Mortimer-Sandilands, Catriona, and Bruce Erickson, eds. *Queer Ecologies: Sex, Nature, Politics, Desire*. Bloomington: Indiana University Press, 2010.

Morton, Donald, ed. *The Material Queer: A LesBiGay Cultural Studies Reader*. Boulder, CO: Westview, 1996.

Mouffe, Chantal. *The Democratic Paradox*. London: Verso, 2000.

Moyo, Sam. "Perspectives on South-South Relations: China's Presence in Africa." *Inter-Asia Cultural Studies* 17, no. 1 (2016): 58–67.

Mullaney, Thomas. *The Chinese Typewriter: A History*. Cambridge, MA: MIT Press, 2017.

Muñoz, José Esteban. *Cruising Utopia: The Then and There of Queer Futurity*. 10th-anniversary ed. New York: New York University Press, 2019.

Muñoz, José Esteban. *Disidentifications: Queers of Color and the Performance of Politics*. Minneapolis: University of Minnesota Press, 1999.

Munro, Donald. *The Concept of Man in Early China*. Ann Arbor: University of Michigan Center for Chinese Studies, 2001.

Murthy, Viren. "Imagining Asia and the Chinese Revolution: Takeuchi Yoshimi and His Transnational Afterlives." In *East-Asian Marxisms and Their Trajectories*, edited by Joyce C. H. Liu and Viren Murthy, 193–213. London: Routledge, 2017.

Murthy, Viren. "Resistance to Modernity and the Logic of Self-Negation as Politics: Takeuchi Yoshimi and Wang Hui on Lu Xun." *positions: asia critique* 24, no. 2 (2016): 513–54.

Nan Fan. "A Difficult Breakthrough: On Representing Subaltern Experiences." In *Debating the Socialist Legacy and Capitalist Globalization in China*, edited by Xueping Zhong and Ban Wang, 183–204. London: Palgrave, 2014.

Naughton, Barry. *Growing out of the Plan: Chinese Economic Reform, 1978–1993*. Cambridge: Cambridge University Press, 1995.

Nealon, Christopher. *The Matter of Capital: Poetry and Crisis in the American Century*. Cambridge, MA: Harvard University Press, 2011.

Nealon, Christopher. "The Price of Value." In *The Values of Literary Studies: Critical Institutions, Scholarly Agendas*, edited by Rónán McDonald, 91–104. New York: Cambridge University Press, 2015.

Nesbitt, Nick. "Value as Symptom." In *Concept in Crisis: Reading Capital Today*, edited by Nick Nesbitt, 229–79. Durham, NC: Duke University Press, 2017.

Ngai, Sianne. *Theory of the Gimmick: Aesthetic Judgment and Capitalist Form*. Cambridge, MA: Belknap Press of Harvard University Press, 2020.

Ning Yin-bin 甯應斌. "Yangqi tongxinglian, fankai xin nanse" 揚棄同性戀 返開新男色 [Forget homosexuality, revisit *nanse*]. *Taiwan shehui yanjiu jikan* 台灣社會研究季刊 [Taiwan: A radical quarterly in social studies] 111 (December 2018): 165–229.

Nussbaum, Martha C. "The Professor of Parody: The Hip Defeatism of Judith Butler." *New Republic*, February 22, 1999, 37–45.

Nyong'o, Tavia. *Afro-Fabulations: The Queer Drama of Black Life*. New York: New York University Press, 2018.

Nyong'o, Tavia. "Back to the Garden: Queer Ecology in Samuel Delany's *Heavenly Breakfast*." *American Literary History* 24, no. 4 (2013): 747–67.

Nyong'o, Tavia. "Opacity, Narration, and 'The Fathomless Word.'" *Representations* 158, no. 1 (2022): 45–56.

O'Brien, Kevin J., and Lianjiang Li. *Rightful Resistance in Rural China*. New York: Cambridge University Press, 2006.

O'Donnell, Mary Ann. "*Dagongmei*: Gendered Troubles in the City of Dreams." In *Proletarian China: A Century of Chinese Labour*, edited by Ivan Franceschini and Christian Sorace, 466–76. London: Verso, 2022.

Padgug, Robert. "Sexual Matters: Rethinking Sexuality in History." In *Hidden from History: Reclaiming the Gay and Lesbian Past*, edited by Martin Duberman, Martha Vicinus, and George Chauncey, 54–64. New York: Penguin, 1989.

Paik, Nak-Chung. *The Division System in Crisis: Essays on Contemporary Korea*. Oakland: University of California Press, 2001.

Pande, Amrita. *Wombs in Labor: Transnational Commercial Surrogacy in India*. New York: Columbia University Press, 2014.

Parker, Andrew. "Unthinking Sex: Marx, Engels, and the Scene of Writing." In *Fear of a Queer Planet: Queer Politics and Social Theory*, edited by Michael Warner, 19–41. Minneapolis: University of Minnesota Press, 1993.

Patel, Geeta. "*Gender Trouble* in South Asia." *Journal of Asian Studies* 79, no. 4 (2020): 947–67.

Patel, Geeta. "Seeding Debt: Alchemy, Death and the Precarious Farming of Life-Finance in the Global South." *Cultural Critique*, no. 89 (Winter 2015): 1–37.

Peletz, Michael. *Gender Pluralism: Southeast Asia since Early Modern Times*. New York: Routledge, 2009.

Penny, James. *After Queer Theory: The Limits of Sexual Politics*. New York: Pluto, 2013.

Pereira, Pedro Paulo Gomes. *Queer in the Tropics: Gender and Sexuality in the Global South*. New York: Springer, 2019.

Perreau, Bruno. *Queer Theory: The French Response*. Stanford, CA: Stanford University Press, 2016.

Pickowicz, Paul G. *Marxist Literary Thought in China: The Influence of Ch'ü Ch'iu-pai*. Berkeley: University of California Press, 1981.

Pietz, William. "The 'Post-colonialism' of Cold War Discourse." *Social Text* nos. 19–20 (1988): 55–75.

Pletsch, Carl. "The Three Worlds; or, the Division of Social Scientific Labor, circa 1950–1975." *Comparative Studies in Society and History* 23, no. 4 (1981): 565–90.

Pomeranz, Kenneth. *The Great Divergence: China, Europe, and the Making of the Modern World Economy*. Princeton, NJ: Princeton University Press, 2000.

Popa, Bogdan. *De-centering Queer Theory: Communist Sexuality in the Flow during and after the Cold War*. Manchester: Manchester University Press, 2021.

Postone, Moishe. "Marx, Temporality and Modernity." In *East Asian Marxisms and Their Trajectories*, edited by Joyce C. H. Liu and Viren Murthy, 29–48. New York: Routledge, 2017.

Postone, Moishe. *Time, Labor, and Social Domination: A Reinterpretation of Marx's Critical Theory*. Cambridge: Cambridge University Press, 1993.

Prosser, Jay. "Judith Butler: Queer Feminism, Transgender, and the Transubstantiation of Sex." In *The Transgender Studies Reader*, edited by Susan Stryker and Stephen Whittle, 257–80. London: Routledge, 2006.

Puar, Jasbir K. *The Right to Maim: Debility/Capacity/Disability*. Durham, NC: Duke University Press, 2017.

Puar, Jasbir K. *Terrorist Assemblages: Homonationalism in Queer Times*. Durham, NC: Duke University Press, 2007.

Pun Ngai. "Discursive Dyslexia and the Articulation of Class: A Theoretical Perspective on China's Young Female Migrant Workers (*Dagongmei*)." In *Mapping China: Peasants, Migrant Workers and Informal Labor*, edited by Chongqing Wu, 80–102. Leiden: Brill, 2016.

Pun Ngai. *Made in China: Women Factory Workers in a Global Workplace*. Durham, NC: Duke University Press, 2005.

Pusey, James Reeve. *Lu Xun and Evolution*. Albany: State University of New York Press, 1998.

Qian Liqun. "Refusing to Forget." In Chaohua Wang, *One China, Many Paths*, 292–309.

Qu Qiubai 瞿秋白. *Lu Xun zagan xuanji* 鲁迅杂感选集 [Selection of Lu Xun's miscellaneous essays]. Guiyang: Guizhou jiaoyu chubanshe, 2001.

Raffo, Susan, ed. *Queerly Classed*. Boston: South End, 1997.

Ramo, Joshua Cooper. *The Beijing Consensus*. London: Foreign Policy Centre, 2004.

Rao, Rahul. *Out of Time: The Queer Politics of Postcoloniality*. Oxford: Oxford University Press, 2020.

Razavi, Shahrashoub, and Carol Miller. "From WID to GAD: Conceptual Shifts in the Women and Development Discourse." United Nations Research Institute for Social Development, Occasional Paper 1, February 1995.

Ren Lixin 任立新. *Mao Zedong xin minzhu zhuyi jingji sixiang yanjiu* 毛泽东新民主主义经济思想研究 [Studies of Mao Zedong's New Democracy Economic Thought]. Beijing: Zhongguo shehui kexue, 2011.

Ricardo, David. *The Principles of Political Economy and Taxation*. New York: E. P. Dutton, 1973.

Rocha, Leon. "Xing: The Discourse of Sex and Human Nature in Modern China." *Gender and History* 22, no. 3 (2010): 603–28.

Rofel, Lisa. *Desiring China: Experiments in Neoliberalism, Sexuality, and Public Culture*. Durham, NC: Duke University Press, 2007.

Rofel, Lisa. *Other Modernities: Gendered Yearnings in China after Socialism*. Berkeley: University of California Press, 1999.

Rofel, Lisa, and Sylvia J. Yanagisako. *Fabricating Transnational Capitalism: A Collaborative Ethnography of Italian-Chinese Global Fashion*. Durham, NC: Duke University Press, 2019.

Roh, David S., Betsy Huang, and Greta A. Niu, eds. *Techno-Orientalism: Imagining Asia in Speculative Fiction, History, and Media*. New Brunswick, NJ: Rutgers University Press, 2015.

Rojas, Carlos. *Homesickness: Culture, Contagion, and National Transformation in Modern China*. Cambridge, MA: Harvard University Press, 2015.

Rojas, Carlos, ed. "Method as Method." Special issue, *Prism* 16, no. 2 (2019).

Rojas, Carlos. "'A New Species': Gender, Sexuality, and Taxonomic Logics in Sinophone Communities." *Prism* 17, no. 2 (2020): 277–97.

Rojas, Carlos, and Ralph A. Litzinger, eds. *Ghost Protocol: Development and Displacement in Global China*. Durham, NC: Duke University Press, 2016.

Roscoe, Will. *Changing Ones: Third and Fourth Genders in Native North America*. New York: Palgrave Macmillan, 2000.

Rosenberg, Jordy. "Afterword: One Utopia, One Dystopia." In Gleeson and O'Rourke, *Transgender Marxism*, 259–95.

Rosenberg, Jordy. "The Molecularization of Sexuality: On Some Primitivisms of the Present." *Theory and Event* 17, no. 2 (2014). https://muse.jhu.edu/article/546470.

Rosenberg, Jordy, and Amy Villarejo, eds. "Queer Studies and the Crises of Capitalism." Special issue, *GLQ: A Journal of Gay and Lesbian Studies* 18, no. 1 (2011).

Ruan, Fang Fu. *Sex in China: Studies in Sexology in Chinese Culture*. Berlin: Springer, 1991.

Rubin, Gayle S. *Deviations: A Gayle Rubin Reader*. Durham, NC: Duke University Press, 2011.

Rubin, Gayle S. "Sexual Traffic." Interview by Judith Butler. In *Deviations*, 276–309.

Rubin, Gayle S. "Thinking Sex: Notes for a Radical Theory of the Politics of Sexuality." 1984. In *Deviations*, 137–81.

Rubin, Gayle S. "The Traffic in Women: Notes on the 'Political Economy' of Sex." 1975. In *Deviations*, 33–65.

Ruvalcalba, Héctor D. *Translating the Queer: Body Politics and Transnational Conversations*. London: Zed Books, 2016.

Sakai, Naoki. *The End of Pax Americana: The Loss of Empire and Hikikomori Nationalism*. Durham, NC: Duke University Press, 2022.

Salamon, Gayle. *Assuming a Body: Transgender and Rhetorics of Materiality*. New York: Columbia University Press, 2010.

Sandler, Joanne, and Anne Marie Goetz. "Can the United Nations Deliver a Feminist Future?" *Gender and Development* 28, no. 2 (2020): 239–63.

Sang, Tze-lan D. *The Emerging Lesbian: Female Same-Sex Desire in Modern China*. Chicago: University of Chicago Press, 2003.

Sargent, Lydia, ed. *Women and Revolution: A Discussion of the Unhappy Marriage of Marxism and Feminism*. Boston: South End, 1981.

Sautman, Barry, and Hairong Yan. "Discourse of Racialization of Labor and Chinese Enterprises in Africa." *Ethnic and Racial Studies* 39, no. 12 (2016): 2149–68.

Savci, Evren. *Queer in Translation: Sexual Politics under Neoliberal Islam*. Durham, NC: Duke University Press, 2021.

Schaffer, Kay, and Song Xianlin. "Unruly Spaces: Gender, Women's Writing and Indigenous Feminism in China." *Journal of Gender Studies* 16, no. 1 (2007): 17–30.

Schein, Louisa. *Minority Rules: The Miao and the Feminine in China's Cultural Politics*. Durham, NC: Duke University Press, 2000.

Schroeder, Andrew. *Tsui Hark's Zu: Warrior from the Magic Mountain*. Hong Kong: Hong Kong University Press, 2004.

Scott, Joan W. "The Evidence of Experience." *Critical Inquiry* 17, no. 4 (1991): 773–97.

Scott, Joan W. "Fictitious Unities: 'Gender,' 'East,' and 'West.'" Paper presented at the fourth European Feminist Research Conference, Bologna, Italy, September 29, 2000. http://archeologia.women.it/user/cyberarchive/files/scott.htm.

Scott, Joan W. *Gender and the Politics of History*. Rev. ed. New York: Columbia University Press, 1999.

Scott, Joan W. "Gender Studies and Translation Studies: 'Entre Braguette'— Connecting the Transdisciplines." In *Border Crossings: Translation Studies and Other Disciplines*, edited by Yves Gambier and Luc van Doorslaer, 349–66. Amsterdam: John Benjamins, 2016.

Sears, Alan. "Queer Anti-capitalism: What's Left of Lesbian and Gay Liberation." *Science and Society* 69, no. 1 (2005): 92–112.

Sears, Alan. "Situating Sexuality in Social Reproduction." *Historical Materialism* 24, no. 2 (2016): 138–63.

Sedgwick, Eve Kosofsky. *Between Men: English Literature and Male Homosocial Desire*. New York: Columbia University Press, 1985.

Sedgwick, Eve Kosofsky. *Epistemology of the Closet*. Berkeley: University of California Press, 1990.

Sedgwick, Eve Kosofsky. "Gender Criticism: What Isn't Gender." In *Redrawing the Boundaries: The Transformation of English and American Literary Studies*, edited by Stephen Greenblatt and Giles Gunn, 271–302. New York: MLA, 1992.

Selden, Mark. *The Political Economy of Chinese Socialism*. Armonk, NY: M. E. Sharpe, 1988.

Sengupta, Somini. "Xi Jinping Vows to 'Reaffirm' China's Commitment to Women's Rights." *New York Times*, September 27, 2015. https://www.nytimes.com /2015/09/28/world/asia/china-united-nations-womens-rights.html.

Sheridan, Derek. "Prehistories of China-Tanzania: Intermediaries, Subempires, and the Use and Abuse of Comparison." In *New World Orderings*, edited by Lisa Rofel and Carlos Rojas, 58–74. Durham, NC: Duke University Press, 2023.

Shi, Flair Donglai. "Reconsidering Sinophone Studies: The Chinese Cold War, Multiple Sinocentrisms, and Theoretical Generalisation." *International Journal of Taiwan Studies* 4, no. 2 (2021): 1–34.

Shi, Liang. "Constructing a New Sexual Paradigm: Emergence of a Modern Subject." *Prism* 17, no. 2 (2020): 264–76.

Shih, Shu-mei. *The Lure of the Modern: Writing Modernism in Semi-colonial China, 1917–1937*. Berkeley: University of California Press, 2001.

Shildrick, Margrit. *Dangerous Discourses of Disability, Subjectivity, and Sexuality*. New York: Palgrave Macmillan, 2009.

Shue, Vivienne. *Peasant China in Transition: The Dynamics of Development toward Socialism, 1949–1946*. Berkeley: University of California Press, 1981.

Silver, Beverly J., and Lu Zhang. "China as an Emerging Epicenter of World Labor Unrest." In Hung, *China and the Transformation of Global Capitalism*, 174–87.

Sinnott, Megan. "Border, Diaspora and Regional Connections: Trends in Asian 'Queer' Studies." *Journal of Asian Studies* 69, no. 1 (2010): 17–31.

Sinnott, Megan. *Toms and Dees: Transgender Identity and Female Same-Sex Relationships in Thailand*. Honolulu: University of Hawai'i Press, 2004.

Solinger, Dorothy. *Contesting Citizenship in Urban China: Peasant Migrants, the State, and the Logic of the Market*. Berkeley: University of California Press, 1999.

Sommer, Matthew H. *Sex, Law, and Society in Late Imperial China*. Stanford, CA: Stanford University Press, 2000.

Song, Lin. *Queering Chinese Kinship: Queer Public Culture in Globalizing China*. Hong Kong: Hong Kong University Press, 2022.

Spade, Dean. *Normal Life: Administrative Violence, Critical Trans Politics, and the Limits of Law*. Durham, NC: Duke University Press, 2015.

Spakowski, Nicola. "'Gender' Trouble: Feminism in China under the Impact of Western Theory and the Spatialization of Identity." *positions: asia critique* 19, no. 1 (2011): 31–54.

Spakowski, Nicola. "Socialist Feminism in Postsocialist China." *positions: asia critique* 26, no. 4 (2018): 561–92.

Spivak, Gayatri Chakravorty. "Bonding in Difference: Interview with Alfred Arteaga (1993–1994)." In *The Spivak Reader*, edited by Donna Landry and Gerald Maclean, 15–29. New York: Routledge, 1992.

Stacey, Judith. *Socialist Revolution in China*. Berkeley: University of California Press, 1983.

Stoler, Ann Laura. *Race and the Education of Desire: Foucault's History of Sexuality and the Colonial Order of Things*. Durham, NC: Duke University Press, 1995.

Stryker, Susan, and Paisley Currah. "Introduction." *TSQ: Transgender Studies Quarterly* 1, nos. 1–2 (2014): 1–18.

Stuckey, Andrew G. "Female Relations: Voiceless Women in 'Liuyi jie' and 'Zhufu.'" *Frontiers of Literary Study in China* 11, no. 3 (2017): 488–509.

Sun, Feiyu. *Social Suffering and Political Confession: Suku in Modern China*. Hackensack, NJ: World Scientific, 2013.

Sun, Ge. "How Does Asia Mean?" *Inter-Asia Cultural Studies* 1, no. 1 (2000): 13–47.

Sun, Saiyin. *Beyond the Iron House: Lu Xun and the Modern Chinese Literary Field*. New York: Routledge, 2016.

Sun Yixue 孫宜學. *Jin Yong zhuan: Qian gu wen tan xia sheng meng* 金庸傳: 千古文壇俠聖夢 [A biography of Jin Yong: Dreams of the everlasting champion of the literary world]. Taipei: Fengyun, 2004.

Sun Yonghuan 孙永焕, producer. "Xin xiao ao jianghu" 新笑傲江湖 [New smiling, proud wanderer]. Beijing Enlight Media, 2018.

Sun, Yun. "China's Aid to Africa: Monster or Messiah?" Brookings, February 7, 2014. https://www.brookings.edu/opinions/chinas-aid-to-africa-monster-or-messiah/

Symons, Jonathan, and Dennis Altman. "International Norm Polarization: Sexuality as a Subject of Human Rights Protection." *International Theory* 7, no. 1 (2015): 61–95.

Szonyi, Michael. *Cold War Island: Quemoy on the Front Line*. Cambridge: Cambridge University Press, 2008.

Tadiar, Neferti. *Fantasy-Production: Sexual Economies and Other Philippine Consequences for the New World Order*. Hong Kong: Hong Kong University Press, 2004.

Takeuchi Yoshimi. "Asia as Method." In *What Is Modernity? Writings of Takeuchi Yoshimi*, 149–65. Edited and translated by Richard Calichman. New York: Columbia University Press, 2005.

Takeuchi Yoshimi. "What Is Modernity?" In *What Is Modernity? Writings of Takeuchi Yoshimi*, 53–81. Edited and translated by Richard Calichman. New York: Columbia University Press, 2005.

Tam, Kwok-kan. *Chinese Ibsenism: Reinventions of Women, Class, and Nation*. Singapore: Springer, 2019.

Tan, Jia. "Digital Masquerading: Feminist Media Activism in China." *Crime Media Culture* 13, no. 2 (2017): 171–86.

Tan, Jia. "Networking Asia Pacific: Queer Film Festivals and the Spatiotemporal Politics of Inter-referencing." *Inter-Asia Cultural Studies* 20, no. 2 (2019): 204–19.

Tang, Tao. "Two Portrayals of Chinese Women in Lu Hsun's Stories." *Chinese Literature* 9 (1973): 83–90.

Tang, Xiaobing. "Lu Xun's 'Diary of a Madman' and a Chinese Modernism." *PMLA* 107, no. 5 (1992): 1222–34.

Tansman, Alan, and J. Keith Vincent. "Sōseki Great and Small: Notes on Sōseki's Diversity." Special issue, *Bungaku* (December 2014).

Taylor, Jeremy E., and Lanjun Xu, eds. *Chineseness and the Cold War: Contested Cultures and Diaspora in Southeast Asia and Hong Kong*. London: Routledge, 2021.

Tellis, Ashley, and Sruti Bala, eds. *The Global Trajectories of Queerness: Rethinking Same-Sex Politics in the Global South*. Boston: Brill, 2015.

Teo, Stephen. *Chinese Martial Arts Cinema: The Wuxia Tradition*. Edinburgh: Edinburgh University Press, 2009.

Teo, Stephen. "Tsui Hark: National Style and Polemic." In *At Full Speed: Hong Kong Cinema in a Borderless World*, edited by Esther C. M. Yau, 143–58. Minneapolis: University of Minnesota Press, 2001.

Tilley, Lisa, Ashok Kumar, and Thomas Cowan. "Introduction: Enclosures and Discontents: Primitive Accumulation and Resistance under Globalised Capital." *City* 21, nos. 3–4 (2017): 420–27.

Tinkcom, Matthew. *Working like a Homosexual: Camp, Capital, Cinema*. Durham, NC: Duke University Press, 2002.

Tran, Richard Quang-Anh. "Sexuality as Translation: Locating the 'Queer' in a 1920s Vietnamese Debate." *Annali di Ca' Foscari, Serie Orientale* 56 (2020): 353–78.

Treat, John W. "The Rise and Fall of Homonationalism in Singapore." *positions: asia critique* 23, no. 2 (2015): 349–65.

Tsu, Jing. *Kingdom of Characters: The Language Revolution That Made China Modern*. New York: Riverhead Books, 2022.

United Nations Commission on the Status of Women. *Report of the United Nations Conference on Human Settlements (Habitat II), Istanbul, 3–14 June 1996*. August 7, 1996. https://www.un.org/ruleoflaw/wp-content /uploads/2015/10/istanbul-declaration.pdf.

Valocchi, Stephen. "Capitalism and Gay Identities: Towards a Capitalist Theory of Social Movements." *Social Problems* 64, no. 2 (2017): 315–31.

Valocchi, Stephen. "The Class-Inflected Nature of Gay Identity." *Social Problems* 46, no. 2 (1999): 207–24.

Veg, Sebastian. "On the Margins of Modernity: A Comparative Study of Gao Xingjian and Ōe Kenzaburō." *China Perspectives*, no. 2010/2 (2010): 34–45.

Vincent, J. Keith. "Sex on the Mind: Queer Theory Meets Cognitive Theory." In *The Oxford Handbook of Cognitive Literary Studies*, edited by Lisa Zunshine, 199–221. New York: Oxford University Press, 2015.

Vincent, J. Keith. "Takemura Kazuko: On Friendship and the Queering of American and Japanese Studies." In *Rethinking Japanese Feminisms*, edited by Julia C. Bullock, Ayako Kano, and James Welker, 251–66. Honolulu: University of Hawai'i Press, 2017.

Visvanathan, Nalini, Lynn Duggan, Laurie Nisonoff, and Nan Wiegersma, eds. *The Women, Gender, and Development Reader*. London: Zed Books, 1997.

Vitiello, Giovanni. *The Libertine's Friend: Homosexuality and Masculinity in Late Imperial China*. Chicago: University of Chicago Press, 2011.

Vogel, Lise. *Marxism and the Oppression of Women: Toward a Unitary Theory*. 1983. Leiden: Brill, 2013.

Volland, Nicolai. "Turning the Tables on the Global North: China, Afro-Asia, and Cold War Cultural Diplomacy." In *New World Orderings*, edited by Lisa Rofel and Carlos Rojas, 21–37. Durham, NC: Duke University Press, 2023.

Von Kowallis, Jon Eugene. "Takeuchi's Lu Xun/China's Takeuchi." *Journal of the Oriental Society of Australia* 49 (2018): 1–25.

Walker, Gavin. "The Accumulation of Difference and the Logic of Area." *positions: asia critique* 27, no. 1 (2019): 67–98.

Walker, Robert, and Jane Millar. "Is the Sky Falling in on Women in China?" *Made in China Journal* 5, no. 1 (2020): 50–55.

Wang, Chaohua, ed. *One China, Many Paths*. London: Verso, 2005.

Wang, David Der-wei. *Fictional Realism in Twentieth-Century China*. New York: Columbia University Press, 1992.

Wang, David Der-wei. "Impersonating China." *Chinese Literature: Essays, Articles, Reviews (CLEAR)* 25 (December 2003): 133–63.

Wang, David Der-wei. "Popular Literature and National Representation: The Gender and Genre Politics of *Begonia*." In *Rethinking Chinese Popular Culture: Cannibalization of the Canon*, edited by Carlos Rojas and Eileen Cheng-yin Chow, 209–34. New York: Routledge, 2009.

Wang Hui. *China's New Order: Society, Politics, and Economics in Transition*. Cambridge, MA: Harvard University Press, 2003.

Wang Hui. *The End of the Revolution: China and the Limits of Modernity*. London: Verso, 2009.

Wang Lingzhen. "Gender and Sexual Differences in 1980s China: Introducing Li Xiaojiang." *differences: A Journal of Feminist Cultural Studies* 24, no. 2 (2013): 8–21.

Wang Ping. "Why Inter-Asia? The *Tongzhi* Movement." Translated by Petrus Liu. *Inter-Asia Cultural Studies* 2, no. 1 (2001): 127–31.

Wang, Qi, and Min Dongchao, eds. *Revisiting Gender Inequality: Perspectives from the People's Republic of China*. New York: Palgrave Macmillan, 2016.

Wang, Qin. "Literary Evolutionism and Its Discontents: Between Zhou Zuoren and Lu Xun." In *Configurations of the Individual in Modern Chinese Literature*, 57–114. New York: Palgrave Macmillan, 2019.

Wang, Xiaojue. *Modernity with a Cold War Face: Reimagining the Nation in Chinese Literature across the 1949 Divide*. Cambridge, MA: Harvard University Press, 2013.

Wang Xiaoming. "Introduction: Chinese Cultural Studies in the Utilitarianism-Oriented Age." *Cultural Studies* 31, no. 6 (2017): 735–39.

Wang Xiaoming. "A Manifesto for Cultural Studies." In Chaohua Wang, *One China, Many Paths*, 274–91.

Wang Zheng. "Detention of the Feminist Five in China." *Feminist Studies* 41, no. 2 (2015): 476–82.

Wang Zheng. "Maoism, Feminism, and the UN Conference on Women: Women's Studies Research in Contemporary China." *Journal of Women's History* 8, no. 4 (1997): 126–54.

Wang Zheng 王政. "'Nüxing yishi,' 'shehui xingbie yishi' bianyi" 女性意识, 社会性别意识 辨异 [Distinguishing between "women's consciousness" and "gender consciousness"]. *Funü yanjiu* 妇女研究 [Research on women] 2 (1997): 17–23.

Weed, Elizabeth. "From the 'Useful' to the 'Impossible' in the Work of Joan W. Scott." In *The Question of Gender: Joan W. Scott's Critical Feminism*, edited by Judith Butler and Elizabeth Weed, 277–381. Bloomington: Indiana University Press, 2011.

Weeks, Kathi. *The Problem with Work: Feminism, Marxism, Antiwork Politics, and Postwork Imaginaries*. Durham, NC: Duke University Press, 2011.

Wei, John. *Queer Chinese Cultures and Mobilities*. Hong Kong: Hong Kong University Press, 2020.

Wei, Tingting. "A Look at the Beijing Conference through Lesbian Eyes." *Asian Journal of Women's Studies* 21, no. 3 (2015): 316–25.

Wei, Wei. "Queering the Rise of China: Gay Parenthood, Transnational ARTs, and Dislocated Reproductive Rights." *Feminist Studies* 47, no. 2 (2021): 312–40.

Weiss, Margot. "Queer Politics in Neoliberal Times (1970s-2010s)." In *Routledge History of Queer America*, edited by Don Romesburg, 107–20. New York: Routledge, 2018.

Weiss, Margot. "Queer Theory from Elsewhere and the Im/Proper Objects of Queer Anthropology." *Feminist Anthropology* (May 2022). https://doi.org /10.1002/fea2.12084.

Wen Tiejun. "Centenary Reflections on the 'Three-Dimensional Problem' of Rural China." Translated by Petrus Liu. *Inter-Asia Cultural Studies* 2, no. 2 (2001): 287–95.

Wen Tiejun. *Ten Crises: The Political Economy of China's Development (1949– 2020)*. Singapore: Palgrave, 2021.

Wesling, Meg. "Queer Value." *GLQ: A Journal of Gay and Lesbian Studies* 18, no. 1 (2012): 107–26.

Wilson, Ara. "Queering Asia." *Intersections: Gender, History and Culture in the Asian Context*, no. 14 (2006). http://intersections.anu.edu.au/issue14 /wilson.html.

Wittig, Monique. "One Is Not Born a Woman." In *The Straight Mind and Other Essays*, 9–20. Boston: Beacon Press, 1992.

Wolf, Sherry. *Sexuality and Socialism: History, Politics, and Theory of LGBT Liberation*. Chicago: Haymarket, 2009.

Wong, Alvin K. "Queering the Quality of Desire: Perverse Use-Values in Transnational Chinese Cultures." *Culture, Theory and Critique* 58, no. 2 (2017): 209–25.

Wong, Day. "Hybridization and the Emergence of 'Gay' Identities in Hong Kong and in China." *Visual Anthropology* 24, nos. 1–2 (2010): 152–70.

Wong, Kam-ming, and Chung-min Tu. "Retroactive Lyricism/Eternal Return: Lu Xun, Darwin, and Nietzsche." In *International Readings in Theory, History and Philosophy of Culture*, edited by Luibava Moreva, 215–56. St. Petersburg, Russia: EIDOS, 2001.

Wong, Lily. *Transpacific Attachments: Sex Work, Media Networks, and Affective Histories of Chinese*. New York: Columbia University Press, 2018.

Wong, R. Bin. *China Transformed: Historical Change and the Limits of European Experience*. Ithaca, NY: Cornell University Press, 1997.

Wong, Wang-chi. *Politics and Literature in Shanghai: The Chinese League of Left-Wing Writers, 1930–1936*. Manchester: Manchester University Press, 1991.

Wu, Angela Xiao, and Yige Dong. "What Is Made-in-China Feminism(s)? Gender Discontent and Class Friction in Post-socialist China." *Critical Asian Studies* 51, no. 4: 471–92.

Wu, Chongqing, ed. *Mapping China: Peasants, Migrant Workers, and Informal Labor*. Leiden: Brill, 2016.

Wu, Guo. "Speaking Bitterness: Political Education in Land Reform and Military Training under the CCP, 1947–1951." *Chinese Historical Review* 21, no. 1 (2014): 3–23.

Xiang, Zairong. "Transdualism: Toward a Materio-Discursive Embodiment." *TSQ: Transgender Studies Quarterly* 5, no. 3 (2018): 425–42.

Xiaomingxiong [Samshasha] 小明雄. *Zhongguo tongxing'ai shilu* 中國同性愛史錄 [A history of homosexual love in China]. 1984. Hong Kong: Fenhong sanjiao chubanshe, 1997.

Xinhuanet 新华网. "Xi Jinping wenyi gongzuo tanhui" 习近平文艺工作座谈会 [Xi Jinping's speech at the forum on literature and art]. Oct. 15, 2014. http://www.xinhuanet.com//politics/2014-10/15/c_1112840544.htm.

Xinhuanet 新华网. "Xi Jinping zai quanqiu funü fenghui shang de jianghua" 习近平在全球妇女峰会上的讲话 [Xi Jinping's speech at the Global Women's Summit.] September 28, 2015. http://www.xinhuanet.com/politics/2015-09/28/c_128272780.htm.

Xu, Feng. "Chinese Feminisms Encounter International Feminisms: Identity, Power and Knowledge Production." *International Feminist Journal of Politics* 11, no. 2 (2009): 196–215.

Yan, Hairong. "Neoliberal Governmentality and Neohumanism: Organizing Suzhi/Value Flow through Labor Recruitment Networks." *Cultural Anthropology* 18, no. 4 (2003): 493–523.

Yan, Hairong. *New Masters, New Servants: Migration, Development, and Women Workers in China*. Durham, NC: Duke University Press, 2008.

Yang, Mayfair Mei-hui. "From Gender Erasure to Gender Difference: State Feminism, Consumer Sexuality, and Women's Public Sphere in China." In *Spaces of Their Own: Women's Public Sphere in Transnational China*, edited by Mayfair Mei-hui Yang, 35–66. Minneapolis: University of Minnesota Press, 1999.

Yapp, Hentyle. *Minor China: Method, Materialisms, and the Aesthetic*. Durham, NC: Duke University Press, 2021.

Yau Ching 游靜. *Xingbie guangying: Xianggang dianying zhong de xing yu xingbie wenhua yanjiu* 性別光影：香港電影中的性與性別文化研究 [Gender shadows: Gender and sexuality in Hong Kong cinema]. Hong Kong: Hong Kong Film Critics Society, 2005.

Ye, Min. *The Belt Road and Beyond: State-Mobilized Globalization in China: 1998–2018*. Cambridge: Cambridge University Press, 2020.

Ye, Shana. "The Drama of Chinese Feminism: Neoliberal Agency, Post-Socialist Coloniality, and Post-Cold War Transnational Feminist Praxis." *Feminist Studies* 47, no. 3 (2021): 783–812.

Ye, Shana. "Reconstructing the Transgendered Self as a Feminist Subject: Trans/ Feminist Praxis in Urban China." *TSQ: Transgender Studies Quarterly* 3, nos. 1–2 (2016): 259–65.

Yi, We Jung. "Division Literature and Visions for De-bordering: Ch'oe Inhun, Pak Wansŏ, and Individuals without Belonging." In *Routledge Handbook of Modern Korean Literature*, edited by Yoon Sun Yang, 143–55. New York: Routledge, 2020.

Yin, Zhiguang. *Politics of Art: The Creation Society and the Practice of Theoretical Struggle in Revolutionary China*. Leiden: Brill, 2014.

Yu Hua. *China in Ten Words*. New York: Anchor Books, 2011.

Yu Zheng 于正, producer. "Xiao ao jianghu" 笑傲江湖 [Swordsman]. Hunan Satellite Television, 2013.

Zavarzadeh, Mas'ud, Teresa L. Ebert, and Donald Morton, eds. *Marxism, Queer Theory, Gender*. Syracuse, NY: Red Factory, 2001.

Zhan, Shaohua. *The Land Question in China: Agrarian Capitalism, Industrious Revolution, and East Asian Development*. New York: Routledge, 2019.

Zhang, Amy. "Invisible Labouring Bodies: Waste Work as Infrastructure in China." *Made in China Journal* 4, no. 2 (2019): 98–102.

Zhang, Charlie Yi. *Dreadful Desires: The Uses of Love in Neoliberal China*. Durham, NC: Duke University Press, 2022.

Zhang Guiyang 張圭陽. *Jin Yong yu Ming Pao chuanqi* 金庸與明報傳奇 [Jin Yong and *Ming Pao Daily* legend]. Taipei: Yunchen, 2005.

Zhang, Li. *Strangers in the City: Reconfigurations of Space, Power, and Social Networks within China's Floating Population*. Stanford, CA: Stanford University Press, 2001.

Zhang, Qian Forrest, and John Donaldson. "The Rise of Agrarian Capitalism with Chinese Characteristics: Agricultural Modernization, Agribusiness and Collective Land Rights." *China Journal* 60 (2008): 25–47.

Zhong, Xueping. "Four Interpretations for the Slogan 'Women Hold up Half the Sky.'" *Nankai University (Philosophy and Social Sciences)* 4 (2009): 54–64.

Zhong, Xueping. "Who Is Afraid of Lu Xun? Politics of 'Lu Xun lunzheng' and the Question of His Legacy in Post-revolution China." In *China's Literary and Cultural Scene at the Turn of the 21st Century*, edited by Jie Lu, 81–102. New York: Routledge, 2008.

Zhong, Yurou. *Chinese Grammatology: Script Revolution and Literary Modernity, 1916–1958*. New York: Columbia University, 2019.

Zhou, Egret Lulu. "Dongfang Bubai, Online Fandom, and the Gender Politics of a Legendary Queer Icon in Post-Mao China." In *Boys' Love, Cosplay, and Androgynous Idols: Queer Fan Cultures in Mainland China, Hong Kong, and Taiwan*, edited by Maud Lavin, Ling Yang, and Jing Jamie Zhao, 101–27. Hong Kong: Hong Kong University Press, 2017.

Zhu, Ping. *Gender and Subjectivities in Early Twentieth-Century Chinese Litera-ture and Culture*. New York: Palgrave Macmillan, 2015.

Žižek, Slavoj. "Class Struggle or Postmodernism? Yes, Please!" In *Contingency, Hegemony, Universality: Contemporary Dialogues on the Left*, edited by Ju-dith Butler, Ernesto Laclau, and Slavoj Žižek, 90–135. London: Verso, 2000.

Zwingel, Susanne. *Translating International Women's Rights: The CEDAW Con-vention in Context*. London: Palgrave, 2016.

Index

accumulation, 24, 162; of capital (*see* capital accumulation); China as new center of capitalist, 35; endless, 131; flexible mode of, 2, 66; global imperatives of, 39; interstate competitive, 26; logics of, 48; transnational routes of, 4; zones of, 9. *See also* primitive accumulation

alterity, 25–26, 28, 30, 32, 41, 167n10; ethical, 71–72; gender as dispossessed, 94

Althusser, Louis, 12, 71, 96, 166n20, 179n82. *See also* interpellation

Anti-Extradition Law Amendment Bill Movement, 3, 104, 110

area studies, 109, 116–17, 185n12; US, 58, 63

Arondekar, Anjali, 35, 67, 178n54

Arrighi, Giovanni, 39–41

autonomy, 121; bodily, 73, 151; Hong Kong's, 110; national, 6; sexual, 15, 107

Barlow, Tani, 148, 151

berdache, 31, 34

Berlant, Lauren, 28, 117, 169n17

Butler, Judith, 29, 70–76, 94, 136, 152, 157, 168n13, 175n14, 178n69, 189n6, 190n15; *Bodies That Matter*, 15, 57, 72; theory of gender performativity, 178n62, 179n73, 179n82. *See also Gender Trouble*

capital, 3, 8–12, 17, 23–24, 27, 37, 46, 48–51, 65; as absent cause, 166n20; body and, 56; corporate, 66; cultural, 89; financial, 43, 50; gendered subjectivity and, 99; global, 4–5, 7, 162–63; sexual difference and, 174n10. *See also* accumulation; capital accumulation; labor

Capital (Marx), 8, 10, 24, 64, 74–75, 124, 176n21

capital accumulation, 2–3, 5–6, 13, 38, 40, 44, 161; Cold War and, 15, 105–6, 109; by dispossession, 26, 42, 74; enclosure and, 117; European, 70; four cycles of, 69; geographic process of, 22; global history of, 58; primitive, 122, 163; Taiwan's structure of, 114; uneven, 30, 162

capitalism, 5, 7, 9–14, 22–27, 30, 41, 44, 56–57, 65–70, 74–77, 83, 103, 105, 139, 162, 167n34; agrarian, 4, 43, 45; China's, 128; Cold War, 109, 113, 121–22, 124, 130; East Asian, 106, 121–22, 124, 130; feminized labor and, 61; financial, 49, 174n11; global, 1–2, 13, 17, 26, 34–35, 37, 45, 49, 51, 58, 82, 87, 126, 171n57; late, 37; homosexuality and, 176n29; industrial, 4, 62; neocolonial, 107; neoliberal, 22–23, 26, 54, 66, 142, 159; patriarchy and, 165n8; racial, 1, 29, 48, 114; sexuality and, 159–60; state, 38–39, 105; uneven and

capitalism (*continued*)
combined development of, 116; world, 16, 136; as world ecology, 175n12. *See also* subsumption

Chen Duxiu, 83, 87–89

Chen, Kuan-Hsing, 15, 102–3, 184n89, 184n92, 185n7

Chinese Civil War, 114–15, 130; *Swordsman II* and, 129

Chinese Communist Party (CCP), 83–87, 132, 138, 148, 155, 180n4, 192n45

Chinese Dream, 3, 154

Ching Siu-tung, 106, 118–19. See also *Swordsman II: Asia the Invincible*

Chou Wah-shan, 121, 140

Chow, Rey, 98, 117, 170n33

Chuǎng, 38–39

class, 5, 24, 35, 42, 58, 64, 66–68, 70, 77, 184n92; capitalist relations of, 60; conflict, 78, 87; consciousness, 86, 97; divisions, 56; issues, 64; mobility, 114; politics, 52; queer theory and, 22; respectability, 45; struggle, 59, 84–85, 88, 105

Club 51 phenomenon, 115, 186n21

Cold War, 4, 14–16, 106–13, 116, 118–19, 185n10; in Asia, 186n19; capital accumulation and, 105; discourse, 186n17; as materialist method, 16, 107–9; order, 40; *The Smiling, Proud Wanderer* and, 121–26; strategy of containment, 43; structure of feeling, 103; subsumption of, 14, 106, 109, 130–31; *Swordsman II* and, 128–31; Taiwan and, 115; trans-memory of, 185n8

colonialism, 102–3, 107, 163, 174n11; China and, 2; Chinese, 114, 121, 129; Cold War and, 186n19; gender and, 136; Going Out policy and, 48; homosexuals and, 4; Hong Kong and, 113; Japanese, 114; Taiwan and, 110; violence of, 101

Communism, 38, 107, 113, 122, 125–26, 179n73, 186n17, 186n19; Chinese, 42, 83–84, 121, 124; collapse of, 104, 110; containment of, 106

Confucianism, 83, 90–91, 148

constitutive outside, 16, 25, 27–31, 37, 168n13; capital accumulation as, 38; capital's, 6, 14, 26; China's, 39, 46; identity's, 66; materialism as queer theory's, 63; peasantry as, 42; queerness as, 51; of the subject, 70

Convention on the Elimination of All Forms of Discrimination against Women (CEDAW), 156, 194n80

corporeality, 57, 168n13

Cultural Revolution, 29, 85, 127, 189n3; *The Smiling, Proud Wanderer* and, 124, 188n44; *Swordsman II* and, 121–22, 128, 130; *Swordsman III: East is Red* and, 123

Currah, Paisley, 22, 135, 174n1

dagongmei (female migrant laborers), 3, 14, 44, 46

Dai Jinhua, 15, 192n57

Davies, Gloria, 84, 180n4

deconstruction, 22, 36

D'Emilio, John, 67–69, 177n53

democracy, 8, 42, 113; for China, 87; democratization as, 186n19; Hong Kong, 105, 111; new, 4, 84; radical, 168n13, 175n17; socialist, 43, 48–49, 85. *See also* New Democracy movement

Deng Xiaoping, 2, 42, 105

desire, 4, 51, 62, 73, 167n9; in capitalism, 65; non-Western subjects of, 31; reified, 22, 24; same-sex, 33–34, 188n41; sexual, 168n16

disabilities, 54, 66

dispossession, 5, 22, 24, 118, 162; accumulation by, 26, 42, 74; accumulation without, 46; experiences of, 99; gender and, 72–73, 75 (*see also* Butler, Judith); Indigenous studies and, 179n74; transnational routes of, 4

Drucker, Peter, 16, 70

East Asian Tigers, 41, 106

Ebert, Teresa, 61–62

industrialization, 37, 49, 105; of war, 40
Inter-Asia Cultural Studies, 102,
 183–84n88
inter-Asia cultural studies movement, 4,
 183n88
interpellation, 12, 24, 179n82
intersectional analysis, 14, 66–67

Jameson, Fredric, 61–62, 84, 110, 180n7
jianghu, 122–23
Jin Yong, 118–23, 125–28, 186n28,
 188n44, 188n49, 188n51. *See also*
 Xiao ao jianghu (*The Smiling, Proud*
 Wanderer)
Jones, Andrew F., 87–88

Kong, Travis S. K., 187n34, 188n42
Kuomintang (KMT), 114–15

labor, 2–5, 8, 23–24, 44–45, 56,
 61–62, 75–76, 167n34, 171n57, 175n11,
 186n13; abstract, 22, 64; Chinese, 48;
 colonial division of, 39; free, 67–68;
 gender and, 174n10; gendered, 51, 60;
 immaterial, 66, 177n42; immobility
 of, 161; intellectual, 36, 109, 116–18;
 international division of, 40, 116;
 material, 12; migrant, 172n71; power,
 8, 10–11, 95–96; process, 10–11, 24,
 38, 134; protests, 42, 172n63; rights,
 125; struggles, 16, 41, 46, 109, 128,
 130; subsumption of, 22, 24, 41; theory
 of value, 10, 71, 75–76; unwaged, 26;
 wage, 24, 44, 60, 69, 83, 95; women's
 public, 132
Laclau, Ernesto, 58, 168n13, 175n17
land reform, 42–43
land tenure system, 7, 43
Latin America, 7, 47, 51, 116
Lewis, Holly, 16, 66
liberalism: multicultural differences and,
 167n10; progressive, 17, 22; queer,
 120, 176n38
Li Dazhao, 83, 87–89, 181n33
Lin Ching-Hsia, Brigitte, 119, 121–22,
 188nn42–43

Lin Chun, 153, 180n5
linguistic turn, 14, 21, 52, 71
literature, 81–83, 87, 89, 101, 108,
 116–17, 180n6; Cold War and, 107;
 East Asian, 103; Korean, 113; Marxist approaches to, 24; non-Western,
 168n16; realist, 86; revolutionary, 85,
 88; subsumption of, 14–15, 82; theory
 of, 81, 88
Li Xiaojiang, 142–47, 151
Li Zehou, 88, 143, 181n19
Love, Heather, 117, 168n14
Lukács, György, 65–66, 86, 179n82,
 181n26. *See also* reification
Luxemburg, Rosa, 13, 74
Lu Xun, 15, 42, 82–103, 180nn4–5,
 181n18, 181n21, 181n27, 181n30,
 182n41, 182n51, 182n59, 182n62; irony
 and, 83, 90–91, 98; Maoist appropriations of, 181n17; Nietzsche and, 180n9.
 See also Ibsen, Henrik

McRuer, Robert, 66, 174n5
Mandel, Ernest, 37–38
Manichaeism, 127–28, 188n51
Maoism, 145; discrediting of, 3, 100
Mao Zedong, 7, 39, 88; Cold War and,
 105, 119; *Little Red Book*, 125; Lu Xun
 and, 85–86; *The Smiling, Proud Wanderer* and, 119, 123
Marx, Karl, 8–12, 24, 59, 167n34; Althusser's reading of, 96; Butler and,
 75, 179n73, 179n82; critique of political economy, 5; definition of labor,
 56; on dispossession, 74; Haraway
 on, 60; labor theory of value, 76; Lu
 Xun's knowledge of, 83; on primitive
 accumulation, 74; queering, 63–64;
 real and formal subsumption, 7, 13, 28,
 37; social reproduction and, 175n21.
 See also Capital; Harootunian, Harry;
 Mandel, Ernest; materialism; materiality; Postone, Moishe; Wang Hui
Marxism, 8, 13–15, 22, 24, 26–27,
 52–55, 58–66, 70–71, 74, 76–77, 147,
 162; Asian, 103, 184n92; Black, 48;

Bolshevik, 89; Butler and, 73; Chinese, 15, 81–83, 88, 149, 183n62 (*see also* Lu Xun); cultural, 83; as cultural revolution of everyday life, 180n6; global queer, 7, 51, 162–63; *Inter-Asia Cultural Studies* and, 102; Lu Xun and, 83, 87–88, 92–95, 99–100, 103; post-Marxism, 1475n17; queer, 16, 25, 58, 65, 70–71; transgender and, 56; transexual, 179n73; Western, 63, 88

Marxism-Leninism, 144, 159; PRC's, 101

mass line, 42, 81

material, the, 52, 54–55, 57–58, 62, 70, 175n14; specters of, 72, 77

materialism, 5–9, 12, 22, 174n5; Butler and, 71; combined and uneven development and, 39; cultural, 83; feminist, 61, 134; gender and, 95–96, 100; historical, 33, 59, 61, 67, 85, 102–3, 134; Marxism and, 14, 24, 77, 163; Marx's, 66; queer theory and, 14–15, 27, 51, 54–55, 58, 62, 70, 163, 72, 77; transgender, 56

Min Dongchao, 147–49

Ming Pao, 125–26, 128, 186n28

modernism, 92: literary, 84, 87, 94; queer, 15, 83, 94. *See also* Lu Xun

modernization, 40, 84, 105, 113, 182n37; capitalist, 42, 82; Maoist theory of, 153; postsocialist, 44

money boys (rural-to-urban sex workers), 14, 45–46

Mouffe, Chantal, 58, 168n13, 175n17

Muñoz, José Esteban, 29, 67

Negri, Antonio, 12, 66

neocolonialism, 48; Chinese, 129; US, 110

neoliberalism, 6, 32, 41, 49, 108; China's, 45, 132; developmental logic of, 174n108; sexual politics of, 65

New Democracy movement, 105, 108

new social movements, 52, 58, 175n14

Nietzsche, Friedrich, 84, 90, 135, 180n9

North Korea, 109–10, 116

Parker, Andrew, 63–64, 176n33

Patel, Geeta, 35, 167n9

patriarchy, 60, 95, 97, 150, 165n8; Confucian, 146

peasants, 7, 42–43, 59, 74, 82–83, 103

Penny, James, 61–62

People's Republic of China (PRC), 105, 109, 115, 126, 142, 185n10, 189n3; education system, 91; global South and, 139; interpretations of Lu Xun, 82, 85–87, 100; Marxism-Leninism of, 101; queer culture in, 172n83; Taiwan and, 110, 186n21; trans discourses on, 191n27; women's history, 145

pinkwashing, 17, 25, 176n38

Pletsch, Carl, 116–17

pluralism: American liberal, 58; epistemic, 170n33; gender, 30, 33–34, 36, 139; sexual, 33

political economy, 5, 15, 22, 65, 134, 137, 140; of the Beijing Consensus, 58; bourgeois, 96; capitalist, 63; China's postreform, 85; China's postsocialist, 3, 26, 39, 51, 162; of feminisms, 158; gender and, 133, 136, 138, 146, 160; of heterosexuality, 29; queer and, 190n14; trans, 23–24

Postone, Moishe, 37–38, 167n34. *See also* treadmill effect

postsocialism, 82, 107, 153

primitive accumulation, 10, 22, 43–44, 49, 74, 163; China's, 105, 122; formal subsumption and, 13; production of arms and, 37; social relations and, 83

privatization, 2, 14, 26, 48, 65, 132, 162

proletarianization, 2, 70, 74

psychoanalysis, 22, 62, 168n16, 178n67

Puar, Jasbir K., 53–54, 175n18

queerness, 5, 21, 51, 92, 145; family relations and, 172n83; Marx and, 63–64

queer studies, 21, 25, 33, 67, 94; Cold War and, 108; location-specific approaches to, 171n44; political referent of, 175n18; solidarity politics of, 168n14 queer theory, 4, 27–28, 30; allochronic, 31, 33; antifoundationalist, 56; Cold War and, 118; early, 4, 14, 28, 31, 34, 56, 168n16; liberal, 5, 14, 29, 169n26; materialism and, 76; materialist, 5, 7, 13, 16–17, 24, 27, 51, 94; transnational, 25, 33, 168n16, 171n43; US, 32, 34, 36

Qu Qiubai, 83–84, 88, 182n62
racism, 8, 21, 70
realism, 87, 181n26; critical, 81–83; geopolitical, 117; investigative, 88; political, 125; socialist, 86–87
reification, 12, 65, 179n82; of capital, 9; of social relations, 9, 83
Rocha, Leon, 148, 192n50
Rofel, Lisa, 143, 153, 173n108, 178n56
Rubin, Gayle S., 33, 57, 59, 134–35, 142, 14546, 170n38, 189n12. *See also* sex/gender system

sannong wenti, 7, 42
Scott, Joan W., 55, 137, 142, 145, 191n38
Sears, Alan, 16, 176n29
Sedgwick, Eve Kosofsky, 1, 25, 32, 35–36, 63, 117, 135, 146, 193n59
settler colonialism, 114, 174n11; Chinese, 129
sex, 6, 16, 28–29, 31, 33–34, 55, 57, 59, 63, 133–35, 137–39, 141–44, 146, 148, 152, 156–57, 159, 169n28, 171n43, 174n1, 189n6; Western notions of, 27; *xing* and, 147, 192n50. *See also* gender; Rubin, Gayle S.
sex/gender system, 33, 57, 134–35, 189n6
sexuality, 3–5, 7, 9, 14, 16, 31, 34–36, 41, 45, 58, 62, 65, 70, 72, 76, 77, 82, 135, 137–38, 151–53, 158, 167n9, 168n16, 169n28, 189n6, 189n12; capital and, 26; capitalism and, 54, 83, 159; Chinese modernity and, 94; dispossession and, 73; gay, 187n34; history of, 30, 67, 69, 109, 178n54; Marxism and, 24, 52, 102, 162; queer, 121–22, 171n43; queer theory and, 61, 63–64; race and, 68; regulation of, 190n26; same-sex,

170n41; social construction of, 141; study of, 21, 32, 36, 55, 59, 100, 146, 163, 193n59; subsumption and/of, 13, 24, 50–51, 134, 160; *Swordsman II* and, 129–30; Western notions of, 27; *xing* and, 147–48. *See also* gender
Shih, Shu-mei, 87–88, 185n10
Singapore, 41, 108; creative economy discourse of, 176n38
Sino-Soviet split, 39, 115
socialism, 6, 38, 126; actually existing, 22, 167n34; Chinese, 82, 86, 149; end of, 110, 149, 154; gender equality and, 139, 143; Maoist, 147; transition from, 15, 106, 150
social construction, 31–33, 140–41, 174n9
Sōseki, Natsume, 101, 183n83
South Korea, 41, 105, 109; culture industry of, 185n8
South-South Cooperation programs, 6, 14, 16, 26, 47, 103, 150, 162
Soviet Union (USSR), 1, 105, 126, 130, 167n34; collapse of, 38, 52, 108, 110, 113
Spade, Dean, 53–54
Stonewall riots, 4, 68–69, 178n54, 178n58
Stryker, Susan, 22, 135
subsumption, 3, 11, 134; of the Cold War, 14, 106, 109, 130–31; formal, 7, 10–13, 24, 28, 34, 36–38, 45, 96; of gender, 14, 24, 50, 58, 162; of labor, 22, 24, 41; of literature, 14–15, 82; real, 7, 10–13, 28, 34, 36–37, 96; of sex-gender distinction, 16; of sexuality, 24, 50–51, 58, 159–60, 162; of social differences, 6, 15, 162–36
surplus value, 11, 37, 49, 60
suzhi (quality), 45–46
Swordsman II: Asia the Invincible (Ching), 15, 106, 109, 118–23, 130–31, 187n34, 187n39, 188n42

Takeuchi Yoshimi, 84, 100–103, 183n83, 184n92
Tiananmen Square, 123; demonstrations, 1; massacre, 2, 86

Tibet, 3, 115
tongzhi, 31, 34, 82, 140, 170n42
transgender, 135; commodification of, 23; communities, 119–20; discourse, 28; experience, 56; identities, 125; movements, 135, 141; people, 72, 174n1; rights, 142, 156; subjectivity, 120; subjects, 28, 145, 191n27
transnational queers, 14, 26, 46. *See also suzhi*
treadmill effect, 37, 171n52
Truman Doctrine, 108, 110

Umbrella Movement, 3, 110
underconsumption, 2, 5, 74
use value, 9, 11; perverse, 173n108
United States, 1–2, 7, 49, 111, 167n10; atomic bombing of Japan, 112; China's relations with, 105–6, 126, 161, 165n1, 165n3; Cold War and, 108, 110, 130; crisis of multilateralism and, 159; gay identity and, 68; liberal pluralist paradigm of, 77; neoliberalism and, 49; queer theory and, 4, 16, 32, 52; Seventh Fleet, 110, 114; Taiwan and, 106, 115

valorization: of capital, 37; process, 11; of value-forming labor, 23

value, 2–3, 9, 12, 57, 64–65, 162, 171n57; extraction, 53, 71; labor theory of, 10, 71, 75–76; new politics of human, 14, 26, 45; production of, 23–24, 26, 37, 46; value-form theory, 24, 42, 56; women's work and, 44. *See also* surplus value; use value
Vatican City, 136, 156, 157
Vietnam, 110, 170n41
voluntarism, 42, 73, 81, 178n67
waishengren, 114, 129
Wang Hui, 15, 85, 167n34, 184n92
Wang Yanan, 12–13
Wang Zheng, 142, 144–47, 191n41
Warner, Michael, 28, 117
Washington Consensus, 47–48, 50, 136, 138
Wen Tiejun, 42, 49
Wittig, Monique, 169
World Trade Organization: China's accession to, 2, 42
world-systems analysis, 39, 41
wuxia (marital arts) movies, 118, 122

Xiang, Zairong, 56, 174n9
Xi Jinping, 3, 46–47, 82, 84, 154–56
Xinjiang, 3, 42; human rights abuses in, 104

Zhou, Egret Lulu, 119–20

www.ingramcontent.com/pod-product-compliance
Lightning Source LLC
Chambersburg PA
CBHW071737270326
41928CB00013B/2713